995

IN SORCERY'S SHADOW

Koda Mounmouni, Sorko of Mehanna

In Sorcery's Shadow

A MEMOIR OF APPRENTICESHIP
AMONG THE SONGHAY OF NIGER

Paul Stoller and Cheryl Olkes

THE UNIVERSITY OF CHICAGO PRESS
CHICAGO AND LONDON

PAUL STOLLER is professor of anthropology and chair of
the Department of Anthropology-Sociology at West
Chester University. CHERYL OLKES is director of
Harmattan, a gallery of African arts in Washington, D.C.

The University of Chicago Press, Chicago 60637
The University of Chicago Press, Ltd., London

Library of Congress Cataloging-in-Publication Data
Stoller, Paul.
  In sorcery's shadow.

  1. Songhai (African people) 2. Witchcraft—Niger.
3. Ethnology—Niger—Field work. 4. Stoller,
Paul. I. Olkes, Cheryl. II. Title.
DT547.45.S65S76 1987   306'.08996   87-10746
ISBN 0-226-77542-9
ISBN 0-226-77543-7 (pbk.)

Bundu si te kaare
"The (floating) log never becomes a crocodile."

SONGHAY PROVERB

"We see the straight highway before us, but of course we cannot use it, because it is permanently closed."

WITTGENSTEIN

CONTENTS

CONTENTS

PROLOGUE

From 1976 to 1984 I was the apprentice to Songhay sorcerers living in the villages of Mehanna and Tillaberi in the Republic of Niger. The Songhay, inhabitants of the region since the eighth century, were once the fierce rulers of an extensive, powerful empire; now they are subsistence millet and rice farmers. My apprenticeship, which was spread over five field stays, took me also to Wanzerbe, which is situated in the far northwestern corner of Niger. The inhabitants of Wanzerbe, most of whom are descendants of Sonni Ali Ber, the Magic King of the Songhay Empire (1463–91), are feared and respected for their feats of sorcery.

As an apprentice I memorized magical incantations, ate the special foods of initiation, and participated indirectly in an attack of sorcery that resulted in the temporary facial paralysis of the sister of the intended victim. As I traveled further into the world of Songhay sorcery, practitioners attacked me, causing on one occasion temporary paralysis in my legs. After that experience in 1979 I learned to eat the powders and wear the objects that would protect me from the will to power of antagonistic sorcerers, and I felt secure enough to return to Niger for subsequent lessons. After Cheryl Olkes and I visited Niger in the summer of 1984, I could no longer pursue my personal quest for comprehension and power; the world in which I had walked was too much with me.

The Representation of Sorcery

My experiences as an apprentice are by no means unique in the community of anthropologists. It is altogether likely that sorcerers have attacked other anthropologists in other societies. And yet, those anthropologists who have observed or experienced something beyond the edge of rationality tend to discuss it almost exclusively in informal settings—over lunch, dinner, or a drink. Serious anthropological discussion of the extraordinary, in fact, transcends the bar or restaurant only on rare occasions (e.g., in Jeanne Favret-Saada's *Deadly Words: Witchcraft and Sorcery in the Bocage*; or Larry Peters' *Ecstasy and Healing in Nepal*). In formal settings anthropologists are

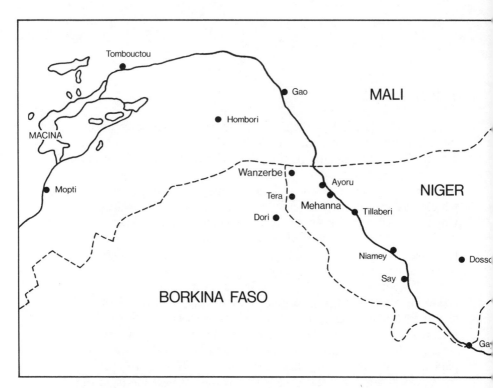

Principal Villages in Songhay Country

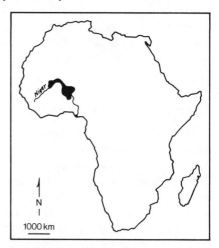

Songhay Country

supposed to be dispassionate analysts; because our confrontations with the extraordinary are unscientific, we are not supposed to include them in our discourse. It is simply not appropriate to expose to our colleagues the texture of our hearts or the uncertainties of our "gaze."

Should I write about being paralyzed in Wanzerbe? Should I describe how a priestess sent spirits to attack me? Is it appropriate to include in ethnographic discourse personal and bizarre accounts? In 1979 my first inclination was to answer these questions with an emphatic "No!" Indeed, in my first article on Songhay sorcery, I scrupulously avoided mentioning the fact that I had learned much about Songhay sorcery as an initiated apprentice. In that text the only mention of my involvement was relegated to a footnote in which I described how a sorcerer in the village of Mehanna came to accept me as his student-apprentice. Why did I edit myself out of that account? The answer is that we do not usually write what we want to write. In my case I had conformed to one of the conventions of ethnographic realism, according to which the author should be unintrusive in an ethnographic text. There are many other conventions of ethnographic representation to which ethnographers tacitly adhere. Writers like Rabinow, Favret-Saada, Crapanzano, Dumont, and Riesman, among a few others, have tampered with some of these conventions in their works.

In *Tales of the Yanomami* Jacques Lizot has suggested a relationship between the length of fieldwork and the form of ethnography. Lizot spent six generally uninterrupted years among the Yanomami Indians. The result is an ethnography in the form of stories about life, death, hunting, love, jealousy. These stories involve explicit dialogue and vivid description—techniques that sweep the reader into the Yanomami world.

Like *Tales of the Yanomami*, this book is the result of a long and intense association with one people, the Songhay in the Republic of Niger. For personal reasons Lizot refused to include himself as a character in his Yanomami stories even though in his book's preface he acknowledges his central presence in the ethnographic situations he describes. In this book I am a character in the text; it is an account of my experiences in the Songhay world.

Every ethnographer is a character in the story of his or her fieldwork. In some stories, the best narrative strategy is to distance the narrator from the text; in other stories the presence of the narrator is a source of narrative strength. Michel Leiris is present in the text of his monumental *Afrique Fantôme*, a personal journal that is also an ethnography. The same might be said of Favret-Saada and Contreras' *Corps Pour Corps* or Read's *High Valley*, Agee's *Let Us Now Praise Famous Men*, or even Lévi-Strauss' *Tristes Tropiques*.

In Sorcery's Shadow is a memoir fashioned from the textures and voices of ethnographic situations. This book is not a standard ethnography; it is a memoir. There are no Songhay informants in this story—there are individuals who behave in very particular ways. Woven throughout the text is the theme of confrontation—the clash of two worlds of reckoning. How far can we go in the quest to understand other peoples? Is it ethical for ethnographers to become apprentice sorcerers in their attempt to learn about sorcery? And what are our motives as ethnographers? Are we seekers of knowledge? Self-actualization? Power? *In Sorcery's Shadow* attempts to explore these questions.

The Nature of the Book

The book follows the chronological sequence of my apprenticeship among Songhay sorcerers and is divided into five parts, describing events in 1976–77, 1979–80, 1981, 1982–83, and 1984. A key feature of the book is dialogue. Longer narratives like those of Adamu Jenitongo were tape-recorded and translated. Other scenes in the book involving dialogue are reconstructed from my fieldnotes. Generally, x would occur and Olkes or I would record in our notebooks the occurrence, including the dialogue. Sometimes we could not write notes during a given rite. In those instances we recorded the event as best we could as soon as we were able. There is no foolproof method for reconstructing subjective experience. Tape-recorded conversation is better than reconstructed conversation. But even tape-recorded conversation must be transcribed and translated. And as linguists well know, even tape-recorded texts suffer from the "exuberances and deficiencies," to use A. L. Becker's apt phrase, of the transcriber and the translator.

The deeper our experiences in the field, the more sensitive we are to distant texts and our reconstructions of them. For my part, I have known some of the characters in *In Sorcery's Shadow* for more than seventeen years; others are more recent acquaintances. We have learned about one another's talk; we have learned about one another's motivations—good and bad—as human beings. We have

xiii

been pleased with one another and we have been disappointed, and these myriad experiences are the foundation of our reconstruction of the episodes of *In Sorcery's Shadow*.

The idea of writing *In Sorcery's Shadow* was conceived by Stoller and Olkes in 1981. After many false starts and discarded drafts, we completed a first version in June 1984, but we found it unsatisfactory, as if it lacked some subtle micron of an ingredient. After we returned from Niger in August 1984, Olkes suggested that we rewrite the manuscript. In collaboration with Olkes, Stoller expanded considerably the text of *In Sorcery's Shadow* in the fall of 1984. In the winter of 1985 Olkes rewrote substantial sections of the manuscript. Through the spring of 1985 we worked together to produce the final version.

ACKNOWLEDGMENTS

This book is the result of the collective efforts of many people. We could not have traveled to Niger without the support of numerous foundations and institutions. Fieldwork in 1976–77 was financed through generous grants from the Fulbright Doctoral Dissertation Program (G00-76-03659) and from the Wenner-Gren Foundation for Anthropological Research (No. 3175). Research in Niger in 1979–80 was made possible through a NATO Postdoctoral Fellowship in Science. Stoller's work among the Songhay in 1981 and in 1982–83 was made possible through grants from the American Philosophical Society and West Chester University. Grants from the Wenner-Gren Foundation for Anthropological Research and West Chester University made possible field studies in the summer of 1984. Among the many things Stoller's anthropological mentors, Annette B. Weiner and Joel Sherzer, taught him at the University of Texas was how to write a fundable research proposal. In Niger we must thank S.E. General Seyni Kountché, President of the Republic, for granting us numerous authorizations to conduct ethnographic field research among the Songhay. At the Institut de Recherches en Sciences Humaines of the Université de Niamey we have received warm encouragement and support from Djouldé Laya, Djibo Hamani, and Harouna Sidikou—past directors—and Boubé Gado, the present director. After months in the bush, Jean-François Berger, Tom and Barbara Hale, and Jim and Heidi Lowenthal invited us into their homes and treated us with graciousness and kindness. Paul Riesman, Jeanne Favret-Saada, Martin Murphy, Dan Rose, Judith Gleason, Jim Fernandez, John Chernoff, and Theresa and Chris Soufas all read the manuscript and made useful comments. John Chernoff's comments were especially helpful. Customarily, ethnographers thank their informants in a section of acknowledgments. We hope that the text that follows demonstrates their contribution to this book.

PERSONAE

Tillaberi People

Adamu Jentitongo:	a powerful sorcerer and ritual priest
Kedibo Jenitongo:	sister of Adamu Jenitongo
Moru Adamu:	son of Adamu Jenitongo; a drummer in the Tillaberi possession troupe
Moussa Adamu:	son of Adamu Jenitongo; a tailor
Djebo Zeinabou:	the wife of Moru Adamu
Djemma:	wife of Adamu Jenitongo
Hadjo:	wife of Adamu Jenitongo, also known as Moussa Nya ("Moussa's mother")
Daouda Godji:	the monocord violinist of the Tillaberi possession troupe
Djingarey Sodje:	a sorko who is also a soldier stationed at Tillaberi
Halidou Gasi:	the nephew of Adamu Jenitongo and a drummer in the Tillaberi possession troupe
Oungunia Harouna:	the best bus driver in Tillaberi
Salou:	a drunken dispatcher at the bus depot

Mehanna People

Idrissa Dembo:	a gardener and farmer who is caretaker of Stoller's borrowed house
Jitu:	wife of Idrissa Dembo
Harijetu:	daughter of Idrissa Dembo and Jitu
Djibo Mounmouni:	a sorko living in Mehanna and Namarigungu
Zakaribaba:	a herbalist who is Djibo Mounmouni's brother
Mounmouni Koda:	the father of Djibo Mounmouni and Zakaribaba; died in Mehanna in 1980
Maymuna:	wife of Djibo Mounmouni
Moussa Djibo:	a civil servant now living in Diffa, who is Djibo Mounmouni's cousin
Abdu Kano:	a shop owner

PERSONAE

Aboulaye:	an Islamic cleric
Amadu Zima:	a powerful sorcerer and ritual priest; died in 1984
Bankano:	the best cook on the western bank of the Niger River in the Republic of Niger
Fatouma Seyni:	a market woman and diviner
Hamidou:	a Niger boatman who paddles people between Mehanna and Bonfebba
Mamadu Djamona:	owner of a motorized dugout; died in 1984
Tondi Bello:	the chief of Mehanna

Wanzerbe People

Kassey Sohanci:	the most renowned sorcerer in all of western Niger
Hassane Sohanci:	the son of Kassey Sohanci
Mumay:	daughter of Kassey Sohanci and the best cook in Wanzerbe
Dembo Moussa:	the father of Idrissa Dembo. Also known as "Kundiababa"
Dunguri:	a priestess and sorceress
Mossi Sirfi:	the *guunu* or circumciser of Wanzerbe; died in 1984
Djibril:	a driver on the route from Dolsul to Markoy via Wanzerbe

Others

Howa Zima:	the priestess of the possession troupe in Ayoru; died in 1984
Olkes, Cheryl:	wife and collaborator of Paul Stoller; a sociologist and student of the Songhay
Stoller, Paul:	an ethnographer and longtime student of the Songhay
Susan:	a Peace Corps Volunteer who once lived in Ayoru

I · 1976–77

1

MEHANNA

The Berliet truck came down at last off the dune-top road and sputtered to a stop at the western corner of the Mehanna market. Swarms of children surrounded the truck, pointing and chanting, "Anasara, Anasara," the Songhay expression for "European." Undaunted, I opened the door of the truck and stepped down onto the sand. The children encircled me and stared with their mouths open. In my best oratorical Songhay I asked the crowd whether people who stare at other people are different from donkeys. My statement precipitated laughter among the adults who were watching this scene. Although the children continued to stare at me, a rare white man in these parts, the elders came forward and introduced themselves. They told me how pleased they were that an Anasara could speak Songhay so well.

"But I do not speak Songhay, really. I hear a little of it," I protested.

"Ah, but you do, Anasara. You speak it as well as I do," one man insisted.

"No, no, I know only a very small bit of the Songhay language." The men around me laughed with pleasure, and when I told them I wanted to meet the chief, they said they would escort me to his house. As we walked through the market to the chief's house, I greeted people in Songhay, mostly to their amazement. The men with whom I walked explained to others that I was a white man who spoke very good Songhay and that I was going to spend some time in Mehanna.

It was my first visit to Mehanna that market day in August of 1976, but it was a return to Songhay country in the Republic of Niger. I had been a Peace Corps Volunteer in a neighboring village five years before and had become fluent in the language. And through the Songhay language I had learned something of the culture of these people. Accordingly, I knew a little about carrying myself in the Songhay world and faced with confidence my introduction to life in Mehanna.

The chief's house was hidden from the rest of the village by an eight-foot mudbrick wall. We opened the corrugated tin gate and walked into the chief's compound, a nearly barren yard somewhat bigger than a football field. In it were three rectangular mudbrick houses which I estimated as 10 x 20 feet in dimension, one for the chief and one for each of his two wives. The chief himself sat with three other men in the shade of a thatched canopy which shielded them from the fierce Sahelian sun. As we approached, one of the chief's manservants materialized with a pillow for me, and one of my escorts presented me to the chief.

"I greet you, chief Tondi. I greet your wives, your brothers, your sisters. I ask after your health and the health of your house."

"I am in good health, Anasara. How is your health and the health of your people?"

"They are well, praise God."

"Praise be to God." He fixed his piercing black eyes on me. "How did an Anasara learn to speak Songhay so well?"

"I do not speak it well. I have learned what little Songhay I know in Tera and Tillaberi. I taught in Tera six years ago and I taught in Tillaberi five years ago."

The chief was wearing a billowing white robe, and his chiseled face, with its prominent cheekbones, was wreathed by a white turban which continued under his chin. He fingered a wooden cane. "Why do you come here, to Mehanna?"

"I come here to live."

"To live?" He looked at his cronies for a moment. "We have never had an Anasara live here. A Frenchman once visited us many years ago, but no Anasara has ever lived in Mehanna."

"I would like to live here, Amiru [chief]."

"But why would you want to live here?"

"I have come to write a book about the people of Mehanna." I remembered that one of my dissertation advisors had suggested that I tell the people that I was writing a book, that they would understand this statement.

"Wonderful." He smiled broadly, and his cronies, all of whom were also dressed in long white robes, nodded in what I interpreted to be agreement. "We will receive a copy of this book?"

"Oh, yes. I will send a copy to you, to the subprefect, and to the central government."

The chief ran his fingers through his beard. "Tell me Anasara, why—"

"Amiru, please do not call me Anasara."

There was silence among the chief and his cronies.

"And why should we not call you Anasara?"

"Because Anasara is neither a name nor a title. Calling me Anasara is like my calling you *Boro Bi* [Black Man]. Would you like me, every time I saw you, to say 'Hey, Black Man, hey'?"

All the men laughed loudly, and the chief conceded, "What you say has truth. But what is your name?"

I told him.

The chief extended his hand. "My name is Tondi. My father's name is Bello." The other men introduced themselves. The chief spoke to me once again. "How can you live here? We cannot provide you with an Anasara house with a fan and a light. The *campement*, outside of town, might be a place where you could stay."

One of his companions shook his head. "No, the campement is far from town. He must stay somewhere in town."

"How about Boulhassane's compound? Is it empty?"

The chief nodded. "It will be good for you, Monsieur Paul. It is right next to the market in the center of town."

The chief stood up and suggested that we go to the market so I might observe that colorful slice of Songhay life. We did not buy anything; rather we sat on a straw mat at the edge of the market and accepted the well-wishes of townspeople and visitors. A few moments after we had settled ourselves two women started to argue. One of them had accused the other of shortchanging her. The accuser, a tall, thin woman with skin a size too big for her body, began insulting the accusee, who was also tall but obese, dressed in brightly patterned new clothes. The thin woman impugned the dignity of the fat one's mother, father, uncle, grandmother, and grandfather. The fat woman took up the challenge and suggested that the thin one had been conceived in the belly of a donkey. The women were soon screaming and brandishing their forefingers like weapons. Yet no one near them attempted to mediate the dispute. The chief smiled at the women and told me that this sort of thing happened all the time, especially on market days. Suddenly, the thin woman dropped her market bundle and attempted to strike the fat one. But she never landed her intended blow, because a man from the amorphous crowd intercepted her, blocking her fist before it reached its target. Restraining her, he coaxed her away from her opponent. Gradually the thin woman calmed down, and she left the market area. I made a mental note: Could it be that the Songhay have a tacit principle whereby it is appropriate to abuse others verbally, but not physically?

The chief awoke me from my anthropological reverie. His younger brother, he told me, would help to get me settled in Boulhassane's compound. We collected my gear from the truck and asked a number of teenagers if they would carry my stuff to the compound, which they agreed to do for a small fee. Boulhassane's compound was at the north end of the market just opposite the fly-covered butchers' stalls. A green door in a ten-foot mudbrick wall admitted us to a vast space interrupted only by two houses and a sickly acacia tree. The chief's brother took me to the smaller of the houses and introduced me to Idrissa, a little rabbit of a man who was the caretaker of Boulhassane's compound. We negotiated his monthly wage as well as a price for my rent. I moved into the other house in the compound, a larger one with two rooms, a dirt floor, and a roof made of sticks cemented together with daub. Its three windows were holes in the wall with corrugated tin shutters. It was furnished with an iron bed with a straw mattress, a flimsy metal card table, and a rickety school chair.

Idrissa gave me a tour of the compound. He explained the lack of vegetation simply, saying the soil was not good. Indeed, the ground was as hard as rock.

"Where is the outhouse?" I asked with trepidation.

Idrissa pointed to the far end of the compound, but I could not see it. So we walked in that direction—some 50 meters— before coming upon a hole in the ground near the far wall of the compound. One's privacy was insured by a mudbrick wall three feet in height.

"Is it solid? I asked as I peered through the hole into what seemed to be a 15-foot pit. "I won't fall in, will I?" I asked as I was assailed by the gases of decaying human waste.

"Oh yes," Idrissa affirmed, responding to my first question. "It's very strong. You won't fall. But don't come here at night."

"At night?"

"Snakes."

"Snakes!"

"Cobras and vipers. And bats live in the pit. At night they fly in and out."

"Wonderful! What else can you tell me about this shithole?"

"Nothing."

Feeling the need to defecate, I asked Idrissa to leave. As I prepared myself—that is to say, as I squatted to afford myself the privacy of the three-foot wall—I heard giggling. I looked up to discover two boys and two girls watching me from the roof of a neighbor's house. They were pointing, laughing, and I distinctly heard the word "Anasara." I grimaced at the prospect of being observed in the day and bitten by snakes at night. But I was deter-

The Niger River from Mehanna

mined, so I ignored the children and went about my business. When I had finished, I stood up and glowered at the amused children. They abandoned their rooftop observation post, and I returned to my new house, feeling triumphant that I had bested my balky digestion and the neighbor's kids. Perhaps my work would go well in Mehanna.

2

A LESSON IN SURVEY RESEARCH

I spent only a few days getting situated before I began my study. My aim was to investigate the relationship between the use of language and local politics among the Songhay. My first task was to construct a language-attitude survey and administer it to a carefully selected sample of the population of Mehanna.

I designed a twenty-item survey and conducted a pilot test on ten respondents. Since none of the respondents had difficulty answering the questions, I went ahead with my plans to administer the survey to the townspeople. My previous experience among the Songhay had prepared me for the diplomacy needed to make the obligatory arrangements to administer the survey. First I visited the chief, Tondi Bello, who was pleased to see me. The chief gave his blessing to the project, but he instructed me to visit eight neighborhood chiefs in Mehanna before interviewing people in those neighborhoods. Since each visit became a rather long encounter, I spent three days contacting the eight chiefs. Finally, I was ready to begin. After that I should have been prepared to find that each session with a respondent would turn out to be a visit, and of such long duration that I could conduct only six interviews a day. It took me thirty days to reach my goal of 180 interviews. I analyzed the data as I went along and soon discovered that the degree of multilingualism was significantly higher than I had anticipated. A cursory examination of the language attitudes, moreover, suggested a high degree of enmity among the various segments of Mehanna's population.

Toward the end of my survey, I interviewed a shopkeeper named Abdou Kano, a short hunchbacked man with an infectious, toothless smile. Abdou told me, among other things, that he spoke four languages (Songhay, Hausa, Fulan, and Tamesheq). My work with Abdou completed, I walked next door to interview Mahamane Boulla, who, like Abdou, was a shopkeeper. I asked him how many languages he spoke:

"Oh, I speak three languages: Songhay, Hausa and Fulan."

During our conversation about languages, Mahamane asked me how many languages Abdou spoke.

"Abdou says he speaks four languages."

"Hah! I know for a fact that Abdou speaks only two languages."

"What! Is that true? How could he lie to me!" I stood up abruptly. Red in the face, I stormed back to Abdou's shop. Abdou smiled and greeted me.

"Ah, Monsieur Paul. What would you like to buy today?"

"Abdou, Mahamane has just told me that you speak only two languages. Is it true?"

"Yes, it is true. I speak only two languages."

"Why did you tell me you speak four languages?"

Abdou shrugged his shoulders and smiled. "What difference does it make?" He looked skyward for a moment. "Tell me, Monsieur Paul, how many languages did Mahamane tell you that he spoke?"

"Mahamane told me that he speaks three languages."

"Hah! I know for a fact that Mahamane speaks only one language. He can speak Songhay and that is all."

"What!"

I stomped back to Mahamane's shop.

"Abdou tells me that you speak only one language. But you just told me that you speak three languages. What is the truth?"

"Ah, Monsieur Paul, Abdou is telling you the truth."

"But how could you lie to me?"

"What difference does it make, Monsieur Paul?"

I spent the next week frantically consulting the other 178 people whom I had interviewed in the previous month. To my disgust, I discovered that everyone had lied to me and that the data I had so painstakingly collected were worthless. I had learned a lesson: Informants routinely lie to their anthropologists for any number of reasons: What's the difference? We do not know you. We know you, but we do not trust you. Since you are too young, we cannot tell you the truth, but we are too polite to tell you to go away. And so on.

Perhaps I was one of the lucky ones. After only one month in the field, I had discovered that people were lying to me. Many of my col-

Abdoulaye Cisse, an Islamic Cleric in Mehanna

leagues in anthropology have perhaps not been so lucky. Further luck brought me to Abdoulaye, an old *marabout* (an Islamic cleric) who was willing to advise me on learning about the Songhay.

"Monsieur Paul, you will never learn about us if you go into people's compounds, ask personal questions, and write down the answers. Even if you remain here one year, or two years, and ask us questions in this manner, we would still lie to you."

"Then what am I to do?"

"You must learn to sit with people, Monsieur Paul. You must learn to sit and listen. You must learn the meaning of the Songhay adage: One kills something thin in appearance only to discover that inside it is fat."

3

DISCUSSION GROUPS

I could not stop thinking of the proverb the elder had recited to me. "One kills something thin in appearance only to discover that on the inside it is fat." Did the statement refer to my failed survey, to one entire month of wasted time, to my inability to see, to think? Did it mean I was defeated so soon? I decided to take the advice of my friend, the Islamic cleric. I would sit and listen to people like an obedient child, and somehow in the process I would learn their ways. However much the unstructured technique of conducting research violated every methodological principle I had learned in graduate school, what was I to do? What choice had I other than to leave Mehanna and return to Niamey, where I could drink beer, eat hamburgers, and interact with my countrymen? But the Songhay fascinated me. They were proud. They were stubborn. Like the warriors of their imperial past, they were hard and aggressive. These qualities drew me to the Songhay, for I wanted to be more like them. Attracted by the ethos of these people, I decided to let the Songhay lead me along their path.

The discussion group is the centerpiece of everyday life for the Songhay man. I was invited to join a number of these groups, which seemed a promising way to learn about Songhay culture. One group I sat with consisted of a handful of older men who were either nobles or the clients of nobles. A Songhay noble is a descendant, through the father's line, of Askia Mohammed Toure, also known as Askia the Great, who was King of the Songhay Empire from 1493 to 1527, its greatest period.

Each morning these men would gather in the shadow of the Mehanna Friday mosque, a large one-story mudbrick structure some hundred meters from the Niger River. The Friday mosque is the most sacred place in any Songhay town. The men usually discussed Songhay history, especially the history of the local branch of the nobility, and national politics, usually cued by a broadcast of national news on the ever-playing radio.

I learned of their reverence for the old days, when men were hard and fierce and unrelenting in their quest to vanquish their enemies. I also learned of their views about life in contemporary Niger. About two weeks after I had begun to sit with the men in this group, the newscaster on the radio announced a student strike at the national high school in Niamey. The old cleric who was my advisor suggested that the students were foolish. Another person described how the Malian government had brutally dealt with a similar situation in Bamako. Several of the discussants could not understand why the students would strike. Did they not have the privilege of attending such a fine school?

The same cleric, however, suggested why students could be so foolish as to strike. He said that students are people who do not know the virtues of patience. The students, he continued, study the white man's talk and as a consequence they think like white men. When one of these students talks to you, he tells you that he knows everything. But know-it-alls know nothing. The students, the cleric stated, do not understand that a person must grow old and study the Prophet's books in order to know just a little bit about the world. These students, he told the group, have no mind; they are doing the white man's work. They do not respect those who are wise. The children of today, the cleric concluded, will not do. Most of the members of the group seemed to agree with the cleric's analysis.

On other days I listened to discussions on kinship, questions of Songhay law, theories about the nature of the cosmos, and criticisms of features of the pre-Islamic religion: spirit possession and sorcery. From the vantage of these men, Songhay was a thoroughly Islamic society, and the problems of contemporary society were attributable to the withering of Islamic belief—especially among the young people.

As the cleric had counseled, I sat and listened and learned from the men. Beyond the specific teachings on Songhay kinship and cosmology, they instructed me that one can learn only when he or she is of an age such that the brain is ready to receive knowledge. The mind of a child is not developed; he is therefore not ready for serious study. The mind of an adolescent is not developed; he is therefore not ready for serious study. The minds of women never develop fully; they are never ready for serious study. A man's mind can begin to receive important knowledge when he is forty years of age, but it is not until a man reaches the age of sixty that he is truly ready to learn. As the cleric suggested, the student of things Songhay must, above all, be patient.

A second group I attended consisted mostly of merchants and their coteries of workers. The most respected member of this group was a man called Larabu, a short, portly man with smooth ebony skin and small black eyes. The richest man in Mehanna, Larabu claimed to be a *sharif*, a direct descendant of the Prophet Mohammed. Given the merchant's wealth and influence, it was no wonder that this group met informally every afternoon in front of Larabu's shop, which, with the other shops in Mehanna, bordered the market area. While business was being transacted in the shop, the group sitting outside would discuss the price of kerosene, the price of cloth, the conditions of transport, and other matters of concern to businessmen. Through such conversations I learned about the Songhay economic system. I came to know Songhay entrepreneurial style as it was expressed in language and comportment—an economic expression of the ethos of the Songhay warrior. Merchants were hard, unrelenting, and merciless in dealing with everyone, even members of their families. Close association with Labaru—we became friends—convinced me that although the merchants had gained great economic power, they had yet to gain the respect of their fellow Songhay. The Songhay reserved respect, I gathered, only for people who had the blood of the Askias—kings of the Songhay Empire—running through their veins. Still, the local nobles, most of whom did not participate in economic affairs for reasons of pride, envied the economic success of the lowborn merchants. The nobles were spiteful.

There were other discussion groups. One group, made up of young men, met in front of the grain warehouse on the western edge of the market. These men would invariably play cards, discuss their dreams of the future, and talk vituperatively about the old ways of the Songhay past. They detested the nobles and their assumptions about the old Songhay social order, which was built on slavery. Most of the participants in this group were of non-Songhay origin. They welcomed me into their group with great enthusiasm, perhaps a tacit recognition of our common status as strangers in a Songhay town.

During one particular card game under the acacia just outside the grain warehouse, one of the card players, Moussa, condemned with uncustomary vigor one of the nobles who lived in town. Issaka, a farmer, had just mentioned that the noble had been slandering Moussa. But Moussa, a government grain agent, dismissed the accusations, for, as he told everyone, the noble in question was a crazy man. He then related an anecdote which underscored his point. One day the noble came to him and asked whether a grain truck was going to Kokoro (the village of the paramount chief). As it turned out, Moussa had been expecting a truck that day, so he told the noble that the truck would leave Mehanna after it had been loaded with grain. The noble then asked Moussa if his niece could have a seat on the truck. Moussa said that she could and asked the noble how much he was willing to pay for his niece's seat. The noble became angry; he told Moussa that he should not have to pay because he was an aristocrat. Moussa laughed at the noble and told him that everyone who wants to travel on the grain truck must pay for his or her seat. The noble lost his temper. He called Moussa a worthless foreigner. He told Moussa to have sex with his mother. Moussa, however, did not return the insults. But, Moussa told us with a smile, "the noble's niece did not leave town that day." Issaka said that he did not give a damn about the nobles. Djibo added that the nobles amount to nothing today.

These kinds of incidents taught me about ideal expectations. Nobles were supposed to be laconic, dignified, and generous, and commoners were supposed to be undignified, avaricious, and loquacious. Somehow, events had scrambled their behavior.

Sometimes women would invite me to sit with them as they pounded millet in mortars. As they thumped the millet with their pestles they would talk about men, the plight of women, and the difficulties of raising children in a world full of changes. One woman told me of her three husbands, each of whom had been cruel to her. Another women told me about her husband who beat her. The husband of a third woman, I was told, had beaten her while she slept the previous evening. They talked of their wealth and their children, of their families and their antipathies for their husbands' families. Among the Songhay, a person's allegiance is to a lineage, a grouping of kin related exclusively through father's blood. In many ways, a man or woman is more attached to a brother or sister (of the same mother) than to a spouse. This is especially true of women, who do not share their possessions or their wealth with their husbands. In the case of divorce, which is very common among the Songhay, a woman loses her children to her husband's lineage. Often the women talked with sadness about children they had not seen for a long time. For some reason, the women were not embarrassed by my presence. Perhaps they saw my silent patience as an invitation to tell their stories. Maybe they thought that I was a powerful white man who could improve their situation.

I listened to people in all of these groups, rarely making many comments of my own. But I could not escape the feeling that although these people had told me a great deal, they had revealed little of themselves. They spoke in generalities, and they refused to let me write notes or tape-record the various discussions. When my level of frustration reached its peak after about two months of attendance at these discussions, I again asked people if I could tape-record the conversations. The response to my request was the same in each of the groups:

"No. We listen to you, we see you, but we do not know you yet."

"But I will not misuse the tapes," I insisted.

"We do not care what you say. We have watched you and we have seen that we do not want you to write notes or open your machine when we talk."

I admired this Songhay hardness and pride, but what was I to do in light of this unequivocal opposition? My passive attendance continued for more than four months. I would sit with a group for thirty minutes or an hour and then run home to write down my recollections. Were these data any better than the stuff I had collected with my ill-fated questionnaire? Or, to quote my friends Abdou and Mahamane, "What is the difference?" Although I had learned much about the sociopolitical dynamics of Mehanna, I nonetheless felt as though all the villagers were holding back, trying to shape my perceptions of them.

Meanwhile my life in Mehanna settled into a routine. I would wake up at dawn, the sun rousing me from my mosquito-net-shrouded bed in the middle of my empty compound; it was simply too hot at night to sleep inside. And so, I would get up and light my Camping Gaz stove to boil a pot of water for Nescafé. Sometimes Idrissa would go out and buy a bowl of fresh milk, which I would boil before adding it to the coffee. This made for an extremely rich café au lait. While I was making the coffee, Idrissa would go out a second time for a loaf of Mehanna bread, usually a baguette peppered with a few baked mosquitoes and other varieties of black insects. When the coffee was ready, Idrissa and I would break bread and slop guava jam on it. Then we would dip some of it into our plastic mugs of coffee. We would take our second cups of coffee with us to chairs just outside our compound's walls. There we would sit and watch people as they walked to market, to the Imam's house, which was next door, or to the Niger River, only 100 meters south of our compound. Songhay etiquette, I knew, required that passersby greet us, and I was obsessed with getting to know everyone in town. Some people were courteous and would greet us; a few people would walk by briskly as though we did not exist. Sometimes I said hello to these people and they refused to respond. Many of these Songhay did not give a damn if a white man was in their town; some people were no doubt angry about my presence.

In the beginning months I was a curiosity. Delegations of men and women would come to my compound and welcome me formally to Mehanna. As the months passed, however, fewer people came to visit and I no longer received invitations to visit other compounds. I began to feel isolated and despaired of accomplishing my goals.

Many of the little boys seemed to sense my despondency and attempted to take advantage of it. In Mehanna and other Songhay towns there are swarms of troublesome children, mostly between the ages of three and five, who roam at will the village paths. The behavior of these children no doubt inspired the Songhay maxim about children: "Children are animals. They eat anything, they say anything, and they do anything." While these children had impressed me as being surly from the beginning of my time in Mehanna, I noticed now, five months after my arrival, an escalation of their beastly behavior. Some of the little buggers would sneak into my compound before dawn, creep up to my bed and pull my hair. Each time, I would claw my way out of my mosquito net, spring from my bed and scream at them. Then I would begin an oration in Songhay addressed to no one, decrying their uncivilized antics and cursing their negligent mothers. They would squeal in delight and then run away. I would not run after them. I suppppose that my lack of aggressiveness encouraged them to continue to pester me. If only I could be like a Songhay warrior and catch one of them and slap some respect into him. But I did not dare, for I had already sensed the Songhay abhorrence of physical violence. The children continued to bait me, and I continued to restrain myself.

But one cool afternoon, when the fine dust of the Harmattan filtered out the hot rays of the sun, I crossed an invisible social threshold. On that day a young child threw a good-sized rock which hit me in the shoulder. On impact I lost all sense of my cultural self. I ran after the little brat and grabbed him. His small round faced grimaced in terror when he saw my clenched teeth. Possessed by rage, I abandoned my lifelong moral training and slapped him on the face so rapidly that I lost count of the number of times I hit him. I felt triumphant. When I let go of the child, who ran away screaming, I noticed a group of men gathering around me. Some were elders; others were thickly built young adults who at the time reminded me of the beefy tackles of professional football teams. As they surrounded me, they seemed to suck up the air from my space. I had trouble catching my breath. One of the football players grabbed my upper arm.

"We wondered," he said, "how long it would take you to understand."

"Understand what?"

"We wondered how long it would take you to understand how Songhay deal with children."

The football player laughed. So did the others.

"You mean?"

"You white people are as slow-witted as donkeys. The children will not bother you again."

The old cleric who had previously given me such good advice broke through this circle of humanity.

"Monsieur Paul, you have listened, which is good. But now you have acted and have become a person in this village."

4

GUIDED INTERPRETATIONS

My work took off. No one seemed to mind now whether I brought my notebook with me to discussion groups. On some occasions the old men of the group which met by the Friday mosque actually would tell me to fetch my notebook. Important words, they explained, should be recorded without errors. I willingly agreed to their requests. And when I recorded their important words about Songhay myth and history, they asked me to read what I had written to be certain that their words appeared correctly on my pages.

These discussions with the old men made me aware of the important role that Islam had in Songhay politics. The great king Askia Mohammed Toure had used Islam as the major weapon in his successful coup d'état in 1493. Askia Mohammed convinced the Army that if Songhay continued to be governed by non-Islamic infidels—the descendants of Sonni Ali Ber—Songhay was doomed. With his growing army of the faithful, Askia defeated Si Baru, Sonni Ali's eldest son, at the battle of Tondibia and established a new Islamic dynasty of Songhay, the Askyiad. On a much smaller scale, the role of Islam in Mehanna politics was evident in the Imam's weekly sermon in the Friday mosque during the *Jumah* (sabbath) services.

Although they stressed a variety of themes from the Koran, the Imam's sermons always covered the same essential points. He consistently began his sermons by insisting that all people—noble, slave, and foreigner—must pay homage to Allah. And why this homage? The reason was simple. Long ago the angels swooped down to earth to choose a great chief—the Prophet Mohammed. The angels brought with them power and gave it to the chief, who gave it to his sons, who, in turn, became great chiefs. All chiefs receive their special powers from the heavens. When one follows the chief Mohammed, the Imam always said, he or she shall be sustained, for along the path of Islam one is guaranteed peace and tranquility.

But the promise of salvation constituted only the beginning of the Imam's usual sermon. In each sermon he would tell us of how Allah, after great thought, gave his hat (*fula*) of power to Mohammed. "In the shadow, his own shadow, Allah sent him to us. We prostrate ourselves and ask for mercy. We give you piety. . . . Great Allah spoke and gave us work, and spoke again and gave us protection from evil. You, Allah, acted and gave us bravery, and then you gave it the chief, Mohammed the Prophet, who gave it to his sons and to our chiefs of today."

In many of his statements, I realized, the Imam used religion as a metaphor for Songhay politics. He referred to the Prophet Mohammed as a "chief." The Imam also spoke of fula, the hat of power, which Allah gave to Mohammed. The Songhay, too, give the hat of power to their chiefs when they are invested. Once they receive the hat of power, chiefs are imbued with its attributes—an inner determination and the will to make difficult political decisions. The Imam also spoke consistently of a salvation reserved for those who follow the path of Islam. Those who follow this path, he stressed, must do everything they can to maintain the harmony of their communities. It is therefore imperative to obey the political decisions of the chief.

The most revealing political event I observed during my residence in Mehanna, however, was the settlement of a major dispute. Well before my arrival, a fundamentalist Islamic sect called the Hebenci had constructed a second Friday mosque in Mehanna. In Islamic communities, the presence of a rival Friday mosque is a symbolic statement of political defiance and a threat to the harmony of the community. This kind of religious insolence angered the Imam and his cronies. The chief considered the presence of a second Friday mosque politically intolerable. The conflict was allowed to fester for a year, but after the Imam and the leader of the splinter group almost came to blows over questions of religious heresy, the chief called for a public resolution.

A large crowd gathered in the shade of a cluster of acacias between the southern edge of the market area and the river. The chief of Mehanna seated himself and three neighborhood chiefs in front of the gathering of some 300 men. The Imam and his cronies sat to the left of the chief's panel; the Hebenci leader and his supporters sat to the right. The chief nodded and one of the Imam's cronies rose to speak.

His white boubou billowing around his long, gaunt frame, the old man claimed that if the sect were allowed to practice Islam sacrilegiously, it would ruin Mehanna. He recounted how the Hebenci had been expelled from Mali and how they had come to settle in one neighborhood of Mehanna. The sect members, he complained, did not pray in Mehanna's Friday mosque, and when they did pray in their own Friday mosque, they refused to recite the Prophet's name. More serious still, they had brought evil to the village. If a village cannot pray together, this man said, what can it do? These people, he stated with finality, are no good here. They should be cast out.

The Hebenci leader stood up slowly and addressed the crowd. He asked the people of Mehanna whether a group of people had the right to pray and worship as they wished. In the land of the white people, he told them, any person can follow any road he or she desires. It should be this way in this country, he said. Then he described the sect, suggesting that his people were men, all of whom were equal under the eyes of Allah. "We do not recognize the social order of the chief," he told a shocked audience. "We do recognize the Prophet as a human being, but he is not first in the family of saints. Our only allegiance is to Allah."

The Imam reacted at once to this blasphemy. He sprang up, and his white boubou fell in folds over his girth.

"No, no! What you say is worthless as the sand!" he cried as he threw a handful of sand in the direction of the sect leader. His students and cronies restrained the Imam and coaxed him into sitting down.

One of the allies of the Imam continued the tirade against the Hebenci. He told the throng that the sect had brought shame to him and his fellow countrymen. "My mind boils like water because of their behavior." He declared that the sect had spread lies about the teachings of the Prophet and its members were therefore worse than nonbelievers. They were agents of Mounakoufi, the devil of discord, the most evil of all devils in Songhay belief. "Either they become pious Moslems like ourselves," he concluded, "or they must leave our country."

One of the sect members recoiled at the idea of expulsion. He pleaded to everyone that the Hebenci wanted to live in harmony with the other villagers of Mehanna, but they should have the right to believe in whom and what they wanted. He insisted that the sect brought no harm to the other members of the community and reiterated that they wished only to live in peace and harmony.

The speeches finished, the chief conferred with the neighborhood chiefs, whom he called forward. After barely five minutes, he stood to announce his decision. He said that the existence of a Hebenci Friday mosque was intolerable, and that like the other Moslems in the area, the sect members would be obliged to pray in the Friday mosque of Mehanna. But the sect members would be free to pray as they wished in their own neighborhood mosques on the other days of the week. This compromise satisfied both parties; even I admired the chief's skillful diplomacy.

My work was proceeding exceedingly well. I noted in my field journal that the dispute settlement demonstrated how religion served as a metaphor for Songhay politics and showcased the strategic devices orators could use to persuade other people about such and such a political point. After six months in Mehanna, I grasped the fundamental processes of Songhay politics. The more involved I became, the more I attracted knowledgeable men who wanted to work with me. We created our own discussion group which met every other night. We talked for hours about the Songhay past, the history of the principality of Kokoro of which Mehanna was originally a slave settlement. We talked about the Songhay language and about how the paramount chief of Kokoro distributed land. Maybe the people of Mehanna had finally accepted me.

5

TWO BIRDS IN THE RAFTERS ARE BETTER THAN ONE IN THE BUSH

February in Mehanna meant cool mornings and evenings and hot afternoons. During the day the sun inched northward in the sky and the shadows its rays cast at midday grew shorter. The Harmattan filled the air with fine Saharan dust which penetrated everything. As the heat increased, so did Mehanna's colony of flies. They buzzed about people's heads in black swarms and landed in convoys in their food, leaving dysentery in their wake.

During these increasingly uncomfortable afternoons, I remained in my house and worked on my field notes and journal. Toward the end of February, on a particularly stifling afternoon, Bankano, my neighborhood cook, brought me my afternoon meal—rice with a spicy fish sauce. Despite the hardships of living in Mehanna—my alternating diarrhea and constipation—I had gained some weight. Bankano often told me, in fact, how pleased she was that her white man had filled out a bit. Had I left Mehanna looking as rotund as she, she would have been jubilant.

Despite my six months of residence in Mehanna, the people still referred to me as the white man. The avoidance of my personal name might have been an intrinsic part of Songhay custom, but the substitute they chose annoyed me. When people introduced me to strangers, they invariably grasped my elbow and said: "Hey, this is our white man."

The strangers invariably responded: "Mehanna white man, how are you? How is your health?"

The people of Mehanna adopted me as their white man; however, I did not claim Mehanna as my village. I had made friends and enemies in Mehanna. I lifted Mehanna's veil of civility as I learned more about Songhay language and culture. Enemies now insulted me openly and suggested to the chief that I be expelled from town. I read the emotions sparked by my presence as indicators of progress; perhaps I was uncovering sensitive, important issues. Although the people of Mehanna professed their eternal friendship, I was a stranger, and like the other strangers in Songhay towns, I knew that I would never cross the invisible threshold to become an insider.

This realization did not inhibit my notetaking. I wrote down my impressions of the political orations I had observed earlier in the week and compared what I had observed to what I remembered from the literature on political oratory.

Someone clapped his hands outside my door. Clapping one's hands at a threshold is the Songhay way of knocking on a door. "Enter," I said, without turning around to see who had come for a visit.

"How are you today?" asked Djibo, a six-footer with bulging biceps who could never sit still. A prominent scar, one mark of Zerma ethnicity, stretched in a single straight line from just below the inside corner of Djibo's right eye to the center of his cheekbone. Like me, Djibo was a stranger in Mehanna. Being a son of Zerma parents, Djibo spoke the Songhay language from birth, but his people lived east of the Niger River some 100 kilometers from Songhay country. While the Zerma share the same worldview—the same culture—as the Songhay, their social history is distinct. The Songhay and the Zerma, in fact, consider themselves to be cousins, a mutual recognition which places them in a joking relationship. When Songhay see Zerma, or vice-versa, they insult one another. But these are ritual insults, not taken seriously.

I wasn't surprised to see Djibo; he visited me frequently. Being strangers in a Songhay town created solidarity; Djibo even called me by my name. Even so, I sensed that Djibo was wary of me. He never looked me in the eye; rather his eyes darted about the room, taking measure of the situation.

"How are you this afternoon, Paul?"

"I am in good health," I said. "And you?"

"My wife and son are in good health. My brother and brother's wife and child are in good health. We give thanks."

"And your father? How is your father, Djibo?"

"Praise be to God. He too is well."

Djibo picked up the only other chair in my house and placed it next to mine. He knew that I worked in the afternoons and he came to my house to watch me as I typed and to look at my possessions. Sometimes Djibo sat silent and motionless for hours while I typed.

My concentration was soon broken, not by Djibo, but by a rustling in the rafters. It was those damn birds again. I continued to type, but soon I felt something like a large drop of rain splatter on my head.

"Oh shit, those goddam birds have finally done it!" I tentatively touched my hair. "Birdshit! Goddam birds! Goddam country! Goddam village!" I screamed in English as I jumped off my chair and kicked the dirt floor of my house.

Ever since I moved into my house the birds had tested me. I first noticed them a week after my arrival. They had built a small mud nest between the mud-daubed sticks which consitututed my ceiling. I did not mind their presence, but I did not like the fact that they had been shitting on my dirt floor. Although part of me was willing to adjust to the social, cultural, and ecological circumstances of Songhay country, I was not yet willing to relinquish all my standards of American cleanliness. To be blunt, I was not going to allow two small birds, one black and one white, to shit all over my house, and I did not care what the Songhay thought about my attitude. Thus motivated, I borrowed from a neighbor a long wooden pole, the kind that Niger River fishermen use to push their dugouts upstream, and with it I knocked down the birds' nest. Nothing could have been easier. Two weeks later the birds quietly built another nest in my ceiling. Again they shat on the floor under their nest. Worse yet, they now liked to fly around my two rooms and defecate in areas some distance from their nest. This activity had to be stopped. I again borrowed the pole and knocked down the second nest. But the birds were as persistent as I. They returned at night and built another mud nest among the sticks of the ceiling. And they continued to shit all over my house. After more than two months of battle, I gave up. Feeling much like weary Sisyphus, I resigned myself to having a bird-infested house. The birds continued their dirty duty; I responded by sweeping the dirt floor every day. But when the birds began to defecate on my pots and pans, on my books, my notebooks, and on some of the pages of my field journal, I resolved to stage a last campaign. I knocked the new nest down, they returned, and so on, until I acknowledged the futility of the battle and surrendered to them. My capitulation: If they shit on my pots and pans, I would clean them; if they shit on my papers, I would wipe them clean. In this way I coexisted with my conquerors until that day in February when, in the presence of a farmer named Djibo Mounmouni, one, perhaps both, of the birds shat on my head.

Djibo laughed so hard that his entire body twitched. Having used my last Kleenex the day before, I had nothing suitable to wipe the bird poop from my hair. I ripped a page from my composition book and scraped the bird droppings from my hair.

"Praise be to God," Djibo chanted loudly, raising his hands skyward.

"How the hell can you say that at a time like this!" I snapped.

"I am not laughing at you, Paul. I feel joy in my heart."

"Joy! What joy can there be in this?"

"Yes, joy. I have seen something here today."

"No kidding."

"Yes, I have seen a sign. You see, Paul, I am a *sorko*. My father is a sorko. And my grandfather, and grandfather's grandfather—all have been sorkos."

"What does that have to do with me?" Despite my frustration I was intrigued, for I had heard and read about the powers of the sorko, one of three kinds of Songhay magician-healers.

"Until today, my being a sorko had nothing to do with you," Djibo continued, "but today I have seen a sign. You have been pointed out to me. Yes, I am a sorko and now that you have been pointed out to me, I want you to come to my compound tomorrow after the evening prayer so that we might begin to learn texts."

"What are you talking about?"

"I am saying that I want you to learn to be a sorko," Djibo said as he cracked his knuckles. "The choice is yours to make. If you choose my path, come to my compound tomorrow." Djibo walked toward the door, stopped at the threshold and looked back toward me. "Praise be to God."

Afternoon had crept into dusk in Mehanna. It was time to leave the stale and dusty confines of my house and sit outside to enjoy the cool breezes of the approaching night. The breezes carried the pungency of freshly pounded ginger. Soft monotonous thumping reported that Songhay women were pulverizing dried peppers, leaves, and roots with their pestles to make zesty evening sauces. Clouds of smoke from cooking fires rose in the air to mix with the thick dust kicked up by cows returning from a day in the bush. Aside from the echoes of pestles meeting the bottoms of mortars, dusk was a quiet time in Mehanna. Weary from the trials of the day, people sat silently in their compounds waiting for the evening meal. For me, dusk was a time of peace, reflection, and some self-satisfaction. Like the people of Mehanna, had I not withstood another day when the sun had blistered the countryside and its inhabitants? Somehow, I had defeated the heat, the sun, and even the flies. Frequently, dusk brought a smile of victory to my face.

The antics of the birds on this day, however, had left me with more than bird droppings on my head. I had to make a decision. Should I study with Djibo? He had declared that the birds were a sign, but he had not said from whom. I tried to imagine what the great anthropologists would have done. Evans-Pritchard would give me unequivocable advice. Faced with a similar dilemma among the Azande of Central Africa in the 1920s, Evans-Pritchard refused to become personally involved with what he called a witch doctor. Such personal involvement, he reasoned, would compromise his objectivity. Since he still wanted to learn about Zande witchcraft, magic, and sorcery, he sent his cook to study with a witch doctor. Each evening the cook reported to Evans-Pritchard the progress of his apprenticeship.

The Evans-Pritchard option, however, was quite impossible. My cook was a woman, Bankano, and as far as I knew, women could not become sorkos. My friend Idrissa was a possible candidate. Tense as taut wire, Idrissa was still preoccupied with marital and economic difficulties; he would certainly not be excited by the prospect of becoming the apprentice of a sorko. Poor Idrissa. He was slow and made up in sincerity what he lacked in talent. The father of his first wife forced upon him a divorce even though he and Jitu cared very much for one another. Alone in Mehanna, he married another woman whom he grew to detest. She bore him a child he did not want. This second wife drained Idrissa of his meager financial resources. Idrissa was out of the question.

Should I risk becoming an apprentice? I thought of Castaneda, with whom I did not want to be compared. In general anthropologists frown upon subjective accounts of anthropological fieldwork. And the questionable authenticity of Castaneda's work made subjective accounts of supernatural acts even more risky in the profession. If Castaneda's work proved to be an elaborate hoax, a brilliant effort to make a lot of money as a best-selling author, what would my colleagues think of a descriptive account of my West African apprenticeship to a sorko? But my internal debate about Idrissa, Evans-Pritchard, and Castaneda only masked the real reason I was waffling about becoming Sorko Djibo's apprentice: I was afraid, and not only of what Djibo might teach me. I anticipated widening ripples of consequences, not the least of which was danger—physical and psychological—to myself. And there were certainly social issues: How would becoming a sorko's apprentice change me as a person? Would other sorkos accept me, a white man?

The aroma of Bankano's peanut sauce freed me from my existential conceits. She was standing next to my straw mat and beaming at me.

"Open the large casserole."

I opened it to discover a small mountain of millet paste capped with melted butter which had been flavored with onion flour. I looked up at Bankano and smiled back approvingly. Without looking, I knew the peanut vapor came from the small casserole blooming with the same enamel flowers as the millet-laden pot. Idrissa, who never arrived home before Bankano made her tasty deliveries, slid into the compound to join me for dinner. He sat down with me on the straw mat and we ate with our right hands. We each took some millet from the mound, rolled it into a ball, and holding the small ball of millet with our thumbs and first two fingers, dipped it into the peanut sauce. And so we ate, until, satiated, we said, *A wasa*, "It is enough." We washed down the millet with water and burped. Our meal finished, we could talk.

"You were at your garden today, Idrissa?"

"Yes. Soon I harvest lettuce and manioc."

"May Allah lighten your burden, Idrissa." I paused to swipe at a mosquito. "Djibo Mounmouni came to visit today."

"You let him in again?"

"Yes. Why should I not let him in?"

Idrissa wagged his finger at me. "Djibo is a worthless Zerma. Do not trust him. He's after your money. He lies. He rapes women. Paul, do not see him."

"He seems to be quite a decent fellow. And besides, he tells me that he is a sorko."

Idrissa nodded and leaned toward me.

"He is a bad sorko," he said, his voice quavering. "Be careful. If you see him, it will be bad for you."

"What will be bad for me, Idrissa?"

Idrissa refused to elaborate. He sprang toward the door and left the compound to talk with his friends or to seek some womanly comfort. I remained on the mat. Not knowing much about sorkos and their motivations, I was both frightened and fascinated. The moon, so full and bright that evening that one could read in its light, calmed me. In the distance I heard the gravelly voice of a BBC disc jockey announcing a requested song. I walked to the door of my compound to survey the Mehanna market in the night. The dim glow of kerosene lanterns outlined the open doors of the shops which bordered the market area. Young men gathered in clusters at rough wooden tables, drank coffee, and murmured—probably about young women. My thoughts returned to Djibo and his invitation. Why would Djibo reveal himself to me now? If I questioned his motives, I had to examine mine as a human being and as an anthropologist. I had arrived at a crossroads. I couldn't refuse an opportunity to learn magic from the inside. I couldn't deny my private desire to become a more powerful person. Slowly I walked back into my house and saw the two birds perched in the rafters near their nest.

6

SORKO DJIBO

Sorko Djibo's family compound was located atop a sand dune at the edge of Mehanna in a neighborhood of people who had recently arrived in Mehanna from the Songhay-speaking regions to the east. The least desirable neighborhood in Mehanna, it is situated next to the spot at the edge of town where many people defecate, and the stench is a constant reminder.

Walking to the compound was arduous. I found that while picking my way around the fresh animal droppings and jagged chicken bones strewn over every part of the path, it was difficult to get good foot traction in the soft, deep dune sand. And sandaled feet had to contend with the ever-present *kram-kram*, a grass spore with skin-piercing needles which seemed to wait in ambush for vulnerable toes.

The family residence consisted of four straw huts shaped like beehives. The compound was separated from the bush by a three-foot fence of dried millet stalks which had been attached to tree branches anchored in the sand. Sorko Djibo lived in the compound with his wife Maymuna, his father, the master sorko Mounmouni Koda, Djibo's unmarried sister Hampsu, and his brother Zakaribaba, also a practicing sorko.

I clapped my hands three times at the compound's entrance. Djibo bounded out of one of the huts, followed by his father and his sister. They all greeted me, and Djibo bade me sit down on a worn mat of woven palm fronds. After some small talk about the weather, Mounmouni Koda and Hampsu left Djibo and me alone.

"My heart pounds strongly. It is good that you come here today, Paul. We shall begin to learn about my heritage."

"Yes, I am here. Are you in good health? And your family's health?"

The Ethnographer's Office in Mehanna

"May God be praised." Djibo hesitated for an instant and then asked. "Why did you come?"

"I don't know."

Djibo laughed. "Ah, that is the best answer. If we do not know then we must search for answers. Is this not true?"

I shrugged.

Djibo continued. "I have talked to my father and told him what happened yesterday in your house. He said it will be good to teach you about us, but you must learn as we learn."

I was still troubled by questions of ethics. "How could you or your father teach your secrets to a white man?"

Laughter shook Djibo's body. "What difference does it make?"

There was so much bluster in Djibo's talk that I wondered if I could trust him. "Djibo, I need an answer, a reason. I cannot walk aimlessly in the world."

Djibo's face froze. His eyes narrowed into a penetrating stare that was directed away from me. "I cannot give you the answer. I cannot give you the meaning. You must discover these things for yourself. And this can occur only when your heart is clean and strong. First we must teach you to hear."

"To hear?"

"Yes, to hear." Djibo stood up, his sign that our meeting was at its end. We walked hand in hand, as do all good friends among the Songhay, to the entrance of his compound.

"Come to the grain warehouse tonight," Djibo told me.

In a black, moonless night the malodor of generations of urine identified the grain warehouse. Located inside a large compound, the warehouse was a big three-room mudbrick house which had been whitewashed. Mountains of hundred-kilo sacks of millet filled the warehouse itself. Djibo's cousin Moussa, the government civil servant who managed the grain operation in Mehanna, had at one time lived in the warehouse. Early in his tenure at Mehanna he built a small one-room mudbrick house in a corner of the compound. He then hired his cousin, Djibo, to guard the compound at night. Djibo's job, for which he was paid $40 a month, made the sorko one of the more prosperous people in Mehanna. He at least had a steady monthly income.

During the day the warehouse compound hummed with activity. The government had built many such warehouses in the major market towns in Niger. In case of drought, which is not an uncommon occurrence in Sahelian Niger, surplus millet could be sold to hungry peasants for a price lower than the market rate. On most days local merchants came to visit Moussa with offers to sell grain. The merchants talked, sipped green tea, and left. Between these visits Moussa enjoyed the company of his family: his wife Fado, the three cousins for whom Moussa was responsible, and his daughter Biba. Despite the relative spaciousness of the warehouse compound, its location near the market disrupted Moussa's family life. Soon after his arrival in Mehanna, Moussa moved to a neighborhood far from the market. Djibo now had the warehouse to himself at night and had moved his most precious possessions into the small one-room house.

I crossed the market area on my way to the warehouse that night. Groups of men sat around their market tables and mumbled about market prices, the Songhay nobles, and women. They said hello to me as I passed their tables. Finally, I reached the entrance to the warehouse yard and clapped my hands three times.

"Enter."

I pushed the door open and entered the compound. It was quiet and cool inside. February in Mehanna means cool windless nights with skies embroidered with thousands of twinkling stars and hundreds of meteors streaking white in fleeting moments of disintegration.

"Come into my house," I heard Djibo say.

The door to Djibo's house was open. A lantern flickered inside the house. I approached and stepped inside. He unrolled a woven palm-frond mat for me to sit upon and, once I had sat down, pointed to a low stool. The stool was roughly constructed of cast-off wood and rusty nails. Djibo had covered its seat with a piece of black cloth. Toward the front edge of the stool, Djibo had arranged fourteen small vials of perfume in a semicircle. Within the space of the semicircle there were three large objects. The first was a shallow rectangular can which had once held shotgun shells. The second object was a round tin can, the kind in which hard candies might be packed. The third object was a vial of perfume. The cork of this vial had a nail sticking through it, and the entire object had been wrapped in black thread. Djibo had draped this black-coated vial of perfume with a string of metal worry beads.

Djibo noticed my intense observation. "These are my things."

"What are they?"

"No questions," he said firmly. "Remember your mind and heart are empty. They must be filled with strength so that you learn how to ask good questions."

How I wanted to tell Djibo that my work was too important to dillydally over what is and what is not a good question. I wanted to tell him that I was an anthropologist and that I could never learn his way. If I was so ignorant, I needed to ask questions from the beginning. But I refrained from communicating these thoughts to Djibo. Instead, I played Djibo's game. "This is very difficult for me, Djibo."

"Oh yes, it is very difficult. It is dangerously difficult. But somehow, with patience, you will become a hard man."

"Hard?" I asked, knowing full well what Djibo intended.

"Never mind," Djibo replied. "We must begin with sound. Let us begin with a simple text."

Djibo's method of teaching texts was simple and straightforward: the student repeated the text until he had memorized it. Once he had memorized the text, he had to reproduce it rapidly without flaws in pronunciation. Passing this examination, the student began the next text. Such a pattern of learning, I was told, might continue a lifetime; Djibo admitted that he was still learning texts from his father.

My first text, an incantation for a reddish powder called *korombey*, consisted of six lines. Djibo recited each line and instructed me to repeat what he had recited. We spent about thirty minutes working on this text. I mastered the text quickly, which surprised Djibo. From the body of the text I divined that korombey is used to protect people from injury, for in the text it is said that the powder prevents all parts of the human body from injury. If one had an accident some time after ingesting this reddish powder, he or she would avoid breaking a neck or an elbow. Or if injuries were inevitable, they would not be as serious as those suffered by the unprotected. But there were unfamiliar words in the text. Somehow they might be potent; they might carry the magical force of the incantation. I asked Djibo about these words.

"Come back tomorrow," was Djibo's answer.

7

AN APPRENTICE'S FIRST MISSION

When I knew Djibo only as the Zerma farmer who came to my house to watch me type my field notes, he never talked about his own life. Even after I had been his apprentice for some time, he talked little of his past. He was born in the Zerma town of Ouallam, which is situated in a dry windswept plain known as Zermagunda, "the belly of the Zerma." He did not talk about his mother, but he enjoyed recounting his father's exploits. Moumouni Koda, I was told, could immerse himself in the waters of the Niger River and emerge completely dry. The old man also spent as many as three days under the Niger visiting the domain of the water spirits. When Djibo was ready, he, too, would learn how to perform these incredible feats. Djibo burned to learn these secrets, but he told me that he would have to wait until his father lay on his deathbed, for no sorko would reveal such precious secrets to his successor until he was about to die.

On the second night of my apprenticeship, when Mehanna was dark and quiet, I slipped through the night and entered Djibo's house in the warehouse yard. We greeted one another, and Djibo said:

"I am running short of korombey. You must go to the bush tomorrow and find some for me."

"What? You show me a powder and I am supposed to go and find the plant in the bush tomorrow. Are you crazy?"

Djibo ignored my protests. "I need korombey, and I want you to find some for me," he snapped. He took out a black vinyl bag which was filled with dusty cloth pouches. He opened one pouch which held a reddish powder—and put of pinch of it in my open palm. "Taste it."

I winced at the bitterness. "Echhh!" I spit it out.

Djibo smiled and slapped me on the back. "This is korombey bark. Bring me some tomorrow."

"But how?"

"You will find a path." He turned his head away from me and searched through the bag for another powder. Finding what he was looking for, he opened the pouch to reveal a gritty powder which was brownish green; it had an acrid smell. "This is diggi, our special powder." He then taught me the incantation which would imbue the powder with power.

The text, a poem with a complex set of bizarre metaphors, was not too difficult to memorize. Whenever I stumbled, however, Djibo barked that I was slow-witted. I let him play his game. Meanwhile I attempted to uncover the meaning of the text. In one line of the text one recites, "They say bam, bam, bam. They say bum, bum, bum." I had never heard these Songhay terms, which reminded me of the

"Bams" and "Booms" of Batman. And then there was the mention of war in the text. What did the reference to war indicate? Was war a metaphor for something else? If so, what? In another part of the text one recites: "When the war comes they will become kokoro leaves. . . . They become red beetles. . . . They will become cow droppings." Who or what became a cow dropping? And who, as the text suggested, would become invisible? Who would never be taken by whom? With my curiosity so piqued, I failed to concentrate on the task at hand—memorization. I forgot this line. I mispronounced that word. I skipped another line, omitted one word, or mangled another.

"Can I bring a tape-recorder and use the tape to memorize the text?" I asked, concealing my real intention, which was to be able to study the text and discover its meaning.

"No," Djibo said without raising his voice. He stood up abruptly, turned his back to me, and informed me that it was time to leave.

After a restless night I ate the breakfast that had become my custom during the previous six months in Mehanna: instant coffee, stale bread (except on market day), canned margarine, and mango jam. Idrissa joined me. In silence we heaped margarine and jam on the bread and then dipped it into our coffee. My first assignment as an apprentice was much on my mind that morning. Although Djibo had not cautioned me, I knew that I could not reveal to anyone the purpose of my mission—to procure medicines for a sorko. Since I knew nothing about the trees and the vines of the Songhay bush, I enlisted the aid of Idrissa. Since Idrissa was a native son and a gardener, I reasoned that he would know a great deal about the flora in and around Mehanna.

"Do you know about the trees in the bush, Idrissa?"

"Yes," he said timidly.

"That is good. I want to learn about the trees and bushes."

"Good," he muttered.

"Tell me, can one find the korombey tree in Mehanna?"

Idrissa frowned. "We have it near Mehanna. It is very tall. We have all the good trees in Mehanna."

"That is good, Idrissa." I stood up. "Let's go to the bush and look at the trees."

Idrissa seemed less than enthusiastic about walking through the bush and introducing me to trees. With an air of resignation, he went into his house and put on his plastic shoes. I put on my hiking boots.

"Idrissa, maybe we can find a korombey tree." As we were leaving the compound, I told Idrissa to bring his large knife. "I will need to bring back some samples."

So began our ramble. As we walked through town, I wrapped a white turban around my head, for the sun's rays would certainly be intense on a morning in late February. We marched down the Kokoro road, which takes the traveler west through dune country to the regional administrative center of Tera, some eighty kilometers to the west. Following the road, we climbed the hundred-foot dune which marked the western edge of town. Like most roads in the Mehanna region, this one consisted only of deep truck tracks in the soft sand. At the crest of the dune we had a magnificent view of Mehanna and the Niger, which sparkled in the bright morning light. Most of the Mehanna compounds were obscured by the sweeping green of acacia trees. This mass of green stood in sharp contrast to the brown expanse of the surrounding Sahelian countryside.

We walked westward past millet fields, which were distinguished by rows of stumps of millet stalks. We saw many such fields and stumps, but only a few trees. In the distance, two indigo-garbed Fulan women approached us on foot. With large jugs of sour milk balanced on their heads, they plodded every day from Gukko, their village in the bush, to Mehanna. I greeted them in their language, but I must have butchered the phrases, for they returned my greeting in Songhay.

We had trudged through the sand for more than an hour when we reached a cluster of straw huts. "This is Gukko, Monsieur Paul."

My legs ached. "I've been to Gukko before. But why did we come here?"

Idrissa pointed to a shrinking pond. "Over there. Your trees are over there."

After greeting the people in Gukko, he led me to the drying water hole. Idrissa chose a rather tall tree which had many thorns on its branches; its green leaves were rounded, thick, and waxy. "This is korombey, Monsieur Paul."

Perhaps the six-kilometer trip had been worth the effort. I would not return to Djibo's house empty-handed. "Give me the knife, Idrissa." I cut off some bark. Idrissa took it from me and we started back to Mehanna.

Thirsty and hungry from the twelve-kilometer walk in soft sand and hot sun, we dragged ourselves into our compound. I entered the house and deposited myself in my folding chair. I noticed that Bankano's daughter had brought the blessing of lunch in our absence. Idrissa and I ate with gusto a meal of rice and fish in zesty tomato sauce. At mid-afternoon Idrissa left the compound to pray. I fingered the piece of bark we had brought back from Gukko. What would it look like in powdered form? Driven by this great empirical question and a lack of confidence in Idrissa's skill as an herbalist, I placed a small piece of bark in a mortar, took up a pestle and pulverized it. It was the wrong stuff; it was a greenish-brown powder. What was I going to tell Djibo that night?

Powder in hand, I bolted from the compound and ran to the marketplace. There was a man who frequented the market area who sold multicolored powders on market day. I found this man sitting in his market stall, talking to another man. The man who sold powders gazed at me and smiled. The skin of his hands was like sun-baked leather, but when he touched my hand it was with the gentleness of a child.

"Sit down, Monsieur Paul. What brings you here today?"

I opened my hand to show him the powder. "What kind of plant is this?"

The man touched the powder with his forefinger. He tasted a pinch of it.

"Well?"

"That's garbey, Monsieur Paul."

Oh, Idrissa, how could you! Given my previous experience with questionnaires and information in general, I should have learned that people, even if they know nothing about something, will give an answer or theory, just to be polite. "Garbey," I muttered to the man. "I was looking for korombey. Do you have any?"

Without answering me, the man rummaged through a pile of assorted pieces of bark and threw one piece into my lap. "That's it, isn't it?" the man asked.

"Sure it is," I murmured, hiding my ignorance. "How much do I owe you?"

"Give me 50 francs (15 cents)." With the guilt of a schoolboy who has cheated, I gave the man his money and prepared myself for another evening session with Djibo.

Long after my after-dinner guests had left my compound, I walked to the warehouse compound. Along the path, I greeted the shop owners and their cronies. Seated, as usual, on the mudbrick stoops of their two-room shops, they reminded me of the denizens of the row houses of south Philadelphia on a hot summer night. Since all of the shops had virtually the same stock—salt, canned sardines, soap, cloth, bubble gum, dates, batteries and kerosene—I wondered why a client would trade at a particular shop. There were no special sales in Mehanna.

There was a group of deaf people seated at a table near the grain warehouse. Like the other men in town, they would pass their evenings together, discussing with animation the events of the day. Over the months they had taught me a few of their signs, especially ones with sexual connotations. One man, who was tall and strong with a chiseled face as perfect as the work of a fine sculptor, taught me ritual insults in sign language. Each time I saw him I would proclaim myself a woman who lusted after his fine body. He would say that I was a man. I would protest. He would proclaim his lack of interest. I would counter that he was impotent. He would say that his potency shrank with the sight of a woman with no breasts, and so on.

Having declared myself a woman to the deaf man once again, I entered the warehouse yard. Sitting on the sand floor of his house, Djibo was wearing a pair of tattered green trousers with one remaining belt loop and a sleeveless black-and-white striped tunic made from locally spun heavy cotton. The room was dark except for the dim glow of the lantern. Djibo's round black face glimmered. His bloodshot eyes were like beacons of light.

"You look awful," I told him. "Haven't you been sleeping well?"

"I never sleep well," Djibo said morosely. "My father never sleeps well. My grandfather never slept well."

"But why, tell me?"

Djibo ignored my questions. "Show me the korombey."

I pulled a small cloth pouch from my pocket and put it on the sand. I opened the pouch slowly and pushed it toward Djibo. He felt it with his forefinger, tasted it, and told me that what I had brought was indeed korombey.

"Recite the text," he ordered.

I recited it rapidly and made no mistakes.

"Where did you find this korombey?"

I had dreaded this question, but I decided to tell Djibo the truth. I recounted my naive quest for the korombey tree. I told him of Idrissa's identification of a garbey rather than a korombey tree.

Djibo didn't laugh at my story. "I am surprised that Idrissa does not know the bush. His people are hunters and magicians from Wanzerbe, the great magic village of the Songhay." Djibo continued to feel the korombey I had brought him. "Tell me, how did you find this korombey?"

"I went to Saadu the Hausa herbalist and asked him for some."

"And he gave it to you for a price?"

"Yes."

"How much?"

"50 francs."

Djibo stared at the powder. "Not a bad price, Paul. You are clever. You accomplished your mission. You see, one must walk at least twenty kilometers to find a korombey tree around here.

"Aha! I understand."

"Do you?" Djibo paused a few moments and shot me a darting glance. "Let's go to the next step on your path. Recite the diggi text."

I recited the text but made many errors. Djibo told me that I needed to use a system for memorization. He recited one line of the text and then etched a straight line in the sand with his forefinger—a mnemonic tactic. He told me to repeat the text line by line in the same manner. Soon thereafter I was able to recite the text correctly. This segment of the lesson accomplished, Djibo revealed to me the powders which made up the diggi mixture. The green powder he called *wata gaya gaya,* but he did not teach me its incantation. He told me to touch a beige powder, which he called *kafia mallam.* This plant, which grows at the edge of the river, is used only in sorcery potions. The other ingredients consisted of korombey; *siria,* a reddish-brown powder from the siria tree; *kobey,* the mauve powder from the bark of the kobe tree; the fat of a black goat; and *saa nya,* a white powder Djibo refused to discuss.

"Why are all of these plants used?"

"I do not know," Djibo answered. "My father says that I have not yet learned enough to ask correct questions. He does not give answers to wrong questions just as I do not give answers to your bad questions."

"It will take me forever to learn this sorko stuff."

"What is your hurry?" Djibo asked. "My father studied with his father for forty years. I have been studying with my father and other men for almost twenty years. There are many things I will not learn until my father reveals them to me on his deathbed."

I was overwhelmed with the undertaking I had accepted. "How can I ever do it?"

"If you want to learn, you will a find a way. With patience and hardness you'll learn."

Djibo closed his pouches and placed all but one of them carefully into his black vinyl bag. "You must now learn the incantation for this powder." He opened the last pouch to reveal a gritty black substance which looked like pulverized charcoal. "This is *ngimgniti.*"

The incantation spoke to the powers of the substance ngimgniti. One who ate ngimgniti, according to the incantation, could defeat in battle the evil sorcerers, the evil genies, the evil spirits, the evil witches, and even Satan. So powerful was ngimgniti that one who ingested it was protected from the fearsome *Tooru*, the most powerful spirits in the Songhay pantheon. To Djibo's surprise, I mastered this text quickly.

"Are there many more texts?"

"Many more," Djibo said.

"How can I learn them all before I have to return to America? I will be leaving in four months."

"You learn quickly, but you cannot possibly learn everything."

"Then what am I to do?"

"You will have to come back, won't you?"

"But can't I write down the incantations? Will you repeat some of them slowly?"

"No, I won't. Only after you have memorized the words will I allow you to put them in your book."

8

IMMERSED IN TEXTS

Djibo immersed me in memorization. So busy was I with the memorization of texts that I did not have the time to figure out what they meant, let alone how they corresponded to the vagaries of Songhay culture. I worried that I was failing my mission as an anthropologist. I could easily spend more than six months at memorizing texts, and to what avail? How would I justify this waste of time to my dissertation committee or any other responsible professional? Besides, memorizing the texts was boring.

After the initial sessions, however, Djibo's lessons extended beyond texts for specific powders to include praise-poems for the deities of the Songhay pantheon. While each spirit—all 150 of them—had a praise-poem, Sorko Djibo explained to me, he concerned himself with the Tooru spirits, for they were the nobles of the spirit world. The Tooru spirits controlled the great forces like thunder, lightning, the winds, and the formation of clouds. Dongo, the deity of thunder, is the most important deity for the sorko. Djibo insisted that I learn the praise-poems for Dongo first.

First the text mentions diggi, the mixture of powders that gives the sorko extraordinary strength. Then the text expounds on the attributes of Dongo. According to the text, Dongo made a great rock in the sky. The rock is called Wanzam. Dongo's magic protects a person from lightning. Dongo's knowledge and power exceeds that of the sorko and surpasses that of the sorko's slave. Dongo strikes people and they fall to the left and the right. Dongo strikes people and they fall forward. His work completed, Dongo returns to the sky. Dongo says that the sun is his shadow. Dongo also says his shadow covers the sun.

Djibo told me that Dongo is the father of all the sorko since the first sorko, Faran Maka Bote. He also warned that if I did not learn the text well, Dongo would punish me in some horrible way. Given this kind of encouragement, I learned the text rapidly and recited it to Djibo's satisfaction in short order. My rapid success with the praise-poem to Dongo encouraged Djibo to teach me a text for another powerful spirit, Nya Beri, which translates roughly as "Great Mother." Great Mother is among the most dangerous of the Songhay spirits. She is the mother of the spirits of the cold (Hargay), which cause miscarriages, stillbirths, and other debilitating diseases and death.

The text makes clear that, despite being female, Nya Beri is something of a giant—bigger and stronger than any Songhay man. Nya Beri can stare into the sun and see. She can look at the moon and see. In fresh milk, she can see the future. In blood, Nya Beri sees the past. She sees all and knows all. Since she is so big and strong, Nya Beri inhabits the place of death. She is always in front of a person; she is always behind a person. Nya Beri can also be wicked. The text ends with a list of Nya Beri's children.

Despite himself, Djibo was impressed with my progress. "In time you might learn enough of these texts to be initiated as an apprentice sorko."

Because of my progress, Djibo felt that I was ready to learn what he considered to be the most difficult text that a sorko must master. This difficult text consisted of a series of praise-songs to the Tooru spirits.

The text begins with the genealogy of the spirits of the Songhay pantheon. Someone gives birth to Suntunga, but the text does not specify Suntunga's mother or father. The same mysterious parents give birth to Mantunga, to Banio, to Banio Cirey.

"How am I supposed to learn the genealogy of the spirits," I complained, "if the text does not specify the original ancestors?"

As was his custom, Djibo said: "Memorize first, ask questions later."

And so I memorized the incomplete genealogy. The next section of the text was tougher, for it named a number of trees I did not know. I had never seen the Sah tree, the Dugu tree, the Wali belinga tree, the Kasah Tobe tree, or the Nyama Nyama Koro tree. But the next line touched familiar territory: Harakoy Dikko, the goddess of the Niger River, the queen of the small and great spirit festivals. But the relief of recognition soon dissipated with the next lines of the text, which say simply: "It is the place of the Kogo tree. The great river's Belinga tree. It has the Kwomno Kosi tree. Its hands leave the Sami tree and it hands return to the Sami tree. Wandu will heal and make one strong. There is Wandu, it stands in pure white sand. The sand has food and water. If the initiated take from this Tooru sand, they will go mad. Those who know the Tooru will eat this special food and laugh."

Many of the Songhay terms in the text were new to me. While I was learning the text, I wondered about the meanings of many of the new words. Were some of the terms borrowed from another language? I posed this question to Djibo, who told me to be patient.

And so I continued to learn this long text. We came to the part of the text which discusses the exploits of Maaru, deity of water holes and lightning. I memorized: "Maaru's work is quiet and forceful. Health and God's blessing. They ask: 'What have you taken?' They say: 'Sorcery.' When they speak the words of magic, they eat magic cake. The sorcery is strong. The mother chicken does not clean dirt from her chick's eyes."

I did not understand the passage about the deity Maaru. How was Maaru connected to the practice of magic? Was he the patron saint of the great Songhay sorcerers, the Sohanci, the the descendants through the father's line of Sonni Ali Ber, the Magic King of the Songhay Empire, who ruled from 1463 to 1491?

As my frustrations mounted, Djibo taught me the next passage, a praise-poem to Nya Beri which was considerably shorter than the one I had previously learned. I memorized: "Nya Beri has power in and out of water. She is the guardian of the Tooru behind the house. For them there are prayers only to the spirits, not to Allah. They killed 150 people with their spell. Their sister also killed 150 with her spell."

Djibo continued to work with me day after day. He taught me the part of the text which spoke to the supernatural exploits of Moussa Nyori, the spirit hunter who controlled the formation of clouds. Questions grew in my mind: Who were the Tooru behind the house? Who killed 150 people with their spell? Why was Nya Beri powerful both in and out of water? And what about the part about praying to the spirits and not to Allah? Did this imply a certain anti-Islamic sentiment among Songhay practitioners of sorcery and possession?

Days passed and Djibo continued to drill me on Moussa Nyori. Finally, I recited the entire text without error, including the section about Moussa Nyori: "Moussa Nyori. Men are carried on his shoulders. He carries a man and a horse on his shoulders. He carries a man and steals a man's body fiber, changing it into a black egg. This is how he takes a man and slings him over his shoulder. If he should take a man's head, the man's head-fibers will bubble like boiling water. If he stops in a man's body, the man must not lift his ankle. He is Moussa Nyori. He awakened the angels and sees them. One must not hurt oneself by doing bad deeds. When you take a cowry shell for magic, it is lost to the spirits. The spirits feel sadness from their loss. There is ever more sadness in the sorko's Ndebbi [intermediary between God and human beings] chant."

Upon hearing my flawless recitation, Djibo proclaimed that he and his father would soon initiate me as a *sorko benya*.

"Wait a minute," I said. "Why must I be a sorko benya? That is a sorko's slave, is it not?"

Djibo smirked. "Is your father a sorko? Was your father's father a sorko?"

"No, of course not."

"Well, then you must be a sorko benya. Think about the texts you have learned and you will understand."

What I didn't understand was why Djibo, who seemed contemptuous of me, was teaching me about his heritage.

9

WANZERBE

Idrissa did not like Sorko Djibo. From the beginning of my association with Djibo, Idrissa warned me that Djibo could not be trusted. When I told Idrissa about my apprenticeship with Sorko Djibo, he warned me again about Djibo's character. He was especially worried that Djibo wanted to exploit me. Despite warnings and my own vague suspicions, I continued to study with Sorko Djibo.

After more than one month of my studies, Idrissa tried a different tack. He suggested that we travel to Wanzerbe, the fabled city of Songhay sorcery. He explained that he was born in Wanzerbe and that he knew the greatest Sohanci of all the Songhay. Despite his own lack of talent, Idrissa was from a family of great hunters and healers; Idrissa's mother's kin, however, constituted the greatest of the sorcerer families. In fact, his father's current wife was none other than Kassey, a woman who was a legendary sorceress. If we went to Wanzerbe, Idrissa told me, he would introduce me to Kassey. "If you want sorcery," he told me, "come to Wanzerbe. Only the truth for you, Monsieur Paul." I had heard about Kassey. Other people in Mehanna had mentioned her to me, and Jean Rouch, the French filmmaker and specialist on the Songhay, told me that her knowledge of sorcery was unsurpassed in the Songhay world. How could I pass up such an opportunity?

We made preparations to travel to Wanzerbe. First I informed my friends of our upcoming departure. Second, we arranged our transportation. Since Wanzerbe was so remote, it was not possible to find a ride in a bush taxi or truck. We decided to go there on horseback. I already had a horse that could make the trip, and I sent Idrissa into town to find another horse that we could rent. My friends and enemies in Mehanna told me that I was foolish. "You are an Anasara. How can you hope to ride a horse all the way to Wanzerbe and back?" "It is too hot. This is March. We all know that the sun is merciless in March. You will fall off your horse and die."

I paid no attention to these doomsayers. Idrissa maintained a anxious silence. When our preparations had been completed, we saddled our horses, put blankets over the saddles, attached our water bottles to the pommels of the saddles and mounted. We trotted out of Mehanna. People asked us where we were going. "Wanzerbe," I told them.

"May God protect you on your journey," they invariably told us.

As we rode up the dune, I turned around and looked at Mehanna. The air was still cool, and a fine dust hung over the village like fog. Soon we could no longer see Mehanna. We rode to the northwest over tracks in the soft sand. Lugi was to be the first village on our itinerary. The tracks passed through a long range of sand dunes.

Then we came upon a vast plain of laterite, the surface of which was so hard that few plants were able to emerge from it. In March the Songhay bush is parched. We saw no grass along the road and no evidence of plant growth. We did see many dead trees and vast stretches of rock, which I realized was petrified wood. After three hours of continuous riding we came upon Lugi, a village of Bella farmers and herdsmen, the former slaves of the Tuareg people, the famous Blue Men of the Sahara. For the first time in three hours, we dismounted. My whole body ached, but I said nothing. Already it was hot, and I had drunk most of my water. We sat for a while in the cool shade of Moussa's house. Moussa, who was Idrissa's friend, told us it would take at least five hours to travel from Lugi to Bankilare, where we expected to spend the night. "You should rest first, and then leave for Bankilare." Moussa filled our water bottles. "There is very little water between here and Bankilare. Travel slowly, and if you are weary seek the shade of a tree."

We left Lugi at noon, having eaten a tasty lunch of rice, sauce, and meat. We headed northwest into a wide, sandy plain devoid of trees and even scrub brush. In the distance we saw Amara, another Bella village, which sat like a cluster of bee hives shimmering in the noon-day sun. Ahead of us loomed a large dune, the end of which could not be seen. Idrissa's worry made him look back at me repeatedly; he didn't want his white man to fall off a horse and die in the bush.

"You all right, Monsieur Paul?"

"Yes."

"Good. We go up the dune and ride for a long time."

Once up the dune, we looked out into the vast expanse of the region. Thrusting up from the flat emptiness of the barren brown plain, the dunes broke the monotony of the landscape. The brilliance of the noon light reduced our vision to only a few kilometers. We both sweated profusely and drank a great deal of water. Idrissa pointed ahead of us. "Look," he said, "Abdu Kwara."

I saw a cluster of straw huts. "Is that Abdu Kwara?"

"Yes. There are Fulan [Peul] there. They will give us water, maybe milk, too."

We arrived in Abdu Kwara. Three Songhay-speaking Fulan women greeted us. They asked after our health and asked us where we were going.

"Bankilare is very far from here. You must drink some milk before continuing," one of the woman suggested.

Another woman walked into her straw hut and brought us a bowl of milk. Idrissa and I drained the bowl. Then the women gave us more water for our bottles. We thanked them for their generosity and left.

The trail curved to the west. We passed a number of ponds that were nearly dried up and a grove of trees and looked ahead to an endless plain which seemed as barren as a moonscape. "Don't drink too much, Monsieur Paul; no water ahead."

I nodded, and our trotting horses carried us inexorably westward. The heat of the day reached its peak now. The sun scorched the rocklike surface of the plain and swallowed our strength. We saw not a living thing in this bush. I grew weak from overexposure to the sun. Idrissa kept looking back. Two hours passed. Finally, we saw a group of straw huts in the distance. Excited by the prospect of seeing other human beings in this desolate region, we kicked our tired horses and cantered up to the dwellings. A Bella man emerged from one of the huts and greeted us in halting Songhay. He explained that his wives had gone off to a distant well, but he could refill our water bottles.

"Are you headed to Bankilare?" he asked.

"We are," Idrissa answered.

"How much time will it take?" I asked, wondering if our trip would ever end.

"It is far from here. You might get there at sunset."

Idrissa agreed and suggested that we get back to the path that led to Bankilare. We continued to ride to the west, into the burning sun. In the late afternoon we entered an area of scattered water holes surrounded by thick brush, plants, and trees. For every water hole we saw, there was a corresponding village of Bella. "They're slaves of the Bankilare Tuaregs," Idrissa told me.

"Slaves?" I responded. "How could there be slaves in this day and age?

"They still give millet to the noble Tuaregs in Bankilare."

"Hmm."

Even as I was becoming dizzy atop my horse, Idrissa announced that we were approaching Bankilare. My dizziness faded. I kicked my horse and we cantered into the village, which consisted of one large mudbrick house, the residence of the *chef de poste*, and an assortment of smaller two-room mudbrick houses and nomadic tents made from camel hide. We rode down past the residence of the district administrator and made our way to Hamidou's house, the very last house on the western edge of town. Like Idrissa, Hamidou, who was Idrissa's cousin, was a native of Wanzerbe. Unlike Idrissa, Hamidou could read and write and was a corporal in the Border Guard.

He patrolled on camel the Mali-Niger border, which was only twenty kilometers north of Bankilare.

Hamidou greeted us warmly and gave us cool water to drink. He called his son, who removed the saddles from our horses and took them to the pond for a long-awaited drink. "I will give them millet to eat when they get back," Hamidou said. He asked Idrissa about people in Mehanna, and Idrissa asked him about the people in Wanzerbe. While they continued this small talk, I went off to the residence of the district administrator to pay him a courtesy call.

The district administrator, a Hausa from the eastern region of Niger, was about my age. He spoke impeccable French and welcomed me enthusiastically. We sat down on comfortable canvas chairs and his servant brought us two Coca Colas that were ice-cold. We discussed my research project, which piqued his interest. He invited me to dinner, but I declined respectfully. "Hamidou has already invited us to eat." He understood Songhay protocol. I suggested that we might dine together when I passed through Bankilare on my return to Mehanna. "By all means, Monsieur Paul. Come to dine with me when you return here."

When I returned to Hamidou's house, he was butchering a sheep he had slaughtered in honor of our visit. I was overwhelmed that a man who was obviously poor would slaughter an animal that was worth more than his meager monthly salary. Meanwhile, Hamidou's wife was busy making millet paste. She sat over her cooking pot, holding a large wooden spoon which she used to stir the thickening mixture of millet flour and water.

The sun went down and cool night breezes swept into Bankilare. Hamidou's face glowed in the light of the fire over which he was roasting mutton. Hamidou's wife brought us a heaping bowl of millet paste and sauce and gave us two wooden spoons. Hamidou cut the mutton into manageable pieces and served us the meat. We ate with gusto. Sensing our fatigue, Hamidou brought us two cots. Idrissa talked with his cousin, but I undressed, lay down on the cot, looked up at the star-filled sky, and fell into a deep sleep.

I woke at dawn to find Idrissa preparing the horses for our departure. My muscles were so stiff that I rolled off my cot without bending a joint. Hamidou prepared a quick cup of Nescafé and checked to see whether our saddles were fastened securely. We mounted our horses and left Bankilare.

Our afternoon destination was Tegeye, some thirty kilometers to the west. Our path took us through still more desolate plains of laterite strewn with thousands of volcanic rocks. We passed occasional water holes, but we no longer saw Bella villages, for we had left the Tuareg territories and had reentered regions governed by Songhay. From time to time, we would sight other solitary travelers—the unmistakable tall, spindly figure of a Fulan walking along with only a hardwood baton and a small gourd for water. After four hours of riding we came upon Tegeye. Like most villages in the region of Wanzerbe, Tegeye is situated on a small dune which is proximate to a water hole and wells.

Idrissa knew many people in Tegeye, whom he greeted. He directed us to a small mudbrick house which belonged to his paternal aunt, Kom. We dismounted and Kom told her son to water and feed the horses. Kom was a tall wiry woman whose tied-under-the-chin braids suggested an earlier era. She greeted both of us and insisted that we stay for lunch. "Idrissa, I will make you your favorite sauce."

Turning to me, Idrissa said: "We eat sesame sauce, Monsieur Paul. It is the best sauce anywhere." Then Kom trapped a chicken and slit its throat. Again, I felt a little guilty. Here was a woman even poorer than Idrissa's cousin in Bankilare, and she had just slaughtered a precious chicken in honor of our visit. I had not yet observed this kind of honor and hospitality in Mehanna. I mentioned this to Idrissa.

"In Wanzerbe, Monsieur Paul, you see the true Songhay. We are pure."

These were the Songhay for whom I had searched. They were proud, bound by codes of honor and hospitality, and they were hard. These qualities lured me deeper into the Songhay world, for they were traits that I admired, traits that I wanted to emulate, traits which would make me a forceful person.

We spent the afternoon at Kom's house and left for Wanzerbe after the late afternoon prayer. Idrissa said that we would reach Wanzerbe in three hours. We headed out to the west and immediately came upon a breathtaking panorama. The tracks took us through mountainous terrain covered by rocks so black that it seemed they had been scorched by fire. There were so many rocks across our path that the horses had to walk slowly to keep their footing. The gray and black mountains with their jagged outcroppings and rounded peaks were magnificent. More striking than the scenery was the silence, broken only by the sound of our horses' hoofs.

At dusk we passed the last mountain, Surgumeye, which overlooked Wanzerbe. Each year the people of Wanzerbe sacrifice a cow to the genie of the mountain, which protects the people of the village from famine and disease. From the vantage of Surgumeye, we saw Wanzerbe, which straddled two dunes. A line of trees meandered like a stream just beyond the village. Idrissa told me that they marked the Garuol River, which flowed only during the summer months.

Slowly we descended toward the village, veering toward the north side of town, which was divided by one road into two neighborhoods. Idrissa's family lived in Karia, the neighborhood to the north of the road, but Kassey, the famous sorceress, lived in Sohanci, which was south of the road. We rode into Karia, entering a large plaza bordered by a horseshoe of small two-room mudbrick houses. This was the compound of Idrissa's family, in which about seventy-five people lived. At the center of the plaza was a round house. This structure, Idrissa explained, was the cooking house. Wanzerbe was unlike any village I had ever encountered among the Songhay. The architecture was distinctive. The women wore the hairstyles of another age. We dismounted and were surrounded by well-wishers. Idrissa's father, Kundiababa, showed us to our lodgings.

We ate a hearty dinner of millet paste and sauce. Grilled mutton materialized. We ate a few pieces of the meat and passed the rest along to others. Then we received visitors, each of whom brought us a gift. One of Idrissa's uncles from the Sohanci neighborhood brought us a sheep. Idrissa's sister brought us three chickens. Idrissa's father gave us four chickens and a goat. Idrissa's neighbor brought one chicken and a gourd filled with millet. Someone else brought us honeycombs. We had more than enough food for our visit.

When our visitors finally left, I asked Idrissa about Kassey.

"Tomorrow, I'll go to her. She knows that you are here, Monsieur Paul."

In the morning we heated some water for coffee and ate some fried millet cakes. Idrissa left early to see his "mother," Kassey. Meanwhile, the children of Idrissa's huge compound came to sit in my house and stare at me. I jotted some notes, trying to reconstruct the two-day voyage on horseback. People from other compounds in Karia and Sohanci paid their respects to me and asked after Idrissa.

Idrissa returned with bad news. "Kassey will not see you, Monsieur Paul. Today she leaves Wanzerbe. She comes back next month."

"What! I came all this distance on horseback to see this woman, and she refuses to see me. Why, Idrissa, why?"

Idrissa looked down at the floor of our house; his body stiffened.

He burrowed his feet into the sand. "She said that she doesn't know you. There's no confidence in you. She says that one does not step over the snake hole if he is not confident."

"What does that mean?"

"She won't see you. She's going to Markoy. A boy there has spirit sickness. The cure will take a month."

"One month! We cannot spend one month here. We will not be able to see her, will we?"

"No. We can see other people."

Although I had fallen prey to another one of Idrissa's half-baked schemes, I decided to remain in Wanzerbe for one week. We met hundreds of people. I recorded some oral histories. One old man recited a magic incantation. I recorded some folksongs. We traveled ten kilometers to the north and visited Youmboum, a lake in which resided a crocodile. At Youmboum we met some hunters, two brothers in fact, whom I had seen in Jean Rouch's film, *The Lion Hunters*. Issiaka was a fearless hunter and a virtuoso on the monocord violin. His brother Wangari was a renowned praise-singer. They performed for Idrissa and me. I gave them a thousand francs and they gave us some smoked fish so that we might eat well that evening.

Our week passed quickly. We prepared for our return to Mehanna. The trip home was much easier than our trek to Wanzerbe. The horses seemed to be walking faster. Perhaps they knew that we were headed back to Mehanna. Idrissa was pleased that we were returning. I was still seething from Kassey's refusal to see me after our 120-kilometer trip on horseback. The hospitality of the people along our route home soothed the sting of Kassey's refusal. In Tegeye, in Bankilare, in Lugi, our friends extended to us the traditional Songhay hospitality. They also told me that they respected my courage. They had never seen or heard of a European who had ridden such a long distance on horseback. They had also never heard of a European who had spent as much time—one week—in dangerous Wanzerbe. In the late afternoon of our second day on horseback, we saw the waters of the Niger River glistening in the golden sunlight. Downstream we saw the rapids just north of Mehanna and we could hear the rush of water cascading over rocks. The hot Harmattan wind burned our faces, but we were home, at last.

We rode into town triumphantly. People greeted us. Children came up to shake our hands. "You are coming from Wanzerbe." "You have been to Wanzerbe." " Did you get sorcery in Wanzerbe?" " We must be careful around Monsieur Paul now that he has been to Wanzerbe."

We entered my compound and dismounted. Although I was disappointed about Kassey's rude refusal, I had completed a 240-kilometer trip to a fabled village to which most Songhay were afraid to travel. People in Mehanna now began to treat me with a degree of respect, as though my trip to Wanzerbe had demonstrated my fortitude, my hardness, my perseverance. I liked that. I liked that a lot.

10

INITIATION

After I returned from Wanzerbe, I resumed my studies with Djibo. So immersed was I in these studies that I failed to notice the change of the seasons in Mehanna. The fleeting heat of March had given way to the skin-blistering rays of April—discomforts which I never could have imagined. The French call April, May, and June in the Sahel *le soudure*. Soudure in French refers to making a joint—with solder—where there is a gap. In the Sahel, soudure refers to that time of the year when farmers run out of food and are waiting to harvest their crop. This gap in food reserves combines with the heat to make the soudure, which begins in April and ends only with the the first rains in early June, a dangerous time for Songhay. The heat is as scorching as the welder's torch. Even in the shade of a tree the air burns one's skin.

In April the sun, now a blazing orange disk, rises due east of Mehanna and sets due west. At midday all becomes still as people seek shelter from the sun, which is in the very center of the heat-bleached sky. There are no shadows at midday in April. Some people go outdoors early on April mornings when they might catch a soft cool breeze coming off the river. But with its unblinking April face, the sun soon heats the wind to blast-furnace intensity. This hot wind is relentless during the soudure; it can raise enough hot dust to obscure the islands some four hundred meters east of Mehanna. By midday and the afternoon meal, the heat is debilitating, sometimes reaching temperatures of more than 150 degrees in the open and more than 110 degrees in the shade. Eating the usual meal of rice and sauce seems to increase the flow of salty sweat. Sometimes it runs into a person's mouth and ruins the taste of the food; sometimes it streams into the pot containing the food. Normally, at the close of a meal, people drink water and take a siesta. During the soudure, however, a siesta affords no refreshment, for one falls asleep early in the afternoon only to awaken two hours later with a throbbing headache.

Like most people in Mehanna, I would spend my April afternoons gazing at the sky, observing cloud formations. In April one begins to see on the southern horizon the fleecy cumulus clouds which eventually bring rain. Would they float silently northward toward Mehanna? Would they bring a rare rain today? Mehanna people were also keen observers of the April winds. If the hot wind blows from the east, one knows that there is virtually no chance of rain. But if the cooler wind from the west is sweeping across town, perhaps it would create the climatic situation which would bring on a thunderstorm.

The pace of life in Mehanna, already slow by Western standards, eases to a crawl during the soudure. Given the relentless heat and lack of food it is a time of physical weakness. The cows produce no milk, there is little rice, and stocks of millet have dwindled. The pernicious wind from the east raises dust which carries in April the meningitis bacillus, which kills scores of children every hot season. Old hearts flutter and die in a profusion of heat and sweat. A miraculous rain could drown that murderous bacillus.

In April my pace of work slackened. Heat stifled people's willingness to talk. This state of affairs suited me well, for my willingness to work had melted.

Toward the end of April on an especially sultry day, I received in my compound Djibo's cousin, Karimoun, whose oval face was smooth and unexpressive. Karimoun, a short boy of fourteen, was wearing a pair of khaki shorts made for a man twice his size. He had come with news from Djibo. I was to go to the grain warehouse in the late afternoon.

"Does this mean that I am to be initiated today?" I asked Karimoun.

"Djibo told me to give you this message, that's all."

Karimoun left me a troubled man, for I sensed I was at a crossroads. In almost three months with Djibo, I had learned virtually nothing about the craft of the sorko, save for a few generally incomprehensible texts which I had memorized and recorded in my notebook. Was I wasting my time? Doubts about my involvement with Djibo persisted. I was uncertain whether he was sincere about initiating me. I knew that his father had agreed to let Djibo initiate me; he would be present at the ceremony. But why me? Was the dirty business of the birds a pretext? How could I be sure that Djibo and his father were not schemers who planned to manipulate the white man for some hidden purpose? I had no answers to these troubling questions. Worse yet, my objectivity had been compromised. I reflected now, as I had from time to time before, on what I called the "Evans-Pritchard Question." In a similar circumstance the great Africanist ethnographer Evans-Pritchard had sent his cook for instruction in "witch-doctoring," believing that his own involvement would prevent him from uncovering the elementary truths of Azande witchcraft. Although no red-blooded modern anthropologist would send a proxy, the question still stood: When does the anthropologist say: "Enough. I cannot become more subjectively involved"?

My doubts notwithstanding, I trudged to the grain warehouse on that hot afternoon in late April. The dusty market stalls shimmered in the heat. The shops were closed, and no one sat at the tables where I had in passing exchanged gestures with the deaf. As Djibo had instructed me, I carried under my arm a gourd of filtered water. In my tunic pocket, I fingered a tin of magarine.

I entered the compound of the grain warehouse. Djibo and his father, Mounmouni Koda, stared at me for an instant. As I approached, they inspected three stalks of millet in a mortar.

Mounmouni Koda greeted me. Although he was about seventy-five years old, Mounmouni Koda was still a powerfully built man. His body was firm; his gait was rapid and sure. His short stature did not detract from his air of great power and profound comprehension of the world. This comprehension was expressed through the deep furrows in his forehead. His power streamed from his deep-set eyes, which seemed to read the innermost secrets of my being. Mounmouni's quiet power epitomized the Songhay notion of the "hard" man.

Djibo grabbed my arm, freeing me from the mesmerizing gaze of Mounmouni Koda. "Two black stalks. One white stalk. Today you begin to understand."

"Good," I said, brimming with confidence.

Djibo turned toward his father. "You see, he is resourceful, but despite his confidence, it will take him a long time to learn."

"It takes all of us a long time to learn," Mounmouni Koda said. "I am still learning and I am at the end of my path."

This brief exchange convinced me that I was beginning something on that afternoon in April which would affect me for the rest of my life.

"Paul," Djibo said. "Do you see the three millet stalks?"

"Yes."

"What do you notice?"

"Two of them are black and one is white."

"Does that remind you of anything?"

I thought about the opposition of black/white. Remembering that the sorko frames propositions in the form of questions, I asked: "Would the black and white birds in my house be important?"

Djibo turned toward his father and nodded. Mounmouni Koda beamed with delight. "Paul, two stalks are black; they stand for Dongo, the father of all sorko."

"Then what about white?"

"Dongo is always with his mother, is he not?"

"Is his mother Harakoy Dikko?"

"Yes." Djibo admitted. "Dongo and his mother Harikoy Dikko are always together to protect the sorko and the sorko's slave."

I chanced another deduction. "Are there three stalks of millet in the mortar because three is the number for men?"

"That I cannot answer now," Djibo said. "We must begin the ceremony."

Djibo took a pot and coated it thoroughly with a ball of the butter the Fulan women sell on market day. From a coffee tin he poured some fine sand on the ground and shaped a small hill, upon which he placed the pot. "The spirits like pure sand," he told me. He added water to the pot and said: "Bismiallahi." He motioned for me to sit next to him. Mounmouni Koda remained standing. Djibo dipped his hand into his black vinyl drawstring bag and removed a number of pouches. He opened one and took out some greenish powder and pointed to it. "What is it?" he asked.

"Is it wata gaya gaya?"

Djibo's nod indicated that I had guessed correctly. Then he recited the text for this spirit powder—a text which he had not previously taught me. He said: "Wata gaya gaya, wata gaye. It has known the seven heavens. It has known the seven hells. It has known the north. It has known the south. It has known the east, and it has known the west."

After he recited this incantation three times, Djibo spit lightly into the powder three times. He took three pinches of the powder with his thumb and middle finger and sprinkled it counterclockwise on the surface of the water. Djibo opened another of his pouches to reveal to me a reddish-brown powder. "And what powder is this?" he asked.

"Is it kobe?"

I had guessed correctly again. Djibo recited the kobe incantation in the same manner as he had performed the previous text. "Kobe is above the earth," he chanted. "The kobe root is below the earth."

Djibo worked quickly now, as the ceremony would have to be completed before sunset, the end of the Moslem day. He recited another incantation for the reddish powder which I correctly identified as siria. "Siria, siria it will [take care of?] sorcery. It must [take care of?] the evil genies. It must [take care of?] the evil [un-translatable]. It must [take care of?] the evil witches. It must [take care of?] the evil enemies."

Djibo continued the rite, taking out some korombey powder, the object of my earlier errand. He chanted the now familiar text and spit three times into the pot. He took out yet another powder which I identified by its greenish color.

"Why are you adding wata gaya gaya a second time?" I asked feeling very proud of myself.

Djibo glanced at me. "You are a young man in a hurry, are you not?"

"Of course I am."

"But you do not know as much as you think. This powder is not wata gaya gaya. It is *kafia malam*." Without further explanation, he recited the short incantation associated with this powder. "Kafia Malam, it is more rapid than the Alfa [Moslem cleric]."

Deliberately, Djibo opened a pouch containing a brownish powder which I had never seen. "This is *sah nya*, the sorko's special powder." Saying that, he repeated the phrase, "Sah nya, dugu nya," three times.

Maymuna, Djibo's wife, emerged from the two-room house in the compound. While Djibo had been reciting his incantations, she had taken the three stalks of millet he had put in the mortar, stripped them, and pounded the seeds into a fine flour. Silently, she brought us the dish of flour. Djibo sang the praise-song to Dongo, protector of all the sorko, and spit three times into the flour. The pot was ready; the flour was ready. Djibo put the pot over a fire, and when the water boiled he added the flour in handfuls and stirred the ever-thickening mixture with a long wooden spoon. The gruel gradually stiffened into paste. When Djibo let go of the spoon and it remained upright in the mixture, he pronounced the stuff ready for consumption.

Carefully, Djibo lifted the pot off the fire and carried it inside his small house. From under his bed, he fetched a coffee tin from which he poured fine sand. Again he molded a small hill upon which he set the pot. He told me to sit on the floor with my back to the east and face the pot. He and his father sat facing me with their backs to the west. Djibo placed his forefinger on the rim of the pot. As he chanted a very long and complicated text, he moved his finger back and forth along the rim of the pot. I floated on the vibrations of the words of the initiation incantation.

Djibo spoke: "Harakoy Dikko. You must understand this well. It is for Paul that I am preparing this sorko food. I am Djibo Moun- mouni who is in Mehanna. Paul is becoming a sorko. He is putting himself in the hands of the sorko in order to learn as they do. I want Paul to enter the sorko's house."

Djibo had taken me seriously and had made me aware of the difficult tasks involved with becoming a sorko benya. Djibo moved on to sing praises to the Tooru spirits, a series of praise-songs which I knew. He spoke of Harakoy Dikko, the goddess of the Niger River, of Dongo, of Maalu, the deity of lightning, of Moussa Nyori, the hunter who controls the formation of the clouds, of Hausakoy, the deity of iron, of Mahamane Surgu, the deity of war, of Faran Baru Koda, the spirit child who controls the fate of millet fields. He sang praises to other spirit families. He spoke of the white spirits, who are great scholars and who advise mortals about the proper way to con- duct social affairs. He also sang of Nya Beri, the great mother, who engendered the spirits of the cold, the spirits of death.

Djibo followed his praise-singing to the spirits with an incanta- tion to Ndebbi, the High God's messenger, whose responsibility it is to relay magical messages from human beings to the supreme deity. Djibo recited this text almost inaudibly; I could not distinguish the words.

Unaffected by the heat and the rigors of his performance, Djibo concluded more than fifteen minutes of chanting: "Paul will become a sorko. Paul will become a sorko. I am speaking thus. I am doing work for Paul. Now Paul is a sorko. I am preparing him food which will enable him to engage in the craft of the sorko. The eyes will not see Paul. The hands will not grab Paul. Paul is with the sorko who are above. Paul has returned and is the hands of the sorko benya."

Djibo spit into the pot one last time. Mounmouni Koda gazed at me with burning eyes. We sat silently for a long moment. Djibo broke the frightening silence. "First, I, Djibo, will eat three measures of the food. Then you must eat the rest."

Djibo scooped up three small measures of the greenish paste, ate them quickly, and passed the pot over to me. Not knowing what to expect, I ate my first handful. The food was gritty and tasteless. Concealing my fear, I ate the paste slowly. Djibo and his father watched me. I found that eating even a small amount of this food filled me. After six handfuls, my stomach distended. "I cannot eat any more of this." I protested.

"You must eat all of this sorko food," Djibo said sternly.

Mounmouni Koda watched me impassively as I struggled to finish the two handfuls of sorko food that remained in the pot. Fighting back waves of nausea, I ate the last two helpings. Gas stretched my stomach to the point of explosion. Djibo stood. Mounmouni Koda stood.

"Are you not going to get up?" Mounmouni Koda asked me.

However much I tried, I could not stand up. Djibo helped me to my feet.

"Now you know the meaning of what it is to be full," Mounmouni Koda laughed. He took his forefinger and pushed it three times into my distended belly. How I avoided vomiting on him I do not know. "You are full," he said, "just like other sorko and sorko benya. When other sorko see you they will know you have eaten and that you are full. But they will never say so. Perhaps they will befriend you more quickly and more genuinely than other people. They may simply press their forefinger three times into your belly and say, 'I am full and so are you.'"

"You are a sorko benya," Djibo proclaimed.

Swollen metaphorically as well, with my good fortune and my new status, I said with the pride of the newly initiate, "I am a sorko benya."

Djibo nodded. "Yes, you are a sorko benya who knows nothing. You are only at the beginning of your path. Do not touch any woman today, as that will weaken the force of your sorko food. And beware of the treachery of others. Now that you have set foot on the path of the sorko, you have entered a new world. In this world you will discover wonders and dangers. Always be careful and protect yourself."

Djibo escorted me to the door of the warehouse compound. I waddled out. "Go home and rest. The sorko food will remain in your belly for the rest of your life."

11

WITCHES

On market days Mehanna bubbled with the sounds of barter and sparkled with a rainbow of costumes. From the east Bella people came to market. Once the slaves of the desert nomads, the Tuaregs, the Bella were the farmers who grew millet in such abundance that they sold their surplus at market. Each market day the Bella women, dressed in coarse indigo dresses made of locally spun cotton, arrived atop their donkeys, which were further burdened with 100-kilo sacks of millet. The Bella men, dressed in bright print robes and white or black turbans which stood stiff and tall above their foreheads, rode to market on donkeys or camels. From the north, Kurtey men and women came to market. These people spoke Songhay from birth, but unlike the Songhay I knew, they refused to farm millet and sorghum, preferring to fish and cultivate rice. The Kurtey also distinguished themselves from the Songhay physically—scarring both cheekbones with a small cross. In the nineteenth century they were feared slave-raiders on the river; now they sold rice at the market. Wogo also came to Mehanna's market. Like the Kurtey, they were Songhay speakers who lived on islands in the Niger. They cultivated rice, grew millet, herded cattle, and raised and sold a cash crop—tobacco. At the request of the sixteenth-century Songhay kings, they had come to the Mehanna region of the middle Niger to keep an eye on rebellious elements of the imperial population. The Tuaregs, too, came to the Mehanna market. Dressed in white robes and their famous indigo turbans, these "blue men" of the Sahara surveyed the market throng from the height of their prized camels.

On market day, Mehanna filled with people, dust, and smoke. Pathways normally wide and empty narrowed with the crowd on market day. The throng made it difficult to walk even short distances. The dust they kicked up seemed to catch the various smells of the market: the mouth-watering aroma of roasting mutton mixed with the nose-crinkling stench of fresh camel dung; the sweet and sour pungency of a bubbling stew combined with the stomach-churning odors of putrid fish; the spicy fragrance of burning resins at odds with the residue of stale urine.

Although I enjoyed the Mehanna market immensely, I could take its frenzy only in small doses. I spent many market afternoons in front of the grain warehouse at the western edge of the market area. Djibo and I often sat on a log in the shade of a giant acacia and observed the comings and goings of people on market day. Next to us, Songhay and Zerma women, seated above small fires, sautéed and seasoned slithery Niger River fish to delectable perfection.

On a particular day in May, Djibo and I sat on our log in silence. Occasionally, people came by to greet us. The short greeting completed, we lapsed back into silence. Perhaps the silence resulted from Djibo's mood. Perhaps the silence came from a heat-induced weariness.

"Do you know that woman?" Djibo spoke at last. He pointed to a willowy middle-aged woman dressed in a bright purple and blue tie-dyed dress which was embroidered about the neck in gold thread.

"No, I don't."

Djibo sniffed the air as though he were attempting to pick up a scent. "Are you sure?"

The woman turned so that I saw her face. "Oh, I do know her. She is my neighbor. She lives in the compound next to mine."

"That is what I thought. Come to my house early in the morning before people are up and about."

"But why? I don't understand."

"That woman is a witch. Can't you smell her scent?"

"She is a witch! Oh, come on, Djibo." I sniffed the air. "The only thing I smell is frying fish."

"Don't be a fool. You are in danger with that woman living so close to your compound."

"What do you mean?" I asked, dumbfounded.

Djibo ignored my question. "Do you have a silver ring?"

I had purchased a silver ring two weeks earlier. "Yes, I do."

"Then bring it with you tomorrow."

"What is this all about?"

"Come tomorrow. Come early."

I had read about witchcraft in African societies, but I had never seen passages that had discussed the scent of witches. Most writers on the subject of African witchcraft had focused their attentions upon the relationships of witchcraft accusations—someone claiming publicly that someone else was a witch—to the various schisms created by the social structure. The great Evans-Pritchard considered witchcraft a kind of religion, a system of belief which in some societies accounted for a person's inexplicable misfortunes. But Djibo had thrust me into a situation in which I could not consider witchcraft dispassionately as a sociocultural process in Mehanna. Songhay witches were supposed to eat the souls of their victims. They were the most maleficent force in the Songhay cosmos, continuously causing illness and death along their path. How could I consider the subject dispassionately when I had a witch living next door to me! The notion of the witch now struck me not as an abstract category, but as a concrete entity—a person who could do me great harm.

My skepticism persisted, however. That evening I decided to make inquiries about the situation. I started at Mounkaila's compound. A shopkeeper of modest means, Mounkaila had only recently moved to Mehanna from the Anzuru, a barren plateau east of the Niger on which a decreasing number of Songhay lived. Mounkaila had spent many of his formative years in Ghana, where he had been a policeman for thirty-three years. In addition to his native Songhay, Mounkaila spoke Ghanaian Pidgin English.

When I arrived, Mounkaila was chatting with Moussa, a former soldier in the Ghanaian army. Both of these men left Ghana in 1969 when President Busia expelled all resident foreigners who had jobs in the public or private sectors of the economy. Both men enjoyed talking to me, for it gave them the chance to show off their considerable abilities in English.

They welcomed me in Songhay, but continued the conversation in a mixture of Pidgin and Songhay.

"How is your work coming along?" Mounkaila asked me in Pidgin.

"Fine. No problems. You know, I'll be leaving in two months."

"Already! You have not been here that long," Moussa said in Pidgin.

"Hey," Mounkaila disagreed in Songhay, "he has been here for more than nine months. That is a long time for a white man to stay in a place like Mehanna."

"That's true," Moussa conceded in Songhay.

Since I talked with these men frequently, I dispensed with formalities and introduced the sensitive subject of witchcraft.

"Listen," I began in Songhay. "I have heard that Boubakar's first wife is a witch. Is it true?"

"Shhh!" Moukaila cautioned me. "We can't talk about this in Songhay. We must speak in English [Pidgin]. This way we will not be overheard."

"Very well. Is is true then? Is Boubakar's first wife a witch or isn't she?"

Tondi, Idrissa Dembo's Sister in Wanzerbe

Mounkaila beckoned me nearer. Moussa, too, leaned forward, to close our small circle of three men seated on a straw mat in the darkness. "We must be very careful with this one."

"Why?" I asked.

"Because they say she is so evil that she eats souls during the daylight."

"True?" Moussa wondered.

"It is true in Allah's name," Mounkaila stated. "That is why we should never talk near her in Songhay. She might overhear us and attack."

"But what about Boubakar?" I asked.

"Boubakar is a noble," Mounkaila told me, "and a fool. He married her, but only later did he find out about her evilness. When he had his children by her, he had to find a wet nurse."

"A wet nurse? Why on earth a wet nurse?"

"If a woman is a witch, she will pass witchcraft on to her children through her milk. You see, a long time ago, there was a woman named Howa, who founded a village of women. She did not like men at all! These women farmed, herded and did all kinds of men's work. One day a handsome man came to the village when only Howa was there. She invited him into her hut and seduced him. Then, when the man was asleep, Howa hit him on the head and he turned into a sheep. The women returned and Howa killed the sheep and roasted it. The women ate. Howa became pregnant from the interlude and gave birth to a little girl. The girl became the first witch and went out into the world of men and gave birth to sons and daughters, and the daughters bore more and more witches."

Mounkaila doodled in the sand and looked at me. "Don't worry. Just behave affably toward her and nothing will happen to you, even though she sleeps in the next compound."

"I'll try to do what you say, but it will be difficult."

"You must behave in that way," Mounkaila warned me. "If this is any consolation, Boubakar's first wife is one among many in Mehanna."

"What do you mean?"

"Mehanna has more witches than any other Songhay town."

"This is true," Moussa concurred.

It was late at night. The roar of the river churning over rocks overpowered the dull murmur of talk. I bade my friends goodnight. Despite my unwavering skepticism about witchcraft in Mehanna, the discussion had persuaded me to bring my recently purchased silver ring to Djibo's house the next morning.

That night I did not sleep well. Donkeys brayed in the early morning hours. Two cats hissed and growled at one another in my compound. I heard a woman screaming. Babies cried.

When I went to Djibo's early the next morning, he, too, seemed tired. His eyes were bloodshot and the mask of sleep had not yet lifted from his face.

"Did you sleep well, Djibo?" I asked ritually.

"I never sleep well. A sorko never sleeps well."

"I am beginning to understand what you mean. I did not sleep a wink last night."

"So, you're learning a bit."

Djibo slipped on his black tunic and asked me for the ring. He told me to sit on the dirt floor of his house.

"Djibo, why are there witches in the world?"

Djibo told me the same story Mounkaila had recited the previous evening.

I overflowed with questions. "What is it about the milk that gives witches so much power?" I began.

Djibo stopped me. "Be very quiet. I am going to open my *baata*."

Djibo knelt and with exquisite care picked up the rectangular tin box that served as his baata [sacrificial container]. Gently, he placed the box on the floor next to me. He took out a piece of white cloth, the color of purity, unfolded it and spread it on the floor. He placed the tin box on the white cloth.

"Do you see my knife hanging from the wall?"

"Yes."

"Bring it to me."

I handed him the knife, which he placed at the edge of the cloth. The setup still not complete, Djibo took from his altar a small mirror, which he placed next to the knife.

"Stand up," he commanded as he himself stood. "We must face the east."

"Why the east?"

"It is our custom." He turned away from me and called to his cousin Karimoun. "Bring the chickens."

Karimoun, still wearing the tattered, oversized shorts he had worn the day of my initiation, brought the chickens. Our scene was complete: Three men lined up to the west of a sheet of white cloth on which rested the baata, a small mirror, a knife, and three chickens; white, red, and red-and-white speckled.

"We are ready to begin," Djibo announced.

Djibo recited an incantation under his breath. He lifted the lid of the baata, and a strong sickly sweet fragrance escaped. I looked into the container and saw what seemed to be a variety of plants, twigs, and roots covered by a black film— perhaps blood. Djibo informed me that the "works" of his baata consisted of *goronfol*, a plant unknown to me, *wakando*, another unknown plant, a dried bumblebee, scented oils, the blood of a black goat and the blood of hundreds of black, white, red, and speckled chickens.

"Does the black goat's blood stand for Dongo?" I asked.

"Of course it does."

"Does the blood of the red chicken stand for Cirey, deity of lightning?"

"Yes, of course."

"And what does the bumblebee represent?"

"Ah, that one I cannot answer for you today." He flashed me a thin smile. "Give me your ring." Djibo laid the ring in the tin box. "First we prepare a tonic and then your ring will be forced to drink."

"Drink? What do you mean?"

Djibo ignored my question. He took his bag of powders and fished for a number of pouches. He opened one pouch to reveal a small pile of black cinders.

"That," he said pointing to the cinders, "is ngimgniti."

"Of course."

He opened other pouches revealing other ingredients: siria, kobe, and ceeyndi, a resin which produces an acrid smoke when burned. He opened another pouch. "And what is this?"

"That is wata gaya gaya," I responded, correctly identifying the greenish powder.

"Good." Djibo opened two additional pouches. "What are these powders?"

I didn't know them.

"You still have much to learn," he proclaimed. "The yellow powder is called *kwara tombo*, and the green powder is called *genji tombo*. Taste them so that you will be able to recognize them next time."

I tasted them. The yellow powder had the flavor of castor oil. The green powder tasted like dried bird-droppings. I knew about the taste of dried bird-droppings!

From the open pouches he took three pinches of each powder. Using his thumb and index finger, he sprinkled the powders over my ring as one seasons meat with salt. Djibo unsheathed his knife and recited another incantation under his breath. Karimoun held the white chicken's head as he stretched its neck. Djibo slashed the chicken's throat. Blood gushed from the chicken's throat into the baata. Djibo maneuvered the thrashing chicken so that some of the blood dripped onto the mirror. Most of the blood, however, dripped into the container. We watched the chicken die. The chicken's blood in the container dried in a thin red crust on the ring. Djibo sacrificed the other chickens in the same manner.

"It is finished, Paul."

"Now what?"

"We must let the rings, the powders, and the blood remain in the container for three days."

"And then what?"

"And then you shall see for yourself, Sorko Benya."

Late in the afternoon, three days later, Djibo invited me to his house at the grain warehouse. He carefully placed his baata on fine sand—the floor of his house—and lifted its lid. This time I was ready for the strong, sweet fragrance which filled the room. He withdrew my ring with his forefinger and thumb and studied it in the deepening shadow of the afternoon. "Wear this ring forever on the third finger of the left hand, for this is the finger of power."

"Finger of power?"

"Yes, of course. It is the only finger that does not have a name in Songhay. Why do you think it has no name?" he asked rhetorically. "Because this finger has too much power to have a name. When you are attacked by sorcery, the sorcery enters your body through the third finger of the left hand. When the witch attacks you, its force will enter your body through the third finger of the left hand. When the spirit takes the body of its medium, its force enters the medium's body through the third finger of the left hand."

"Why are you telling me this, Djibo? I thought I had to ask good questions."

"This is very true. But you have been initiated. You are on the path. And once you are on the path, you must be prepared to walk on it. Our path can be dangerous. You must be prepared."

"What on earth could happen to me?"

"I cannot tell you. But one day you will understand."

"Yes, of course," I said mockingly.

Djibo frowned at my insolence. "Let's go and sit in front of the compound."

We emerged into the late afternoon light, which made the mud-brick walls glow as though dying fires burned within them. Like two cats, we sat silently, staring into space. Apprehension slowly over-took me. Djibo and his father had plans for me. Perhaps Djibo and his father were playing with me, taking advantage of me? But how could they enhance their prestige by teaching the craft of the sorko to a European? From my readings, I knew that anthropologists often became the pawns of their informants, who involved them in politi-cal schemes totally unrelated to the research missions of the schol-ars. In fact, many people in Mehanna besides Idrissa had cautioned me about Djibo and his father. "They can't be trusted." "Don't give them money." When I protested that Djibo and his father were sorko, my friends told me that they were sorko who had filth in their hearts—people who would willingly betray a trusted friend.

The advice troubled me. What troubled me even more was that Djibo mentioned repeatedly the danger involved in walking the sorko's path. What could happen to me? After all, I controlled my life in Mehanna. And, as a white man, I felt less vulnerable to the dangers Djibo spoke of. If people attempted to cast a spell on me—assuming such things existed—they could get themselves into a lot of trouble, could they not?

Djibo tapped my arm. He pointed to a woman who was walking toward us. Balanced on her head was a mountain of brightly decorated enameled metal pots. "Paul, you have the sorko food in your belly, do you not?"

"Yes, I do," I responded, though for the life of me I could not understand how something that I had eaten three days before could remain in my belly for the rest of my life.

"And," he continued as he watched the woman with the pots, "you are now wearing on the third finger of your left hand a ring which has drunk, are you not?"

"Yes, I am."

"Well . . . ?"

"Does it mean that I have strength?"

"Yes, of course it does."

"But how am I to know it? I do not feel any different, just a bit more constipated."

"I am sorry about your dried-out intestines, but this usually hap-pens when one has eaten the food of strength." He waved his hand in the direction of the woman with the pots on her head. She had stopped to talk with another woman going toward the river. "Go up to that woman with the pots on her head. Look at her eyes even if she attempts to avoid your gaze. When your eyes meet, a tear will roll out of her left eye."

"Sure it will," I said sarcastically. Hoping to prove Djibo wrong, I approached the woman with the pots on her head; she was slowly walking away from the market. When she realized that I intended to intercept her, she quickened her pace. She lost her balance and some of her pots thumped into the sand. Like a conqueror, I stood over this woman as she picked up two of her pots. For a second our eyes locked. A large tear dropped from the corner of her left eye and ran down her cheek. She stood up stiffly and ran away, somehow holding on to her pots. I returned to Djibo, stupefied.

"I don't believe it, Djibo. The woman would not look at me, and when she did, a tear dropped onto her cheek from her left eye."

"Did you smell her?"

"No, I didn't."

Djibo shook his head. "One day you will be able to smell them, but that lies ahead of you on your path."

"Smell what?" I asked.

"Witches, you fool."

12

A TONIC FOR WORK

Because my funding was to run out in two months, the day of my departure from Mehanna was rapidly approaching. Despite my apprenticeship with Sorko Djibo, I would be happy to leave the dusty wastes of Mehanna. My plan was simple. Spend one month in Niamey transcribing my linguistic data and write the final report of my research findings for the government of Niger. Still, I had more than one month to complete in Mehanna.

The heat in Mehanna remained intense. But the approach of the rains now brought to the desert a tropical sultriness. In April, evenings had been a time of resuscitation; people regained their strength and sense of humor when the sun slid below the horizon. But as the rain clouds approached in mid-to-late May, our nightly relief ended. Now we dreaded the setting sun, for nightfall brought on a choking humidity.

These humid discomforts of May affected my work more than the searing heat of April. In the morning I felt dizzy. In the evenings I felt nauseous. At midday my weariness made me listless. I stopped going to Djibo's house for lessons. Djibo did not come to visit me. Occasionally, Djibo sent for me to assist him in a healing rite.

One night about two weeks before my departure from Mehanna, Djibo sent Karimoun to fetch me. I slipped into the compound of the grain warehouse and greeted Djibo's wife and his cousin, Moussa, who was compiling his monthly report to the government agency for which he worked. As was usually the case, Djibo looked terribly tired. He did not complain, however. By now I knew better than to ask whether he had been sleeping well.

Djibo told me that a client had come to visit him the previous evening. The man, a civil servant, had traveled all the way from Tera—eighty kilometers—to see him. The problem, as the client related it, concerned his government job. The man had been in the same dull government position for four years. There was little chance of his moving on to a more responsible position in another jurisdiction. He wanted something which would propel him forward.

"And?"

"We sorko have something perfect," Djibo said, opening his hand to reveal a solitary cowry shell.

"How can a cowry shell improve a man's fortunes?" I demanded. I knew already that the cowry shell was the medium of exchange in precolonial Songhay society. Diviners also used the shells to read the past and the future. During possession dances, one sees many cowries sewn into the costumes of the deities. Reflecting a moment, I answered my own question with another one. "Can a cowry drink?"

"Yes, it can," Djibo said

We entered Djibo's house. Because it was a particularly humid night in Mehanna, the fumes of scented oils filled the air in Djibo's rooms. Djibo sat on a straw mat opposite the stool which served as his altar. He opened the *baata,* which was on the altar. He pointed to another cowry in the container. "That is called Bamba," he said. "That is Bamba. Bamba is Ndebbi's white pigeon. The base of Ndebbi's Kokoro Bah tree. It rides on the head of Ndebbi's Kokoro Bah tree. Therefore it rides on the head of enemies. It rides on the head of sorcerers. It rides on the head of evil verbal sorcery. It rides on the head of evil genies. It rides on the head of the evil Doguwa spirits. It rides on the head of evil Tooru spirits. It rides on the head of evil medicine. Ndebbi presented his bed to all of them. He released his bed and it floated to earth and remained there. Thus, it will sit on the heads of enemies. It will sit on the heads of the agents of Satan. It will sit on the heads of evil spirits. Ndebbi made a small heavy rock. They will never see it. Their hands will never grasp it. Thus, the force of the heavens will be upon the head of the sorcerers."

As with all the other incantations I had witnessed, Djibo recited the text three times, and spat into the container after each recitation. Djibo told me that the cowry shell must remain in the container for three days. "After three days, the Bamba will have drunk the forces of the heavens, and our ancestors will be with my client."

"Will it work?" I was always the skeptic.

"That will depend upon the filth in the man's heart."

13

BETWEEN SOUND AND THE SHADOW

In May people scan the eastern sky in the late afternoon, hoping to see the formation of fleecy cumulus clouds on the horizon. As the cloud pattern develops, the most knowledgeable people among the Songhay can divine whether the clouds will bring nothing, wind and dust only, or, with the grace of the spirits, wind and dust followed by rain.

When a band of storm clouds develops on the eastern horizon, the sleepy tranquillity of a hot afternoon in Mehanna is transformed into a flurry of frenetic activity. The deep orange color of the clouds matches the baked laterite of the Songhay steppe. Before the direction of the wind changes, people scurry about, tethering animals, putting their beds inside their houses or huts. The dust cloud looms large as it approaches Mehanna, until, like an ocean wave crashing onto the beach, it inundates the town, blocking out the sun. The sky becomes solid with reddish-brown dust, which filters the late afternoon light to a dim red, as though a fire were burning in the distant sky. The temperature drops precipitously and the scent of rain is in the air. If Mehanna is fortunate, the wind and dust will be followed by a downpour. If the town is not blessed with good fortune, the dust will blow for hours, bringing discomfort, disease, and another hot grimy day.

Even though it was almost June, Mehanna had not yet been blessed with rain—only the wind and sand of ferocious dust storms. Sand blew into my house and coated everything. My dirt floor resembled the great sand seas of the Sahara. My skin and scalp felt like coarse sandpaper.

Despite my gritty misery, the last four days had been exhilarating. Djibo and I had been treating a pious Moslem who claimed to be a *sherif*, a direct descendant of Mohammed the Prophet. Djibo doubted that this man was a sherif, but he and I both knew him to be an *El Hadj*, a person who had made the sacred pilgrimage to Mecca. The man was thirty-five years old and had been suffering for almost a year from an undiagnosed illness. He complained of chronic lethargy, aching joints and nausea, and had consulted the local Islamic healer, the local state nurse, and the physician in the regional health center. He eventually went to the National Hospital in Niamey where he underwent a battery of diagnostic tests. No one could diagnose his disorder. When the man finally returned to Mehanna, he consulted Sorko Djibo, an act of desperation for such a pious Moslem. Djibo took one look at him and announced that the man had been bewitched.

"I do not believe in your devils," the man said. "You, Djibo, will rot in hell."

Djibo puffed. "One foot cannot follow two paths."

"Your cursed proverbs will not solve my problem," the man retorted. "I am going to die."

"Nonsense," Djibo replied. "If we work quickly, we'll have you on your feet in three days."

Djibo asked me if I would assist him during the curing rite. I agreed to participate only if the El Hadj had no objection to my presence; he welcomed me.

The first day of the ceremony we made a house call to the El Hadj's compound. The compound was half a football field in size and there was one large three-room mudbrick house at the west end of the rectangular space. Three smaller houses hugged the compound's northern wall, one house for each of the El Hadj's wives. In the center of the compound were posts where the El Hadj's cows, goats, and sheep were tethered at night. Toward the east wall and the entrance to the compound there was furniture arranged as an outdoor parlor under a cluster of acacias—a bed made of fastened sticks and a number of canvas deck-chairs which the El Hadj had no doubt purchased in Niamey.

We found the ailing El Hadj outside, lying on his stick bed in the shade of the acacias. We greeted him and asked him to sit at the base of the largest acacia in the compound. With great difficulty the El Hadj rolled out of bed and eased himself down next to the acacia.

Djibo took from his shirt pocket a pouch of *sibitah kaaji*, the fragrant root of a shrub which grows along dry river-beds. These roots had been dried for three days in the sun. He then asked one of the El Hadj's wives, the only other person in the compound at that time, to bring us a brazier filled with hot coals. When the woman brought the brazier, Djibo placed it in front of the El Hadj and put in it some of the sibitah kaaji roots. Ribbons of smoke floated up from the brazier. Djibo told the El Hadj to breathe deeply so that the smoke entered his lungs. As the man took deep breaths, we rubbed the fragrant smoke into his ears, armpits, navel, and all of his other joints and orifices. We repeated this exercise four times during the first day of treatment and four times the second day of treatment.

Thursday was the third and final day of the cure. It was on Thursdays, Djibo reminded me, that the spirits are close to the social world. We walked briskly to the man's compound. As we walked into the compound, another of the El Hadj's wives ran toward us. "Hurry," she said, "my husband is very sick today. He cannot move his body and he is in great pain."

The El Hadj lay in a heap on the stick bed under the acacia trees. We called to him softly and he turned toward us. His limbs were twitching. I touched his hand, which was hot from fever.

We went about our work quickly. Djibo prepared an ablution of twigs, perfume, and water. He recited an incantation over the gourd containing the mixture. The words of the incantation, Djibo told me, would infuse the liquid with the force of the heavens. Through the text, which is called "water container," Djibo spoke to Ndebbi, the intermediary between human beings and *Iri Koy*, the High God of the Songhay cosmos. He sang about his ancestors and their power and how their power had been passed down through the generations, father to son, father to son. He spoke of the world of eternal war, the world of sorcery in which men have thirty points (crossroads) of misfortune and women have forty points of misfortune. He described the inhabitants of the world of eternal war: witches, evil genies, the evil Songhay spirits, sorcerers, and *Iblis*, the Islamic devil. When innocents come upon their points of misfortune, they are in a space between the spirit and social worlds and are vunerable to attack. But when the evil witches, genies, spirits, sorcerers, or Iblis attack an innocent, the innocent can sometimes repel them. The agents of evil can be misled. They can be overcome. They can be defeated.

Djibo recited the text three times, the number which corresponds symbolically to men. Each time, Djibo spat three times into the ablution. In this way, Djibo told me, the force of the heavens, which is embodied in words, enters the potion.

Djibo completed the incantation and beckoned one of the El Hadj's wives. "Wash him with this ablution," he told her, "especially the joints of the body, the ears, nose, and mouth."

Djibo then led me out of the El Hadj's compound. We trudged up a large dune just to the west of Mehanna. On the outskirts of town Djibo spoke to me: "Now we shall find the man's double. A witch has stolen it. The smoke of the sibitah kaaji is with him; his body is ready to receive its double. But we must find the double before the witch transforms it into a animal and cuts its throat."

"And if that happens?"

"The El Hadj will die."

We struggled up to the crest of the dune, where we encountered a pile of *duo*, the husk of the millet seed, for it is upon these dunes that women let the wind separate the precious grain from the chaff. Like an exploring infant, Djibo crawled into the pile of millet husks. He sifted through the pile for a few moments when suddenly he leaped to his feet. He flapped the palm of his hand over his open mouth. "Wo, wo, wo, wo," he cried.

He turned toward me. "Did you see it?"

"See what?"

"Did you feel it?"

"Feel what?"

"Did you hear it?"

"Hear what?"

Djibo shook his head in disappointment, for he expected that I would have sensed the man's double as he, Djibo, had liberated it. He grumbled: "You look but you don't see. You touch but you don't feel. You listen but you do not hear. Without sight or touch," he continued, "one can learn a great deal. But you must learn to hear, or you will learn little about our ways."

Exhausted from the frustration of instructing such a dull-witted student, Djibo lapsed into silence as we plodded down the dune toward the El Hadj's compound. I didn't understand what had occurred on the dune and I wondered whether Djibo had feigned his "discovery." How could he see, feel, and hear something which had eluded my common senses?

Although downhill, the walk back to the El Hadj's compound seemed twice as long as the climb to the top of the dune. It seemed an age before we re-entered the courtyard. To my surprise and Djibo's satisfaction, the El Hadj strode up to Djibo and lavished him with praise. Somehow the man had regained his strength. Djibo turned to me and said: "The words were good for this one."

"What words?"

Djibo did not answer; rather, he expressed his gratitude to the spirits for providing the healing force that cured the El Hadj of his disorder. He pushed me out of the compound.

"Where are we going?" I asked.

"To my house. There is not much time left and you must learn more before you meet your next teacher."

"My next teacher? Who is he, your father?"

"No, no. You will go to Tillaberi on the other side of the river. There, you will ask for Adamu Jenitongo, the *zima* [possession cult priest] of Tillaberi. He is a sohanci."

"Is this Adamu Jenitongo a direct descendant of Sonni Ali Ber [the Magic King of the Songhay Empire]?"

"Yes, of course he is a descendant of Sonni Ali Ber, just as I am a descendant of Faran Maka Bote, the giant who was a fisherman and the first sorko."

"I cannot wait to begin."

"Children know haste; elders know patience."

"There you go with those proverbs again."

"You cannot go to Adamu Jenitongo without knowing the words I used in the treatment of the El Hadj."

Inside his house Djibo drilled me for two hours, till I knew by heart the "water container" incantation. Djibo then gave me another incantation, a text about hearing the Songhay world. Djibo revealed to me the name of the incantation, a non-Songhay word, but insisted that I never reveal it to outsiders. The sound of the incantation's name embodies the power to repel witches. I learned this incantation easily. There is a sound, the non-Songhay word, in the darkness, and the sound is directed toward a rock. And the rock directs the stream of sound toward the genitalia of an evil witch which is flying in the black night air. As the witch flies by, its torch flashes on and off. But the stream of sound has now reached the witch, and when the witch lifts its torch, the torch no longer frightens anyone, for the witch has lost control of itself, and is falling from flight. And when the witch falls from flight, following the incantation, fear escapes from people like steam from a teapot. Men will not fear the witch. Women will no longer fear the witch. Incapacitated and confused, the witch will not know its frontside from its backside. Time will pass and the witch will remain immobilized in the same spot. The darkness will lift.

Satisfied with my memorization of the "water container" text and the text with the secret name, Djibo asked me to visit the El Hadj on each of my remaining days in Mehanna. "Let me know if the El Hadj gets sick again." I welcomed this opportunity, for now I could verify the results of the cure. The El Hadj, I believed, would soon suffer a relapse, proving to me the ineffectiveness of Djibo's cure.

Early each day I hauled myself through the heat and the humidity to El Hadj's compound. Surprisingly, the El Hadj appeared to gain strength on each successive day. One week after the curing rite, the El Hadj dressed himself in his finest white damask boubou, a flowing gown made heavy with elaborate gold-thread embroidery around its neck and on the ends of its sleeves. "Come with me to my shop. This is a great day," he commanded.

"Why is today so important to you, El Hadj?"

"Do you not understand?"

"Understand?"

"I have not been to my shop in more than six months. Today, I want to greet personally all of the people who come to my establishment to buy things. I want to sit outside my shop and pass the hours talking with my friends. How bored I have been. Life without talk, you know, is like a living death."

"I am pleased for you, El Hadj. Very pleased."

And so we went to the shop, greeted customers, and then retired to an empty market stall opposite the entrance to El Hadj's shop. Despite the heat and discomfort of a "dog" day in June, the El Hadj spent hours talking with me and his friends. At midday one of his wives brought us lunch, and six of us ate from a common bowl, a delicious dish of rice topped with a tangy fish sauce. I stuffed myself and burped loudly. The El Hadj appreciated my burp; he and the others followed suit. "I assure you," he said to me, "I will tell my wife how much you relished the meal she prepared."

I stood up. The cured El Hadj seemed impervious to the heat, which by now had evaporated my energies. "Thank you, El Hadj. I must return to my compound now. I am tired and I must begin to make preparations for my departure."

"Ah, Paul," the El Hadj said, "your leaving will make life boring in Mehanna."

14

TILLABERI

At midday in the month of June a quiet hung over Tillaberi. People shielded themselves from the sun as they ate their noon meals in their houses. A donkey brayed. An occasional truck chugged along the Tillaberi road, which was paved all the way to Niamey, Niger's capital, 120 kilometers to the south. I had left Mehanna that morning, the day after the first rains had fallen. Idrissa bade me an anxious goodbye and hustled off to plant his field. He hoped that I would return to bring him good fortune—a salary—in the near future. Other people neither had the time nor the inclination to say goodbye. Although I told Djibo when I was going to leave, I did not expect him to see me off. He once told me that the sorko must be unsentimental, and he was a man true to his word. I also knew that many people in Mehanna were pleased to see me depart. For some of them I was someone who had intruded into the depths of their personal lives. I, too, was happy to be leaving Mehanna. My work there had succeeded beyond my expectations, and I was confident of discovering even more about the Songhay world in Tillaberi.

I wriggled out of the bush taxi which had brought me from Bonfebba, a riverside market town on the east bank of the Niger, to Tillaberi. Realizing that I was uncertain of Sohanci Adamu Jenitongo's address, I walked to the post office. Since Tillaberi is an administrative center, numerous government offices were located in the town. The post office was closed, but a man was sitting outside the building.

"Hello," I said to him. "How is your health?"

"Fine. And yours?" He stared at me for a while. "Don't I know you?"

The man did look familiar, and I had taught secondary school in Tillaberi five years earlier. "Do you?"

"Aren't you Mr. Jim?"

"No, no."

"American?"

"Yes."

"A teacher?"

"I was, and so was Mr. Jim. But he taught here two years before I came."

Adamu Jenitongo, Sohanci of Tillaberi

"You white people all look alike to me," he said scratching his head. "Boy, you speak good Songhay! You have become Songhay."

"Thank you," I said. "but they say that the floating log never becomes the crocodile."

"Great God, you know proverbs!"

"I need some information, and maybe you can help me?"

"Of course."

"Can you tell me how to get to Adamu Jenitongo's compound?"

"Who?"

"He is the zima of Tillaberi."

"Oh, the zima's compound. He lives on a dune behind the secondary school."

How reassuring to know that the zima lived in the compound that he occupied five years earlier when I had been a teacher at the secondary school. At that time I knew him as the old man who organized frequent possession dances in his compound. The echo of the gourd drum had broken the quiet of many hot afternoons in Tillaberi. Even then, Adamu Jenitongo seemed a very old man. He was short and spindly. His thin, neatly trimmed white beard contrasted sharply with the ebony skin stretched taut across his face. He had prominent cheekbones and undimmed black eyes which glowed inside deep sockets.

When I taught in Tillaberi, I visited this old man, the zima. Each time we talked he insisted that I attend one of his possession dances. I steadfastly refused, thinking that my attendance might compromise my position as a teacher in the community. Toward the end of my contract, however, I witnessed a number of the dances he organized. The high-pitched whine of the monocord violin and the clack and roll of bamboo sticks on the gourd drum—the possession instruments—impressed me. The dancers, mostly old women, struck me with their grace and spirit.

But five years had passed and I was returning to this old man's compound, now knowing him to be one of the greatest of all the sorcerers in all of Niger. How could I have been so ignorant, I marveled, as I followed the sandy paths which cut through town. I descended an embankment and sank into the deep sand of a dry riverbank. I waded across that river of sand, up the other bank, and onto the steep incline of the dune. The strap of my duffle bag cut into my shoulder. I rubbed my forehead, gritty with sand. Sweat dripped into my eyes. Determined, I slogged up the dune until I reached its summit. Behind me the bush stretched for miles like a brown canvas, broken only by the outcropping of mesas. To the right, the

Niger glistened in the sunlight. To the left the roof of the secondary school shimmered in the heat. Just beyond the school I saw the Sohanci's compound, a cluster of grass huts enclosed by a three-foot fence of dried millet stalks.

I clapped three times at the entrance of the compound to announce my presence. Walking stiffly and bent a bit forward, Adamu Jenitongo came to greet me. As in the past, he was dressed in filthy drawstring trousers. A sleeveless black shirt with a frayed collar covered his frail torso.

"Pap, pa, pa, pap. I've been expecting you. How was your journey from Mehanna?"

"How did you know I was coming? How did you know about me?"

Adamu Jenitongo, the Sohanci, laughed. "I have known about you from the moment I saw you when you taught at the school."

I stared at the Sohanci.

"You look drained," he said, breaking the silence. "Come into my hut and eat with me. He turned and called. "Moru, come and get Monsieur Paul's things."

A youth of twenty or so, no taller than the old man, bounded out of another hut. We stooped to enter the Sohanci's hut. He unrolled a straw mat. He plopped a pillow—a bundle of his other shirts, trousers, and robes—on the mat and asked me to sit down. He opened the lid of a bright enameled pot of steaming rice and sauce and gave me a wooden spoon. "Eat, you need to regain your strength."

We did not talk while we ate in the midday heat.

"Have you had enough to eat?" the Sohanci asked.

"Yes," I answered.

"But you have hardly touched the food."

"I am full," I told him.

"In more ways than one," he said.

Did this man know everything about me? When his deep set eyes rested on mine, I felt that I could hide nothing from him. His was the gaze of great perception and wisdom, the kind of gaze which cuts through a person's defenses and seizes the true self.

"I have come to sit with you . . . ummm."

"You must call me Baba. All the men who come to sit with me refer to me as Baba."

"Baba, I have come to sit with you and to listen."

"You choose your words well, my son. You must come to visit Baba morning, noon, and evening. We must eat together, for when two men eat together, this builds a confidence bewtween them. But to learn important things, you must come late at night when everyone is asleep."

"I think I understand. If you have powerful words they must not be overheard."

"Great God! How much you have learned." The Sohanci reached into one of the deep pockets in the side of his sleeveless black tunic and pulled out a leather wallet. He opened it and carefully slipped out a tattered card stained with spots of age.

"What does it say?" I asked. In answer he handed it to me.

It was his identity card. "It says you are Adamu Jenitongo, a farmer who was born in Jessey around 1882." I looked at him. "Is that true?"

"Oh yes, they say that I am five years short of being 100 years old."

I was skeptical. Still, he was obviously quite old. "You are very healthy for a man of your age," I told him.

"All the descendants of Sonni Ali Ber are strong people who live long lives. My father, Jenitongo, lived to be 102."

"102?" The longevity of his family reminded me of the longevity in my own family. My paternal grandfather's grandmother, a healer and herbalist herself, lived to be 107. And all the men on my father's side of the family had lived healthily well into their eighties and nineties.

"Oh yes. Let me tell you of my early life."

"My father, Jenitongo, was the most powerful sorcerer of his time. When I was still a young boy, my father chose me to inherit his burden. I would work in the fields during the day and return home to listen to Father tell me of his life. I learned that my grandfather had been born in Wanzerbe, the great magic city of Songhay. But Grandfather came to the lands of the Zerma east of the Niger River. There my father became a man and learned to be a sohanci.

"With his father's magic, our ancestor Sonni Ali made himself impervious to spears and arrows. With the magic of his mother's people, the Faru, Sonni Ali Ber learned how to fly. Like a vulture, the symbol of his ancestors, Sonni Ali soared high in the sky and traveled great distances. The Magic King passed this powerful knowledge to his son, Si Baru, who passed it on to his three sons, who passed it on to their sons, until the knowledge came to me in Jessey.

"Life was peaceful in Jessey until one hot day when the French soldiers came. They attacked our village and killed a few of our people to demonstrate their overwhelming force. I hid from the soldiers in a grotto just outside of town. I heard the crackle of rifle fire and the screams of the wounded. But I did not see the European soldiers.

"The soldiers left soon after their conquest and life in Jessey returned to normal. Because the elders of Jessey submitted to the authority of the French, the soldiers took no prisoners. The officer leading the soldiers promised to make Jessey the seat of a colonial chieftaincy.

"My father, Jenitongo, took little interest in this political business. Jenitongo preferred to probe the depths of the Songhay world of magic. Father continued to instruct me in the ways of Songhay sorcery.

"When I was barely twenty years old, the wanderlust infected me. Each day I gazed southward and imagined the excitement of the southlands. I had heard about the wonders of Accra, where gray clouds, hanging low and heavy in the sky, blocked out the sun. The most wondrous sight in Accra, I was told, was the endless river, a body of water so big that one never saw its distant bank, a river with powerful waves which smashed against the sandy beach. All of this I wanted to see.

"I told my father of my intentions. Father did not want me to travel to a faraway land full of treachery. Although he feared for my safety, he did not stop me from leaving Jessey. As I went further south, the cool mountains gave way to the forest. The thick foliage blocked out the sky. I have never seen so many trees and plants, and I have never felt more uncomfortable. Although the sun of the forest did not wilt a person's spirit, the humidity of this land rapidly sapped a person's strength. Feeling weaker and weaker, I continued walking through the forest until one day I caught a cool breeze from the south.

"My first sight of the ocean was at dusk. It was vast. I stumbled onto the beach and dropped to my knees and stared at the ocean, the waves. I felt the dampness of the ocean spray. Did the beach go on forever? Was there no end to this river? And what was on the other side?

"I went into the *zongo* quarter of Accra, the neighborhood for Moslem foreigners. There I found my countrymen. For more than a month I had passed through villages of peoples unknown to me. Some of these people wore no clothing. Some of these people filed their teeth into sharp points. They ate donkey, dog, and monkey meat. They spoke in strange tongues which sounded more like song than speech. Still, these people were kind to me; they gave me food and provided me shelter. In return I gave them some of the amulets Father had given to me before my departure. But now I was among my own people, Zerma and Songhay from the north.

"Two men from Ouallam, which is near Jessey, invited me to stay in their room, a small cubicle with whitewashed walls. Once I was situated, I accompanied my roommates to the port and signed on as a stevedore. Hauling heavy cargo from the ships to the shore exhausted me. The work was difficult, but I liked the cool climate of Accra. I also liked the foods of the coast: the ocean fish, rice, the flaked manioc, and *fufu*, a paste made from pounded cassava or plantains.

"I was not in Accra long before illness gripped my body. My arms hung limply from weakened shoulders. My legs buckled when I walked. A fever which would not go away blurred my vision. I took to my bed. The men from Ouallam called a ritual priest, a zima, to look in on me. The zima gave me a potion to drink and recited some incantations over my body. This did not help. I grew weaker and weaker. My countrymen persuaded a Ghanaian nurse to examine me. My condition baffled the nurse, who suggested that I go to the hospital. I refused. Three months passed and my condition grew worse.

"One day I awoke utterly exhausted. I noticed the absence of my brass thumb ring. I had never removed the beautiful ring which Father had given me for protection. At that very moment, Harouna, a man from Jessey, came into my room. 'Your father,' he told me, 'says that Accra is not good for you. Your father says that you will regain your health as you make your journey home to Jessey.'

"Suddenly I felt stronger than I had in months. I agreed to return home. I told my friends from Ouallam that I would be leaving. I could not find my thumb ring.

"My friends helped to get to the train, which I rode to the end of the line. As the train rolled northward, I felt myself getting stronger and stronger. From the last stop in the savannah land of northern Ghana, I began my trek home. Each step to the northeast infused me with more energy. My stride grew long, sure and swift. After two weeks I came upon the Niger River near the village of Say. I crossed the river in a dugout and headed for Jessey. Walking at a brisk pace, I arrived in Jessey three days after crossing the Niger. My kinspeople rushed to greet me. My father, Jenitongo, was the last one to greet me.

" 'Adamu, welcome, welcome,' he said to me.

"Father walked away from me and gestured for me to join him at the edge of his compound. 'You were ill in Ghana,' father stated.

" 'Yes, Baba.' I said.

"Father smiled as he put his hand in the deep breast pocket of his robe. He pulled out my brass thumb ring. 'Did you lose this?' he asked as he put it into my hand.

" 'But how did you . . . '?

" 'I flew to Accra to save you.'

" 'Yes?'

" 'And now you know that a true sohanci always brings back evidence of his rapid voyages.' "

"That is enough for today. There is much more to tell. I enjoy having a son who is so good at listening."

"But why are you telling me all of this?"

"Must not a son know the father with whom he sits?"

"Yes, you're right."

"Good. Where will you be staying?"

"I hope to stay with a French teacher that I know."

"That is good. Don't come here late tonight. I'll tell you when to come at night. But come tomorrow. I have much more to tell you."

15

THE YOUNG SOHANCI

I installed myself in the house of J. F., whom I had known since 1971 when I taught in Tillaberi. As bidden, I returned to the compound of Adamu Jenitongo the next morning. Baba sat placidly in the shade of one of his huts as he wove palm fronds into rope.

"How was your sleep, my son?"

"I slept in health and tranquillity. And yours?"

"Good." He looked up at me. "Sit next to me. I have more to tell." He scratched his thin beard. "Where did I stop yesterday?"

"You had returned home from Accra, and your father had given back your ring."

"Ah, yes."

"When I returned to Jessey, I worked in my family's millet fields.

At night, I studied with my father. He taught me about the plants and herbs used by our ancestor, Sonni Ali Ber himself. But my father and I are special sohanci. We are *guunu*. Because our fathers are sohanci and our mothers are witches, we guunu are the most power-ful sohanci. For this reason, the guunu performs circumcisions. When my father went to circumcise a young boy, he asked me to come with him so that I might learn. He taught me how to make the correct cuts and showed me the plants to use to dull the pain, stop the bleeding, and bring on rapid healing. Soon, I was doing the operations and my father was watching.

"While I was learning how to circumcise, the great Swollen Stomach Drought [*gunda beri*] came [in 1911]. There was no rain for two years. Children died. Old people died. We survived by eating the seed of the *kram-kram* [the burrs that cut into bare feet] and the cooked bark of the *haasu kwarey* tree, which burned our throats as we swallowed it.

"God spared my family and the great Swollen Stomach Drought passed. My father told me to go out into the world and circumcise. 'You must travel to the edges of our world, my son, and seek out those who wish to have their sons circumcised. You will not pass through a village in which you will not be needed.'

"Before I left, my father gave me two things: a large satchel which contained the powders that the guunu uses in circumcisions and a *lolo*, a long metal staff. 'Take this lolo which is caked with the blood of a thousand sacrifices,' my father said to me. 'Take it and plant it in the sand before you begin to circumcise. It will mark the place where you will cut the young males of a village. The lolo is the legacy of our ancestors: it enables us to defeat our enemies.'

"For many years I traveled from village to village with my lolo and satchel, but I would always return to Jessey for the planting season. I walked through the lands of the Songhay, the Hausa, the Tuareg, the Bambara, the Fulan, the Gormantche, and the Mossi. I saw the Sahara. I saw the mountains of the Dogon. I saw the palace of the Mossi king. Where I went, I planted my lolo, and the village elders brought me their sons. 'Circumcise these boys,' they told me, 'and make them into men.' In some villages I circumcised 100 boys in one afternoon. When I completed my cutting, the elders of a village slaughtered a bull and brought forth musicians and bards. We feasted, sang, and danced late into the night.

"When I returned to Jessey each year for planting, I sat with my father and learned more incantations. Sometimes he sent me to the bush to search for the plants, roots, and barks he needed. Life was sweet during that time. Millet filled our granaries and children filled our huts.

"My father got very old and frail. He walked only with great difficulty. One day he could no longer get out of his bed. It was during the hot season just before planting that he called me into his hut.

" 'My son, I must now give you my greatest gift, the chain of our power [*sisiri*].'

" 'Yes, Father.' "

" 'Are you ready for it? Is there no filth in your heart?' "

" 'I am ready. My heart is pure.' "

" 'So be it, my son.' "

"My father told his youngest wife, Mintu, to bring me a small pot which was filled with a greenish paste. 'You must eat this, and then you, too, shall have the chain of power,' my father said.

"I ate a small bit of the paste [*kusu*] and my stomach filled with gas. I looked like a pregnant woman. I could not walk very well. And so, I remained with my father that day. The next day my kusu had gone to sleep and my stomach was once again flat. Father sent my younger brother Ali to fetch the drummers. My test was about to begin.

" 'Are you ready, my son?'

" 'Yes, Father, I am ready.'

" 'Then go outside and control your power.'

"The musicians arrived with their double-headed drums slung over their shoulders. They set up and began to strike their drums with great speed. The sound made me dance and dance and dance. I danced for a long time and asked Mintu for some ordinary millet porridge. The drummers again started their playing and I danced and danced and danced until I felt a tingling in my stomach. The tingling moved up from my stomach into my throat. I saw a bright white light and the chain of power came out of my mouth. A crowd gathered around me. The chain dangled from the end of my tongue. Two men helped me to sit down on an overturned mortar, and I began my test. I had to swallow the chain. I took it into my mouth until the last link disappeared. Then I swallowed and it went back into my stomach where it went to sleep. Many sohanci have died when they first try to swallow the chain. They died because they dared to swallow the chain when their hearts were filled with filth.

"I entered my father's hut. He knew I would survive. 'Your chain is now a powder, my son. It will become a chain only when you dance for hours to the beat of the best drummers. When you die, you, too, must give to your most worthy son a chain of power. In this way, we pass on our heritage and keep in the family the power to defeat our enemies!'

"My father died the next day, but people in and around Jessey knew that I had become the bearer of my father's burden."

"And then?" I asked with impatience.

"I am tired now, and people will be coming to see me soon. Stay with me if you like, but we won't be talking to one another until late tonight."

"Late tonight?"

"Yes, when Tillaberi is asleep."

A mountain of a middle-aged woman waddled into the compound. The skin of her melon-shaped face was smooth over her fat. She was so large that she rumbled when she stooped to enter the Sohanci's hut. And when she sat down on one of the straw mats in the hut, she groaned.

"Bismiallahi," she proclaimed to us, trying to catch her breath.

"How is your health, Hampsa?" the Sohanci asked her.

"As you can see, I am in fine health. And your family?"

"There are no problems in my household," the Sohanci answered.

"Why is there an Anasara here?" she asked the Sohanci.

"How are you, beautiful woman?" I asked in my best Songhay, for I knew that Songhay considered obese women beautiful.

"Ahh, Anasara, you speak Songhay?"

"Just a little bit," I said.

"Well, Anasara, how is your health?"

"Beautiful woman, my name is not Anasara. My name is Paul, just as your name is Hampsa."

"In God's name, you are correct, Paul. Now why don't you leave us, anyway," she insisted.

"Hampsa," the Sohanci interjected, "what you say to me you say to Paul, for we are one body, one mind, and one heart. We are on the same path."

"So be it."

The Sohanci took out a leather pouch and opened it. He poured onto the sand eleven cowry shells. Smoothing the fine sand between himself and the woman's mat, he threw the cowries. The Sohanci stared at the configuration of shells on the sand and looked at the woman. "There is trouble in your household, is there not?"

"Yes, Baba."

"The trouble has to do with a co-wife, a woman from the north who is younger than you."

"Yes, Baba."

He threw the cowries onto the sand a second time. "This co-wife had a stillbirth last year, did she not?"

"Yes, Baba.

"And this woman is jealous of you." He pointed to one shell in the configuration. "Don't you see it, Paul? Can you not see the jealousy there?"

"Of course I do," I lied.

"Baba, this woman makes me miserable. My children do not sleep. I have been nauseous for months. I cannot sleep. My husband pays no attention to me."

"Patience, patience." He threw the cowries a third time. "I see the solution. You must bring me a speckled chicken on Thursday, in two days, and I will make an offering to Nya Beri. You have filth in your heart, my child. Have you not betrayed your good friend?"

"I . . . I . . . ." She hesitated. "I have, Baba."

"Then bring me the chicken. Your heart must be cleansed so that life in your house can return to normal."

"Is that all, Baba?"

The woman pulled out a knotted cloth from between her huge breasts. She untied it and gave the Sohanci a 100-franc coin.

"Thank you and may God bless," he told her.

The woman had such trouble getting to her feet that I extended my hand to her. Slowly, I helped this giantess to stand. She took a deep breath, squeezed out of the Sohanci's hut, and lumbered away.

"How many people come to you each day?"

"Between five and ten people come to have me read the cowries for them."

"Will the woman return Thursday with the chicken?"

"If she wants tranquillity in her life, she will be back. If there is too much filth in her heart, she will remain at home."

We sat in the shade of the Sohanci's hut, like two people who had known one another for most of their lives. Neither of us felt the need to converse. Perhaps two hours passed this way before another client—also a woman—approached. She was visible at some distance in a red print wrap-around and top, and she walked steadily toward us. Her eyes were bright and deep-set.

"Baba, we must talk."

The Sohanci did not move from his shady spot. "Talk."

The woman looked at me and frowned. "But . . . ."

"Do not worry, Paul is sitting with me and working with me."

The woman sat down next to us. "My son is to be married next week. But I am afraid. I don't like his bride-to-be. I think she's a witch, and that she'll turn my son's children into witches."

"These are normal fears," the Sohanci told the woman.

"I want my son to marry and to prosper. I want him to bring healthy children into the world."

"It is good to hear this kind of talk." The Sohanci turned to me. "You know, Paul, the young people today have no respect for the old ways, the old values. They don't ask."

"What must I do to insure my son's prosperity?"

"We must stage a possession dance on the afternoon of a Thursday. It is the best time for the spirits. We shall try to bring to earth Serci. Serci will advise you and your son. Serci will tell you what to do to ensure a good marriage."

"What will you need for this dance?"

"I will need 2,500 francs for the musicians and spirit mediums and a white chicken to sacrifice."

"You shall have all of it."

16

ASKING QUESTIONS

Thin night clouds raced past the half-moon as I labored up the dune for my rendezvous with Adamu Jenitongo. My flashlight found the entrance of the compound, which was dark except for the pale glow of a lantern inside one of the grass huts. The Sohanci, who was seated by the lantern, greeted me and invited me in. Four hatchets, each with a bell attached to its head, were wedged between the hut's wooden skeleton and the thatch just above the entrance. Three large poles formed the hub of the round dwelling. The center pole poked through the top of the roof; the other poles were perhaps five feet tall. Red, white, and black twine had been tied around the shorter poles. A black cap had been placed on top of one of the shorter poles. But the most magnificent sight of all was the lolo, which the Sohanci had anchored in the sand near the center of the hut. It was a four-foot iron staff, the surface of which was mottled with the blood of sacrifices. Seven blood-caked rings had been attached to the top of the lolo.

"How was your day?" the Sohanci asked me.

"Fine." In the dim light I noticed for the first time the rings on the Sohanci's left hand. He had seven rings on the third finger of his left hand, the finger of power, a twisted iron and copper bracelet on his left wrist, and a huge brass ring, the one his father had given him, on his left thumb. His right hand bore no rings.

"Recite for me a text."

I recited the korombey text and provided my explanation of it. My view, of course, was that when a sorko or sohanci recites the incantation, the powder, korombey, receives the power to heal every part of the broken body. The incantation, I told him, transfers the force of the sacred words into the powder. But I saw from the expression on the Sohanci's face that my explanation had not satisfied him.

"Is that all? he asked. "Do you have some good questions to ask me?"

"Well . . . ." I hesitated.

"Out with it!"

"What about *asi goun goun ma* [the untranslatable first words of the incantation]?"

The Sohanci nodded. "Ah, *that* is the power of the incantation."

"But what is asi goun goun ma?"

"It is another name for korombey, but the sound of it has the power."

"I do not understand."

"Of course you do not, but you will in time."

"But what am I to do?"

"You tell me that you like the dune in the late afternoon. Go there tomorrow and think. Perhaps the answer will come to you there."

I stood up and bade the Sohanci good night.

"And remember," he said, as I passed into the cool night air, "you must ask to learn. He who does not ask, will know nothing. If you have the knowledge to ask the good question, then I shall answer you. But I will not talk to you unless you ask the correct question."

The next afternoon I stood atop the dune behind the secondary school. The sinking sun cast its light on a dune which hugged the east bank of the Niger River. I turned to the east. The late afternoon light brought into relief the jagged features of *Tilla beri*, the great mountain. A Fulan herdsman followed his cattle back from the bush. No rain tonight, I thought. I pondered the meaning of the text. "Asi goun goun ma!" These words came from another language, perhaps the language of the ancestors. How could their sound be powerful? Geese leaving the river honked as they took to the air to scout sleeping perches in the bush. A theory started to shape itself in my mind. The meaning of the words of the incantation is less important than the sound of those words; it is the vibrations, the sound vibrations, that really matter. That, too, I reasoned, was the significance of the witchcraft text I had learned. Djibo had made me promise not to divulge the name of the incantation. The meaning was important, I theorized, but so was the sound, the sound of words once uttered by the ancestors.

Late that evening while Tillaberi slept, I returned to the Sohanci's hut. This time we dispensed with the elaborate greetings, as we were both eager to learn whether my reflections had been accurately focused. I explained to the Sohanci my theory of sound, that sounds like "asi goun goun ma" carry the forces of the heavens, the force of the ancestors.

"Yes, of course they do," he said in a manner which reminded me of Djibo.

Having mastered my first lesson, I smiled.

"You know nothing yet," the Sohanci reminded me. "Recite another text."

I recited the second text I had learned, Diggi, in which they say "bam, bam, bam," and "bum, bum, bum." It is this incantation in which war is discussed, in which people transform themselves into leaves, beetles, hard clay, and cow droppings. "I believe the words of the text," I told the Sohanci, "enter into the substance and enable the sorko or sohanci to transform himself into various objects. In this way, his enemy will not see him or capture him."

"This is true. Diggi is very powerful," the Sohanci told me.

"But what happens when the sorko or sohanci is seen or taken?"

The Sohanci's face froze. "He becomes sick or he dies."

"Oh come on, Baba, he doesn't really die, does he?"

"A person on the path must always be prepared to meet his enemy. If not, he will die a young man." His eyes held mine for what seemed an endless moment. "What else do you have to ask about this text?"

"What is bam, bam, bam, bum, bum, bum?"

"In America, what are the sounds that one makes when his or her heart has been spoiled with the grief of betrayal? [zamba]."

"I don't know, Baba. Some people carry their grief silently."

"Good. Here, when a man on the path is betrayed, when his heart is filled with the filth of betrayal, his heart is awakened and he says bam, bam, bam, bum, bum, bum. It is a warning to those who could betray him and to those who have betrayed him, that his powerful heart is awake and dangerous."

"Oh?"

"And you," he pointed to me, "who are full. You must be careful not to become angry, not to say bam, bam, bam, bum, bum, bum, for now your heart is powerful. Since you are so young, you do not know what your heart is capable of doing. When I was younger I paid a heavy price for my bullheadedness. You must avoid this kind of folly."

"Oh?"

"Do you have any other good questions?"

I had mused about the metaphoric image of the milkweed falling from the seven heavens to earth. Was the image of the milkweed floating from the heavens to earth consistent with the ritual action of reciting the incantation? The words come from the heavens—above—and are aimed at the substance—that which is below on earth. One spits into the substance—that which is below—from his mouth, that which is above. And when one eats the substance, it travels from above, one's mouth, to below, one's belly. This ritual incantation was an enactment of a kind of heaven:earth/ powerful:powerless metaphor. In my experience among the Songhay, scant as it had been, people talked incessantly about the powers and forces of the heavens. And I had read in the works of Jean Rouch and Boubou Hama that the Songhay consider themselves powerless pawns in the scheme of a powerful and deadly universe, a universe controlled by God, his messenger Ndebbi, various angels, ancestors, and spirits. Like the milkweed, the incantations for diggi, for korombey, kobe, siria, and the other powders came from the heavens. They were passed down from Ndebbi to the ancestors and so on, until these secret and powerful sounds entered the minds of the healers of the present day. "When you recite the sacred words, it fills the powder with the force of the heavens," I told the Sohanci. "Words and the power to recite them come not from the present, but from the past, from the ancestors."

"It is true," the Sohanci said, "that the force comes from the heavens, from the ancestors. They revealed to us the path and we should follow it. And if we follow it, only God has the power to take us from earth. Our enemies cannot touch us." The Sohanci adjusted the wick of the kerosene lamp. "Continue."

17

PRISON YEARS

The day after the Sohanci had guided me to philosophic discovery, heavy rains drenched Tillaberi. Like most of the rains in June, this storm began early in the morning with blasts of sand and dust followed by a stampede of rain on our tin roof. The rain woke me from a short, sound sleep. While the rain cleared the outside air, the dust which still hung like fog in my room made it difficult for me to breathe. The heavy rains soaked the dunes, and the farmers of Tillaberi might at last sow their millet fields. The fields now lured men from the comforts of their homes early in the morning. Men worked hard at sowing, a labor motivated by the expectation of a fine harvest in October.

My heart filled with expectations also, expectations about learning the truths of Songhay philosophy. I ate a quick breakfast, and when the rain had stopped, I climbed a dune made firm by the early morning downpour. Although the lingering clouds obscured the sun, the Sohanci sat to the west of his hut in what would have been the early morning shade.

"Ah, Paul. Did you sleep in peace and tranquillity?"

"In peace and tranquillity only."

After greeting me, the Sohanci returned to his favorite pastime—braiding rope from palm fronds. "Sit down," he said without looking up from his work.

"Have you eaten?"

"Yes."

"Well, we will send my granddaughter out for some bean cakes. Your European stomach can tolerate bean cakes, can it not?" he asked.

"Of course. I like bean cakes."

"Good."

He returned again to his weaving, not bothering to talk to me. We sat silently until Kati, the Sohanci's granddaughter, brought us a bowl filled with bean cakes, which we ate in silence. "Jemma," the Sohanci called to his second wife, "come and get the bean cakes." We had eaten barely half the bean cakes in the bowl.

The Sohanci returned to his rope-weaving, and I stared into space wondering when we might begin to talk about substantive matters.

Two men approached the compound from town. Even from a distance I recognized Daouda Godji, who played the monocord violin, and Halidou, the Sohanci's nephew, who played the gourd drum. These tall, thin men always wore Western fashions—skin-tight trousers and snug cotton shirts with collars. They had come to discuss the possession dance the Sohanci had scheduled for that afternoon.

The Sohanci looked up from his growing coil of rope and greeted the two men. They greeted the Sohanci and me.

"Baba," Halidou said, "We have come to discuss how much we are to be paid for this afternoon."

"How can you discuss payment," the Sohanci asked, "when we have yet to receive money? Besides, if you play well, people will contribute money to us. Be patient. Be patient."

"We want to know our cut, that's all," Daouda said.

"You will both be well paid for your work. Do not worry. And do not pester me with this stupid money business."

The Sohanci looked at me. "You see Paul, all these young people are interested in is money—only money. Do you think they ask good questions? No, they are in a hurry to learn and they learn nothing except treachery." He turned back to the musicians. "Why don't you sit down and listen to me? I have much to tell today, and maybe you will learn something."

"I'm sorry, Baba," Halidou said, "I have to go."

"You see, Paul. Halidou is a worthless person. He has no time to listen to the wisdom of the old."

Halidou got up and left; Daouda, the violinist, remained. The Sohanci placed the palm fronds he had been weaving to one side. "I shall tell you about my time in Mali."

"Soon after my father's death, I took up his burden. People from faraway places came to my compound in Jessey to be healed. I treated people for simple problems like skin infections, sore muscles, broken bones, fevers—things like that. But I also helped people who had been bewitched or people who suffered from an attack of sorcery or from mean spirits. I also made people charms to protect them from witches and sorcerers, and the big people came to buy amulets and knotted belts which might bring them great power.

"My reputation grew in the land of the Zerma. It spread to the lands of the Hausa to the east and to the lands of the Songhay to the west. People became jealous of my power and reputation. Some people sent snakes to my compound. One snake, a puff adder, bit one of my children. She died. I did not seek revenge, however, for my father had taught me to use my power with great care. And so I did, despite repeated attacks upon me.

"I prospered. My clients brought me many gifts: millet, rice, chickens, goats, clothing from market cities. My family was very happy. I remained in Jessey throughout the year. My younger brother Hamani took up the burden of being a guunu. During the nonplanting season, Hamani traveled far and wide offering his services as a circumciser.

"My days of prosperity, however, came to an abrupt end. There had been a death in my family, and the French soldiers came and took me away to Tillaberi, where they threw me into prison. I lost much weight in prison during the three years I remained there awaiting my trial. Sometimes, members of my family came to see me. They brought me delicious food from time to time. But the food lifted my spirits only momentarily. During the day the French soldiers used us as laborers. We built roads. We farmed. We worked in their gardens. We repaired their houses. We worked like donkeys during the hot days only to return to the stuffy prison at night.

"My trial came up and the judge condemned me to a prison term of twenty years. He said I had murdered my wife. This whole business was a series of lies; someone had betrayed me. But the judge believed these lies and he condemned me to Chidal. This military prison was for the worst criminals in the colonies.

"I went to Chidal in Mali when the great war began. My first few years there were very difficult. We worked every day in the fields, building roads, tilling the soil. But I used my knowledge to survive. After only two years as a laborer, the commander of the prison made me a cook. I prepared the officers' mess. I have never seen so much meat, cabbage, onions, milk—more than any man could eat. But the officers ate more than any person I had known. They liked my cooking so much that they made me the head cook of Chidal. After a while they gave me my own house and asked me to look after their children.

"We were all transferred from Chidal to Bidon 5, an army post in the middle of the desert, a place with much wind, no trees, and no water. I remained the cook of the officers' mess, which meant that I had enough to eat and drink. Other prisoners perished in great number. Many of them starved to death. Some of them went mad.

"When I was at Bidon 5 during the great war, I saw General De Gaulle. He arrived there one day in an airplane. He was accompanied by a short fat man who walked with a cane. Commandant

Villey told me to fetch some water so De Gaulle and the other man could take a shower. When I arrived De Gaulle was taking off his clothes. He was the tallest man I have ever seen. I said: 'General, ze vous donne l'eau pour dous.' He thanked me and washed himself. When I saw De Gaulle, I knew he had great sorcery. I had heard that he had secretly gone to Mecca where he had received an amulet which had the power to defeat his enemies. The other man took his shower. Then the men got into their airplane and flew away.

"I spent only one year at Bidon 5. We thanked God when we left that terrible place. How we survived, I do not know. We settled in Tessalit, a prison town in Mali. In Tessalit, Commandant Villey named me the head cook of the officers' mess. He also wanted me to continue to look after his children.

"In God's name, I prospered in Tessalit. I had a fine European house to myself. I ate as well as the French Army officers. I became fat from all of the good food. One day the new head of the prison called me into his office.

" 'Adamu, come in,' he ordered me. 'Come in and sit down.'

"I entered the man's office and sat down in front of his large wooden desk. He held up a piece of paper.

" 'Do you know what this is?' he asked me.

"I had no idea.

"'It says here, Adamu, that you have done your time. You entered prison in 1940 and it is now 1960. Twenty years have passed. You are free to return home.' The Commandant stood up and walked over to where I had been sitting. I stood up. He shook my hand and congratulated me. He gave me 5,000 francs and a ticket for my transportation back to Niger. Before I left, the officers of the prison gave me many gifts—mostly cloth. They told me to take the cloth to the local tailor so that he could make me a beautiful grand boubou. On the day that I left the officers gathered to bid me farewell. The Commandant told me it was now time for me to return home to see my family. He told me that he had sent a telegram to Niger to tell them of my arrival. He also gave me a piece of paper that I had to give to the soldiers in Niger.

"I boarded the bush taxi and left Tessalit forever. My trip to Niger took one day to complete. We stopped in Gao and then in Ayorou, in Niger. When I showed my paper to the soldiers, they said, 'Welcome back, Baba. Soon you'll be in Tillaberi. There you are to report to the Commandant. Get on your bus and go home.' Two hours later I was in Tillaberi. We drove past the prison where I had spent three

years. I stepped out of the bus and recognized no one. A woman
cried out. 'Where is Adamu Jenitongo?'

" 'I am here,' I said.

"The woman threw her arms around me. 'Adamu, it is Kedibo,
your sister. You are so fat! I could not recognize you. Your clothing
is so beautiful!'

" 'They liked me in prison, but I am happy to be home.' "

A man marched into the Sohanci's compound. The Sohanci
looked at the man's face. "My son," he said to the man, "come into
my hut. Your face tells me that I have work to do."

18

THE COMING OF SERCI

In the early afternoon of that same Thursday, men and women associated with the Tillaberi cult of possession came into the compound of Adamu Jenitongo. They greeted him and me and entered
the Sohanci's hut, which they called the spirit house, a grass hut that
was the domain of supernatural beings. The Sohanci instructed his
wife, Jemma, to bring the adepts food to eat. She brought them a
plate of steaming rice which she drenched with a pungent black
sauce. From my vantage under the single tree in the compound, I
heard the mediums chattering as they ate their meal. Soon
thereafter, the acrid smell of the resin *ceeyndi* wafted out of the spirit
house.

"Why are they burning that resin?" I asked the Sohanci.

"They are preparing themselves for the festivities this afternoon,"
he told me.

When the shadows stretched from the thatched canopy to the
spirit house, it was time to begin the ceremony. The drummers sat
behind their gourds and struck up a rolling beat. The violinist took
his place directly behind the drummers on a low stool and played
some of the syncopated melodies from the huge repertory of sacred
spirit music. The cracking echo of the gourd drums carried far in the
still dry air of Tillaberi. Attracted by the music, people trickled into
the Sohanci's compound. Men and women strolled into the com-

pound wearing their most flamboyant clothing, for a possession dance is a dress-up occasion.

As the spectators arrived, so did the vendors, with small tables of goods balanced on their heads. A possession dance gave them the opportunity to sell cigarettes, hard candy, and chewing gum to the audience. The tempo of the music quickened. The buzz of the audience heightened. Some young children sauntered onto the dance grounds in front of the musicians' canopied stand, but they were ignored by the crowd and the major personalities of the possession cult.

But now a number of older women swept onto the dance ground. Holding one-foot-wide strips of cloth horizontally in front of them with both hands, the women formed a circle and danced counterclockwise. Moving to the slow melodious beat of what is called the *windi*, they danced with deliberation, pressing their right feet into the sand three times before taking a step forward. Eventually, these women broke the circle and formed a line at the edge of the dance ground. The musicians picked up the beat and played a tempo called the *gani*, or dancing music. As each dancer moved toward the canopy and the gourd drums, the musicians accelerated the tempo. One by one the dancers came closer and the tempo became faster still. The tempo reached a climax when the dancers, now performing directly in front of the musicians, furiously kicked up sand.

The most talented dancers received tips from the appreciative audience. When this occurred the dancer held up the gift, usually a coin worth 50 or 100 francs, and threw it to one of the drummers, who put the money in a common kitty. When many people come to a possession dance and dancing and music are particularly good, the cult can sometimes collect as much as 5,000 francs ($20).

At the peak of the dance contest, much to the delight of the audience, the aged Sohanci glided onto the dance ground. Inspired by the dancing of his younger colleagues, Adamu Jenitongo danced frenetically to a captivating beat. Several people from the audience, concerned that the dance might strain the heart of this old man, gently urged him off the dance ground.

The dancing continued for about two hours. The musicians played their favorite spirit rhythms, and people who were not spirit mediums danced in front of the musicians' stand. As the golden glow of late afternoon enveloped the Sohanci's compound, an old woman ordered the children to leave the dance ground. The musicians played the music of the *genji kwarey*, the family of spirits to which Serci, the social advisor, belonged. The chief of the Tillaberi

Zakaribaba Sorko Officiating at a Possession Ceremony

mediums, a large old woman whose loose jowls flapped as she walked, entered the dance ground accompanied by two other spirit mediums. They formed a circle and danced, moving counterclockwise. A sorko in an indigo robe leaped onto the dance ground. He sang praises to the genji kwarey, the white spirits. He sang:

"Dugunda's husband. Garo Garo's husband. Zaaje. White salt. Master of evil. You have put us with your own covering of clouds. Mercy and Grace.

"Only God is greater than he.

"He is in your hand. He gave the angels their generosity.

"You are the father of Kangey.

"You are the birth of language. You brought about victory."

The sorko repeated the praise-song as the musicians played the rhythms associated with Serci. The three mediums approached the musicians. The jowly woman took another step closer to the musicians. The sorko stood directly behind her. He screamed into her ear Serci's praise-songs.

Gradually, the tempo increased. Now standing directly in front of the musicians, the large woman moved only her head and arms to the music. She turned her head to the left as she slid her right hand along her right thigh. Then the woman slid her left hand along her left thigh and shook her head to the right. She shook her head from left to right, left to right, left to right. The violinist, sensing that the spirit Serci was just above the dance ground, made his bow fly. Swinging her body and pumping her arms to the music, the woman perspired profusely. The sorko shouted directly in her ear. The woman grimaced and her face cracked like the surface of a dry water-hole. Tears streamed from her squinting eyes and mucus ran from her nose. Something unseen grabbed her body and threw it to the ground. A voice shouted: "Ah di, di, di, di, di, a dah, dah, dah, dah, a dah." A deep groan escaped from the old woman's body. Again animated, the woman squatted on the sand with her hands on her hips and spat at the musicians. The drummers welcomed Serci, for that was the spirit now inhabiting the old woman. "Welcome, Welcome, Dungunda's husband, Garo Garo's husband."

Two attendants gently lifted Serci off the sand and guided him to a newly woven palm-frond mat. There, the attendants washed Serci's feet, ankles, hands, and head as though he were being prepared for Islamic prayer. Meanwhile, another attendant brought Serci his costume, a billowing white robe with gold embroidery around the neck. Once Serci was dressed in his robe, another attendant wrapped a white turban about his head. The Sohanci walked over to the mat and presented Serci with a string of silver worry beads.

The sorko in the indigo robe who had been shouting in the old woman's ear spoke to the woman who was sponsoring the possession dance on her son's behalf. He bade her to come with him to Serci's court. The sorko escorted the woman and her son to the mat upon which Serci sat. Following the lead of the sorko, the woman and her son sat on the sand in front of the spirit. The woman asked the sorko what she had to do to insure the successsful marriage of her son. The sorko, serving as an interpreter, posed the same question to Serci.

"Sorko," Serci began in a quavering and distant voice. "a white chicken, a red chicken, and a red-and-white speckled chicken must be sacrificed."

"Good," the sorko said. "And what else?"

"Sorko. The young boy must take the egg of a white hen and bury it at the base of the gao tree which is at the crossroads at the eastern edge of town."

"Praise be to God," the sorko proclaimed.

"Sorko. If these things are done, the marriage will bring healthy children into the world."

The sorko turned to the woman and her son and repeated Serci's words to them. Serci then beckoned to the son and grabbed the young man's head with both of his hands. Placing his mouth on one of the young man's ears, Serci screamed a word into it three times. Finished with his work, Serci pushed the young man away.

"Sorko."

"In God's name, I am listening."

"Sorko. Tell them that they must never stray from the path of their ancestors, the path of the spirits."

"Okay," the sorko said.

As the sorko communicated this admonition to the mother and her son, the Sohanci slowly placed his hands over Serci's temples. He lightly shook Serci's head from left to right. The body of the old woman slumped; she had lost consciousness. The Sohanci caressed her forehead and her temples. Attendants massaged her feet and legs. She opened her eyes, but appeared dazed. She coughed and asked for water.

"Old woman," the Sohanci said to her. "we thank you for your pain. We thank you for your work."

The woman took a few sips of water. "Sohanci, you have your burden, and I have mine. So it is in this world."

19

WORDS OF PROTECTION

It rained only twice while I was in Tillaberi in 1977. But people in Tillaberi were not yet worried about their millet crop. As they explained to me, it usually does not rain more than two or three times in June. The brief but heavy rain had been pleasant, and I was able to repress the memory of the scorching heat of the Sahel in June. But my respite lasted only a few days, for as the clouds dissipated and the cool west wind diminished, the blazing sun re-emerged to suck the last drops of cool moisture from the land. The dunes once again became powdery and hot. As I trudged up their inclines, the sun's rays made me dizzy. Even the short trip from the secondary school to the Sohanci's compound, a trip I made two or three times a day, made me thirsty, breathless, and fatigued.

The pace of my work did not slacken, however, for my time in Niger was short. Toward the end of my two-week stay, the Sohanci told me more about his life.

"The first thing my family did when I came back to Tillaberi was to arrange a local marriage for me. In this way I married Hadjo, whom I call Moussa Nya [Moussa's mother]."

"How did you come to marry Jemma, the mother of Moru?"

The Sohanci smiled. "While I was in prison, my family moved to a village called Sohanci, which is just outside of the town of Simiri. My family thought it was a terrible thing for the oldest member of our line to marry a woman from Tillaberi. My brother came to Tillaberi and said: 'Adamu, we thank God for your life, but you must come home to Simiri. There, you will farm our lands and marry one of our local women.'"

"And?" I wondered.

"One cannot refuse one's family. And so I went to Simiri, where I farmed the fields of my family and married Jemma, the mother of Moru."

"And then?"

"And then I came back to Tillaberi."

"Why?"

"Because all of the mediums of Tillaberi agreed that they wanted me to be their zima." He reached into his pocket and pulled out his wallet. From the wallet he carefully slipped out a folded piece of paper. He gave me the paper, which I opened. It was dated February 1964. "What does it say?" the Sohanci asked me.

The paper had been signed by the regional administrator of Tillaberi and proclaimed Adamu Jenitongo to be an officially registered healer in the town of Tillaberi.

"I have been here ever since. Right here in this house at the edge of the bush."

The Sohanci stood up and motioned for me to follow him into his hut—the spirit house. "It is time to see what lies on your path, my son." He sat down and took out his cowry shells. "With the help of Wambata [Nya Beri] may I see into past and into the future," he chanted. He threw the cowries onto the sand.

"What do you see, Baba?"

"I see trouble for you on your path. Maybe next month. Maybe in two years. You see this woman here," he said, pointing to a shell which had separated from the others. "She is in the west and she will give you trouble sometime in the future."

"Yes?"

"And I see that you must come here tonight. I must give you the *genji how*, for these words, and these words only, will protect you from the trouble which lies before you on your path."

He threw the cowries again.

"What do you see, Baba?"

"With protection, I see that you will move forward, that you will be hard. You will make your way in the world. People will like you. But beware, for there are people on your path who will attempt to block your way. You must be hard, very hard with them."

"Hard?" I asked. "What do you mean?"

"The meaning will come to you. I cannot tell you what it is. You must experience it as best you can."

"Baba, I have a thousand good questions. . . ."

"No more questions. You must go now and prepare to learn the genji how. Come late tonight."

That afternoon I could not sleep during the siesta hours; I paced in the afternoon heat and wondered what awaited me that evening in the Sohanci's hut. I drank glass after glass of water. I turned on the electric fan, the greatest of luxuries in a place like Tillaberi in the month of June. But the water did not cool me and the fan did not help much; it merely circulated hot air.

The heat dissolved the boundary between fantasy and reality. I saw the trouble to which the Sohanci referred. Some river demon, a serpent fifty feet in length, attacked the dugout which was carrying me across the Niger. We capsized and the demon closed its giant mouth on the pilot, cutting the poor man in two. The demon went off after the other passengers, gobbling them up in one swallow. It lifted its head out of the water and came after me. Its eyes blazed red, and its double tongue lashed out, cracking in the air like a bull whip. I had met my end. But I remembered that the genji how protects people from danger. And so I recited it, and the serpent stopped coming toward me. Instead, it slithered under the water. Fully expecting it to attack me from under the water's surface, I awaited my certain death. But nothing occurred. The serpent had disappeared. I swam to a nearby island where villagers came to my aid and called me *cimikoy*, a keeper of the truth, a person who possesses the knowledge of the ancestors.

The bray of a donkey brought me back to my senses, back to an overheated whitewashed room in Tillaberi. This sorcery and philosophy I had been learning had to be illusion, certainly not something one might reduce to tangible data, to facts. I realized at that moment that I must not relinquish my role as objective observer, no matter how involved I might become in the Songhay world of magic. I must not forget, I told myself, that I am an anthropologist, a scientist of the human social condition. I was certain that after a time I would truly understand the Songhay, perhaps better than they understood themselves.

When the quiet of night settled on Tillaberi, I headed for the Sohanci's compound. My shoes crunched as I inched forward up the dune; no other sound escaped into the moonless night air. My weak flashlight made barely a dent in the depth of blackness ahead of me. Slowly, I climbed the dune, recognizing a familiar foothold, an odd-shaped bush, a particularly tall and thorny tree.

I walked directly into the Sohanci's hut, which was marked as usual by flickering lantern light.

"Come in," he whispered. "We must be very quiet tonight; I will be introducing you to words which have great power. If bad people were to overhear us, they might misuse the words. I know you well enough, my son, to realize that I can trust you with these words."

Despite everything I had learned, I still could not accept that words could have such power, such force. Words might protect me from the vengeance of river serpents in my daydreams, but how could they protect me from a sorcerer bent on poisoning me? "I thank God for your trust, Baba." Indeed, I did not understand why this old man, who had not seen me for five years and was only now getting to know me, wanted to give me one of his greatest treasures, which he had thus far refused to teach his youngest sons, Moussa and Moru.

"Are you ready, my son?"

"I am, Baba."

He touched my hand gently. "Listen carefully. There will come a time, a time that I have seen in the cowries, when you will travel throughout the lands of the Songhay in search of knowledge."

"Yes, if God wills it."

"And when you travel away from me, people will know you. They will know that you are on the path. Many people, for this reason, will not like you. They will want to harm you. And so, when you visit other people, always bring a chicken or two with you."

"Why chickens? They are a burden to a traveler."

"That is correct, but better to carry a burden than to die."

"What are you talking about, Baba?"

"A man on the path can never know what another will do to him. A man on the path does not always know his enemies. A man on the path must be hard; he must be prepared. When you receive food from a person whom you do not know well, or from a person whom you know but in whom you have little confidence, then you must give some of the food to your chicken. If the chicken survives, the food is fit to eat. If not, you know that you will have a battle on your hands."

"A battle, what do you mean?"

"That I cannot say."

"Why would anyone want to poison me?"

"In the world of war, every person on the path is a target for the bad faith of others. There is much filth and betrayal in our world. You must be prepared."

Overwhelmed and perplexed, I promised the Sohanci that if I traveled in the future, I would be sure to take along two or three chickens. The thought that a Songhay would attempt to poison a European researcher, however, seemed out of the realm of possibility.

The Sohanci continued to whisper to me. "Sometime in the future, a woman will bring you trouble. She will do something to you. And you will think that you are going to die. When this happens you must recite the incantation that I teach you tonight. You must recite it until your fear of death has escaped."

His chilling words froze my face. Open-mouthed, I stared at the Sohanci. "I understand," I told him.

He patted me on the back of the hand once again and whispered his genji how:

"In the name of God, Koosh. In the name of God, Koosh. I speak to Ndebbi. I speak to the seven heavens. I speak to the seven hells. I speak to the east. I speak to the west. I speak to the north. I speak to the south. My words must travel until, until, until they are known and understood. Ndebbi was before human beings. He gave the path to Soumana. Soumana gave it to Niandou. Niandou gave it to Mata. Mata gave it to me. What they have given me is better than good. My path is beyond theirs. Ndebbi gave to us seven hatchets and seven picks. He came and gave us speech, and he took it back. He showed us the rock. He made the princes strong. Now the angels will not see. Bullets will not see. All is protected by the force of the heavens."

He laughed. "Oh it is a very mean text; it is a hard text."

I found it a mysterious text, and I flooded him with questions. Who was Soumana? Who was Niandu? To what does the "seven hatchets and seven picks" refer? Why did Ndebbi take back speech?"

"Shhh! Someone might overhear us."

"Explain the text to me, Baba?"

"That I cannot do. You must remember the text. The meaning of the words is secondary. Do you understand?"

"No, I do not," I said in frustration.

The Sohanci found my impudence amusing. "It makes no difference. Let us memorize this text. Quickly now."

Given my previous practice in learning incantations, it did not take me a long time to memorize the Sohanci's genji how. Once I mastered it, he took my hand between his hands.

"Keep this text in your heart, and never recite it unless you must."

"Yes, Baba."

He took out his cowries once again and threw them on the sand. "Aha! Do you see that shell which landed to the south? That, my son, is you. You should not delay your departure from Tillaberi. Go tomorrow, for your path is a clear one, a good one for you and your work."

"But I would like to stay on a few more days. I have so many good questions."

"Which I would not answer," the Sohanci said. "When the shells say you must go, you must. They do not lie. Go tomorrow, and go with God's protection."

"But Baba, when will I see you again?"

"Before you realize."

20

ON THE ROAD

It rained the day I left Tillaberi. Throughout the early morning the clouds hung low and heavy, indicating that the rain might last most of the day. Despite the rain, I knew that I had to leave. And so I stuffed most of my things into a large green duffle and put them into J. F.'s Peugeot. We arrived at the Tillaberi auto depot, which was adjacent to the market along the paved road going south to Niamey. After saying goodbye to J. F., I saw Salou, the manager of the depot. He sat listlessly on a bench under a thatched canopy.

"Ah, Monsieur Paul," Salou said to me in slurred French. "You are going to Niamey?"

I had known Salou since 1970. In those days he and I drank beer together at the Giraffe Bar. On some of those occasions, I kept pace with Salou's consumption. But as the years passed my capacity for beer had decreased arithmetically while that of Salou's had increased exponentially. People told me that there were three certainties in Tillaberi: the sun would rise in the east, it would set in the west, and Salou would be drunk by mid-morning. The rainy day of my departure was no exception. Salou reeked of beer. A small splotch of vomit had dried on the sleeve of his shirt.

"Ah, Monsieur Paul, where are you going?"

"To Niamey."

"You are in luck, Monsieur Paul. Oungunia's bus will depart very, very soon."

"How wonderful! I will go to Niamey with my good friend Oungunia."

Oungunia's skill as a driver was legendary in Tillaberi. Even I can attest to it. In the hot season of 1971, I agreed to travel from Niamey to Tillaberi in the back of Oungunia's bush taxi, a Peugeot 404 pickup truck. Along with twelve other people I squeezed myself into the Peugeot's carrier, which was designed to hold eight people. My cramped position against the door between a 250-pound woman and three bawling infants enabled me to spy Oungunia drinking a 3/4-liter bottle of beer. Straining, I pushed myself out of the taxi and confronted our driver.

"How many beers have you had, Oungunia?"

Oungunia belted down the rest of the beer and burped. "That makes four bottles. When it's hot, I drink beer."

A Vista South of Tillaberi

"But can you drive?" I asked.

"Can I drive, he asks. Well, Monsieur Paul, get into the taxi. Soon you'll know whether I can or cannot drive."

By the time we had reached the midpoint of our journey, Oungunia had consumed three more bottles of *Bière Niger*. The more beer Oungunia drank, the faster he drove along a rough dirt road with precipitous curves and fallen tree-thorns standing upright in the sand just waiting to puncture a tire. The passengers pounded on the back window of the driver's cabin; they thought Oungunia was going too fast. And we all knew that we had yet to pass the Bridge of Death, a one-lane span without restraining barriers which extended over a dry but deep riverbed. The Bridge of Death also spanned the rusted, twisted frame of a truck lying dead on its side in the riverbed. As we approached the Bridge of Death, I heard a loud pop, for Oungunia, laughing wildly, had pried off with his teeth the cap of another bottle of beer. He floored the gas pedal; the engine roared. The passengers in the carrier hammered on the back window of the cab. They screamed insults in Hausa and Songhay. Nonetheless, we whizzed across the bridge. As we were all letting out our breath after our safe crossing, Oungunia came to a screeching halt and jumped out of the taxi. "Am I not the best driver in all of Niger?"

"No, no, Oungunia," one woman retorted. "You are simply the son of a donkey."

The large presence of Oungunia transported me from past to present. He was big, thick, round, and black and wore a "bush suit," matching shirt and trousers. He slapped me hard on the back and greeted me in his throaty voice.

"Monsieur Paul. Are you coming with me to Niamey?"

"Yes, Oungunia."

"Good. The rains will make our trip a pleasant one. You must sit next to me so we can talk about old times. OK?"

"OK."

Despite his drunken restlessness of another time, Oungunia and I had become good friends. Before leaving Niger in 1971, I took a photograph of him leaning on his bush taxi. Later, I sent him a print of the photo.

"You know that photo, Monsieur Paul?"

"Yes."

"I got it in the mail. I bought a frame for it. It hangs on the wall of my house. I'll keep it always." Oungunia turned around and yelled at one of the young men who was loading his bus, a Mercedes, which seated thirty-five people. "Tie it down securely, you monkey.

We can't afford to have something fall on the road." He turned back toward me and smiled. "Ah, Monsieur Paul, the road may be paved now, but nothing has really changed."

"You speak the truth, Oungunia," I said.

The passengers scrambled onto the bus and found seats.

"Are we ready?" Oungunia asked Salou.

"You are ready," Salou responded. "Off with you."

We traveled less than one kilometer when we came to a police roadblock. A young man in green fatigues motioned for us to stop. He asked everyone to get out of the bus. Seeing me, a white man, he gruffly demanded my papers. I handed him my passport and my research authorization, which had been signed by the President of the Republic.

After seeing my papers the young man said: "We are honored to meet you, Monsieur le Professeur."

"The honor is mine, sir, "I told him.

The sergeant, who sat on a wooden bench under a tree, called Oungunia and me over to his office. "White man, where are you going?" he asked me in French.

"My name is Paul. My father's name is Stoller," I told him in my best Songhay. "I am going to Niamey."

"Hah," gasped the sergeant, "you speak Songhay." He was a giant man, bigger even than Oungunia.

"Only a little," I told him.

"More than a little," he said with obvious pleasure. He looked at Oungunia and arched his eyebrows. "Tell me Oungunia, why should I not make you unload all of your cargo?"

"Because," Oungunia answered without hesitation, "if you make me unload everything, how can I return to Tillaberi today with the case of beer that you and your friends want to drink tonight?"

The sergeant scratched his chin. "You know, I had almost forgotten about that, Oungunia. Well, don't stand here looking at me. Get on the road, I am getting thirsty already."

Now we could roll. The road stretched to the horizon, cutting the flat scrub desert in two. To our left lay the sunbaked plains, which were dotted by occasional trees. Mesas broke the monotony of these flatlands. To our right the Niger glistened in the morning sunlight, snaking its way ever southward. Soon we veered to our left and chugged up a mesa which towered over the Niger basin. We stopped at Sansanne-Hausa, a small town which had a tiny medical facility. Young girls balancing trays of mangoes and lemons on their heads converged upon the bus. A young man asked me if I wanted to buy a brochette. I declined, being all too familiar with the consequences of eating meat cooked with too much hot pepper and peanut flour. We soon left Sansane-Haussa, racing down one side of a mesa only to creep up the side of another. We did not stop again until we reached the outskirts of Niamey, the capital of Niger, where we encountered another roadblock. Here, a soldier with a rifle slung over his shoulder stood next to the barrier. While Oungunia presented his papers to the man in charge of this operation, a young soldier swaggered up to me and asked why a rich European rode in a people's bus. I showed him my passport and my letter of authorization from the President of the Republic. The young soldier's attitude changed.

"I wish you a good sojourn in Niamey," he told me.

Since there were no problems at the checkpoint, we headed into Niamey. The outskirts were under heavy construction: government buildings, new mudbrick compounds, and, to the east, a new neighborhood of two-story luxury villas. As we drove into the center of Niamey, a kaleidoscope of urban sensations formed our impression of the city: the breathtaking stench of open sewers; flies hovering over stagnant pools of dishwater discarded over dirt streets; a child squatting over a crack in the sidewalk, green slime emerging from between his buttocks; knots of people dodging scores of taxis which fired down the street like bullets; the wail of a frightened child. Near the market we saw aged men, twisted by poorly set broken bones, shuffling along sidewalks. Toothless lepers inched forward on crutches, thrusting their stubs of hands into the faces of possible donors. Young boys and girls carried enameled bowls, leading their blind mothers and fathers along an invisible beggars' trail. Driving our way through this sea of human misery, we entered the auto depot, which was adjacent to the central market of Niamey. The depot was an asphalt-covered yard blooming with trucks, buses, and taxis. In many of the empty trucks and buses, young men sat passing the time of day, listening to cassettes or to the radio.

Oungunia parked the bus at the west end of the depot, where Tillaberi buses arrived and departed. Clusters of young men swarmed over the bus. Some of them hawked sunglasses tied to a pegboard; others presented their arms, which were ringed with reworked Swiss watches. One young man offered baked rolls; another sold stringy boiled manioc. Those young men who had nothing to sell asked if the passengers needed help with their luggage. Most of the young men of the depot knew me personally or by reputation—as the white man who spoke good Songhay.

"Hey, Paul, hey. Hey, Mehanna Anasara, hey," one called to me.

"How are you?" from another. "Hey, Paul. When you go back to Mehanna, take me with you. I'll work for you."

"Thank you for the feeling in your hearts," I told them. "But in God's name, I am coming to Niamey to stay. Soon I return home to America."

The most enterprising of these young men approached me. His black trousers and sleeveless black cotton shirt fit snugly on his thin frame. "You are going to America?" he asked me.

"Yes. In a few weeks, I will enter an airplane and go."

"So, why can't you take me? Take me in the plane. I will go to America."

"Do you have a ticket?" I asked.

He slapped me on the shoulder. "You will pay my ticket, of course."

I slapped him on the shoulder. "How much money do you think it takes to fly to America?"

"I have never been. How would I know?"

"It costs 300,000 francs for a round-trip ticket."

"God, 300,000 CFA?"

"That's it. And I am a student. My government paid for my trip. I couldn't afford to pay it myself."

"Sure you could," another of the young men chimed in.

"And anyway," I said to the man in the sleeveless black shirt, "how could you go if you do not have a passport?"

"A passport?"

I took out my passport and showed it to the group. "Can you get one of these from your government?"

"I don't know," said the man in the sleeveless shirt.

"And even if you get a passport, you'd have to get a visa to come to America."

"I have heard that that is true," interjected a bystander who was listening to our conversation. In fact, my talk about passports, visas, and airline tickets had in the space of a few minutes attracted a crowd of about fifty onlookers.

One of Oungunia's assistants handed me my duffle bag. Oungunia said goodbye, but he told me before he left that he knew I would be coming back to Tillaberi again. "I can feel it in my heart."

Refusing offers of aid, I hoisted my bags and headed for one of the depot's many exits.

"Monsieur Paul," the young man in the sleeveless shirt called.

"Yes?"

"You know how to talk. In God's name, you know how to talk."

21

VENGEANCE FOR THE POWERFUL

I emerged from the depot on the Avenue De Gaulle, a main thoroughfare in Niamey, opposite the American Cultural Center. I crossed the street, and Ali, a young man crippled by polio, hobbled over to me; he insisted on carrying my bags. We walked by the Cultural Center into one of Niamey's many teeming neighborhoods. I was headed for Moussa's house, which was fairly close to the Cultural Center. Moussa had once worked at the Social Science Research Institute in Niamey. Since Moussa's house was so close to the bus depot, I always stopped there first when I came to Niamey.

Moussa greeted me at the opening of his compound. He was a short man with an extraordinarily large head and oval face. He was one of the few young Songhay man I knew who had a beard.

Moussa introduced me to his cousin Mody, who was visiting. He told us a terrible tale of a person who had abused him. This person, a European who had his own business in Niamey, routinely mistreated his employees. Mody had worked fifteen years for the European; he was a trusted employee. But one day in an unexplained rage, the European fired Mody, accusing him of theft. Mody pleaded with his boss not to fire him. There was a police investigation; Mody was not implicated. The European fired him anyway. Mody vowed revenge.

"It sounds terrible, Mody. What have you done about it?"

"Perhaps you can help?" Moussa wondered.

"Me? What can I do?"

They led me into one of three small two-room houses in the compound. "We know," Moussa said, "that you have been to a sorko's house in Mehanna. We also know that you have sat with a sohanci in Tillaberi."

"How did you know about that?"

Moussa smiled, revealing teeth too big for his small mouth. "Word travels fast down the river."

"So what does it matter that I have sat with these men?"

"It matters a great deal." Moussa took a deep breath. "We thought you could do something to this man to punish him for firing my cousin."

109

Blood rushed to my face. "Moussa! I'll do nothing of the sort. Besides, I know nothing. I haven't even begun to learn these things."

Moussa opened his mouth ever so slightly and said softly. "We need your help. Monsieur Paul, we have suffered greatly because of this man. And Mody is not alone; others are suffering, too."

When I first arrived in Niger Moussa had been kind to me; he had given of himself and had asked for nothing in return. I relented. "In a week's time, I will leave Niamey to consult one of my teachers. If something is done, I will tell you of it. If not, I will never mention it again."

That week I suffered in Niamey. I split my time between the library of the University of Niamey's Social Science Research Institute, where I read French ethnographies of Sahelian societies, and a cubbyhole at a friend's house where I transcribed scores of texts which I had tape-recorded. I filled spare moments drafting a version of the final report of my research activities which the conditions of my research permission required me to submit to the government of Niger before my departure. As a field-oriented anthropologist, I did not enjoy completing these tasks. But I suffered more from guilt than from the chores of transcribing texts and writing final reports. Had I become too involved in the world of Songhay sorcery? Here I was contemplating becoming an accessory in an attack of sorcery, although I doubted that a ritual would bring an end to the European's outrageous behavior. Frankly, I did not believe that a ritual act—no matter what its seriousness—could alter behavior. Still I had agreed to talk to the Sohanci about this case, and I couldn't determine which of my many mixed emotions was the strongest. Was it out of my scholar's urge to learn more about the Songhay world of sorcery, or was I slowly being led into a world in which morality did not exist?

I returned to Tillaberi early one afternoon just one week before my departure from Niger and set out directly for the Sohanci's compound. The school year had ended and the school grounds were empty. I climbed the dune to the Sohanci's compound and found him weaving palm-frond rope in the shade of the spirit house. He was not surprised to see me.

Motioning for me to sit down next to him, the Sohani resumed his rope weaving. We sat in silence as we often had. Then he looked at me. "My son, what brings you to Tillaberi?"

I told the Sohanci about the man who had fired Moussa's cousin in Niamey. "Don't you think it is ridiculous for Moussa to ask for my help? What could I do?"

"Are you not on the path, my son?"

"Yes."

"Are you not full?"

"Yes, I'm full."

"Is your heart not a strong one? Are you not capable of saying, bam, bam, bam, bum, bum, bum?"

"Yes, Baba, I can feel anger, but I don't feel that my heart is dangerous to other people. How could it be?"

The Sohanci ignored my rhetorical questions and returned to his rope weaving. "What you describe is a case of *bankwano foutu* [lit. 'mean chief']. In the old times there were many chiefs who were unjust. Sometimes, the good chiefs asked us to do work for them to fix a chief."

"Fix?"

The Sohanci chuckled. "Yes, to put an end to the man's authority." He stood up abruptly and entered the spirit house. He called me inside and asked me to sit next to him. "In the case of a mean chief, the solution is simple."

"What is the solution?" I asked.

"You take the _____ of a _____ chicken and bury it under the threshold of the mean chief's compound, a place he steps over every day. When you recite the incantation, no one must see you and no one must overhear you."

"What incantation?"

The Sohanci recited it. "Heart for heart, mind for mind. My heart is your heart. My mind is your mind. What is in my heart will be in your heart. What is in my mind will be in your mind. Whatever I want, you want. You have no choice. You cannot escape."

I memorized the incantation in five minutes.

"What must I do now?" I asked.

"You must return to Niamey at once," the Sohanci said, "and buy the _____ of a _____ chicken and say the text over it. Then you take the _____ of a _____ chicken and give it to your friend and have him bury it at the house of the mean chief."

"Shouldn't I do it myself?"

"No, no, someone else must bury it."

"So be it."

The ride back to Niamey passed quickly, probably because I daydreaming as I stared at the darkening western sky. It was professionally unethical for me to intercede for Moussa and his cousin, but, I reasoned, in one measure or another the nature of ethnography is unethical. Is it ethical for anthropologists to pry into the private lives of people in the name of science? Still, my involvement had provided me an inside view of how and why Songhay seek sorcery. How could such a rite work, anyway?

We crossed the barrier into Niamey at dusk, and by the time we reached the center of town, it was dark. A fog of dust hung below the fluorescent street lights near the market.

I met Moussa at his house the next morning.

"Well," said Moussa. "What can you tell me?"

"I can tell you a great deal, but before we do anything, I need some information."

"What do you want to know?"

"First, I want to know the identity of the European boss."

"Okay, he is Monsieur R. Do you know his business?"

"Oh, yes. I have heard of him. He is disagreeable, isn't he?"

"Yes, and he has caused our family great pain." Moussa searched my face. "Anything else?"

"Yes. Neither you nor I will participate directly. Let Mody or someone else from your family get involved."

"But Monsieur Paul, they are *already* involved. They have already tried some work; it has failed."

"Very well." I presented the ＿＿＿ of a ＿＿＿ chicken to Moussa. Earlier in the morning I had recited the incantation over it three times and theoretically considered the object imbued with the forces of the heavens. "Now someone must bury this at a threshold over which Monsieur R steps every day."

"I understand, Monsieur Paul. My whole family thanks you."

"Don't thank me, Moussa. Thank my teacher."

I did not see Moussa again until the day before my departure. I had just turned in my final report to the government of Niger and had reconfirmed my airline reservation for Paris. Walking toward the market, I saw him on the Avenue De Gaulle.

"Ah Monsieur Paul, can we talk?"

I hadn't much time for talking, rushing to tie up loose ends before leaving. "Only for a minute, Moussa."

Moussa leaned toward me conspiratorily. "When the donkey throws a person, the person cannot break the fall by catching the donkey's ear."

"What are you talking about, Moussa?"

"Don't you know the proverb?"

"No."

"Well, it means that once a person has done something, it can never be erased from history."

"Aha! So it is done, is it?"

"It is, Monsieur Paul."

"Good. May God protect us all on our journeys."

"Amin [Amen]." Moussa opened the satchel he was carrying and pulled out a strip of brightly colored cloth. "This is for you, Monsieur Paul. My brother wove it."

I hesitated. "But, I can't . . . ."

"You must take it."

"But, but . . . ."

"You must, Monsieur Paul."

"Thank you from my heart, Moussa."

"May God go with you, Monsieur Paul."

I left Niger the next day, hoping that despite the fervent prayers of many people, the ____ of a ____ chicken would never alter the behavior of the mean chief.

II · 1979–80

22

FRIGHTENING DISCOVERIES

I returned to Niger in November 1979. Despite the official obligations which confront a scholar about to begin fieldwork in a foreign country, I decided to see Moussa directly after clearing customs and getting myself situated in a room at the Social Science Research Institute. And so one hour after my arrival I walked past the American Cultural Center and saw the cripple Ali, who greeted me with praise-songs. I continued along until I reached Moussa's house. I clapped three times at the entrance of the compound. Someone said, "Enter," and so I did. Moussa was sitting on rickety canvas director's chair. He greeted me as if he had seen me yesterday, not a year and a half ago.

"How is your health, Moussa?"

"All is fine," he said casually. "I am thanking God for it." I stared at Moussa for an instant. How could he be so casual?

Gathering my courage, I posed the question I had been waiting to ask for more than a year.

"Moussa," I began. "How is Monsieur R?"

Moussa smiled at me. "Didn't you hear?"

"I heard nothing," I said breathlessly. "What happened?"

"Are you sure you didn't hear, Monsieur Paul?"

"No, I didn't hear."

Moussa leaned over the table. "Monsieur R left Niger."

"When did he leave?"

Moussa scratched his head. "Let's see." He looked up at the ceiling. "He . . . left about one month after you left Niger, almost a year and a half ago."

"How could that be?"

"Well, Monsieur Paul, there are strange things that happen in Africa. Monsieur R has returned home."

"Really?"

"Really," Moussa said.

"But," I wondered, "didn't Monsieur R spend many years in Niger?"

"He had been here for ten years," Moussa told me.

Was it coincidence that the "mean chief" had suddenly left Niger

117

after ten years and had returned to the country of his birth? "What happened? Why did he leave?"

Moussa pursed his lips. "You should know what happened, Monsieur Paul."

"I don't know why I should know anything."

"You should know what happened, Monsieur Paul," Moussa repeated.

I asked the unthinkable question. "Did Monsieur R become sick?"

Moussa answered no. "His sister became seriously ill, Monsieur Paul."

"His sister?"

Moussa described the bizarre circumstances of the sister's illness. One day about three weeks after my departure from Niger, the woman woke up to discover that her face was paralyzed. "Her nose was over close to her ear and her mouth had moved to the left side of her face," Moussa told me. Concerned about his sister's bizarre condition, Monsieur R took her to a private clinic. The doctors there gave her muscle relaxants and a series of sedatives. But this therapy proved ineffective. Monsieur R took his sister to the National Hospital where they also attempted to treat her condition. They, too, failed. Considering the facilities in Niger to be inadequate, Monsieur R evacuated his hysterical sister to their home country in Europe. "When she set foot on the soil of her country," Moussa reported, "the paralysis ended and her nose and mouth returned to the center of her face."

"How do you know that occurred?" I asked.

"Both Mody and I saw her before she left, and besides, this sort of thing happens all the time in Africa."

"But how do you know that Mlle R has recovered?"

"Ah. Sometime ago he wrote someone at his former business that as soon as his sister returned home, she recovered."

I turned away from Moussa and looked toward the door of Moussa's house. I could not accept that I had had anything to do with this event.

"But how could this happen, Moussa?"

"Monsieur Paul, *you* know how this could happen."

"But who would do such a thing to that poor woman?"

"Monsieur Paul, *you* know who could do this."

"But . . . ."

Moussa sighed and pointed at me. "You know who could do this, Monsieur Paul."

"But I do not have the force for such an act. Surely, it was my teacher, or someone else."

"Maybe so," said Moussa, "but I fear you and your mind, Monsieur Paul. You are a hard man with much violence deep in your heart."

"You fear me? I can't believe it. I can't do that. Believe me, I can't." I flung myself out of the house onto the street. I dashed past the American Cultural Center, crossed the Avenue De Gaulle, and disappeared into the bowels of the central market.

23

EVIDENCE OF POWER

Three days later, in search of answers, I took a dugout that was headed for Mehanna. At first my interest in sorcery had been largely theoretical. I hadn't actually believed in the act I had performed. Perhaps Moussa had been playing with me. Surely a conference with Djibo would answer these questions and put my mind at ease. He would tell me that I knew nothing, that I was unnecessarily tormenting myself.

We poled out onto the river. In a matter of moments the dust and grime of the fields and river bank gave way to the enchanting serenity of the river. We glided through narrow canals cut through high rice grasses. Among these swaying green walls the sounds were hushed: the push of the paddle against the water, drops from Haruna's raised paddle, the rustle of the dugout against the river grasses. Over us, calling ducks flew in formation. A fish leaped from the water to snatch a fly from a blade of grass. We passed close to egrets and herons which nonchalantly stood their ground. We emerged from the grasses and coasted into the broad, fast-moving western branch of the Niger River. I took up my paddle, and Haruna and I rowed with the current. As we came nearer to Mehanna, we joined a motley flotilla with the same destination.

We landed on the fine sands of the Mehanna shore and, like Gulliver among the Lilliputians, were surrounded immediately by scores of young children. They chanted, "Paul has come. Paul has come." Far more decorously, some of the elders of Mehanna came to the boat to greet me. Idrissa ran to the dugout and welcomed me back to Mehanna. He took my belongings and headed toward the compound which I had quit more than a year and a half ago. Despite Idrissa's continuing efforts at gardening, nothing new had grown in the compound; it was still barren except for one acacia.

I settled in. After chasing away gift-seekers, Idrissa joined me in my house.

"How long in Mehanna this time, Monsieur Paul?" Idrissa asked.

"I won't be many days in Mehanna, Idrissa. My work is finished here. I came to see old friends."

"And then?"

"I'll go on to Bonfebba on Friday and travel to Tillaberi. There, I'll study with an old man. I should be there about one month, maybe two."

Idrissa frowned. His body twitched with nervous energy.

"Of course, I'll come back once more before I return to America."

Idrissa leaned toward me. "Monsieur Paul. You don't know it, but I divorced my second wife. I want my first wife now."

"Why are you telling me this, Idrissa?"

"You are my patron."

"You mean I'm like your noble?"

"That's it, Monsieur Paul. I still want my first wife, Jitu. Her father didn't want her to leave Wanzerbe. When we married, he spoiled everything and we got divorced. Then I married this Loga woman. She bore me a son. I couldn't live with her anymore. I sent her back to her parents' house and divorced her. Now I want to marry Jitu again."

"You want to marry Jitu?"

"Yes. But I need money, a brideprice."

"Yes?"

"And I need to travel to Wanzerbe to ask Jitu's father for his daughter."

"For his permission?"

"Yes, he has changed. He has agreed to the marriage for a price."

"Which would be how much, Idrissa?"

"5,000 francs [roughly $20]."

"That's not too bad," I told him.

"It's good, Monsieur Paul. Could you make the marriage happen?"

Idrissa's request troubled me. I had been trying to maintain social distance even while I had shared the intimacy of the everyday life of

Idrissa's father's compound in Wanzerbe. I should have known better. "But Idrissa, this is a task for your father or your mother's brother, is it not?"

"Yes, but my father, Kundiababa, is poor. He has no money and you do."

I did not explain to Idrissa my shoestring budget and the limitations it placed upon my research; rather I told him that arrangements would be made, somehow, for a trip to Wanzerbe and that he would have his brideprice. Idrissa beamed, and for the first time in our three-year relationship, he hugged me.

The smoke hanging in the air above Mehanna signalled the arrival of dusk, when women fanned their cooking fires. I stood up and told Idrissa I wanted to walk around the village.

"Going to see the Guardian?" Idrissa asked

"You mean Djibo, the sorko?"

"Yes, him."

"Well, I thought I would say hello to him."

"Say hello to him, Monsieur Paul, but don't give him money. He's a bad man. He'll betray you. I know it."

"How do you know this, Idrissa?"

"I don't listen to what the Guardian says, I watch what he does. The Guardian will betray you. He'll make your life miserable."

I left the compound. Why did Idrissa distrust Djibo so? Was it because he wanted money that might otherwise be given to Djibo? Small children ran up to me, touched my hand, giggled, and ran away. A young mother carrying an infant born during my absence presented her baby to me.

"It has no nose," I said.

"What?" said the mother, smiling broadly. "My baby does have a nose. Are you blind, Monsieur Paul?"

"No, I'm not blind. Your baby has no nose; it is ugly."

The young mother laughed. "My baby is ugly, is it?"

"It is terribly ugly," I said. "How could it be otherwise, when it has no ears?"

"What are these?" asked the mother pointing to the child's little ears.

"Those," I said, "are not ears. Perhaps the baby will grow a nose and grow ears. But as of today, it has no nose; it has no ears."

The young mother moved on. She stopped and talked to another woman and I heard her recount our brief exchange. They laughed loudly and appreciated my compliments, for among the Songhay one never comments on the beauty of the newborn, for fear of the evil eye.

I walked into the compound of the grain warehouse and found Djibo seated under the large acacia which shaded the center of the compound. "I heard that you arrived," he said levelly. "Now I see that it is true."

"How is your health?"

"My health is fine. And how is yours?"

"Fine. And the health of your father?"

"My father died last year."

"What! And you didn't write me to tell me of this horrible news?"

"No, I did not. I knew you would be back. The news of death should be told directly to the face of a person, should it not?"

"What happened to your father?"

"God took him away," Djibo said. "One day he became warm with fever. Then his body shook. And then he called me to him so that I would be at his side when he died."

"What an awful thing. The man had so much knowledge, and now he is gone." I looked intently at Djibo. "Did he pass things on to you?"

"Oh yes. He told me a great deal from his deathbed, for that is the time when a master passes his secrets on to his successor. I am a full sorko now, Paul."

"You will carry on the tradition of your heritage, then?"

"Oh yes, I will." Slowly, Djibo stood up. "Now, recite for me the praise-songs of the Tooru."

I recited them rapidly and correctly.

"Give me the incantation for ngimgniti."

I gave it to him.

"You have remembered. I hope that you will be staying with us for a long time."

I shook my head no. "I am leaving on Friday to travel to Tillaberi to sit with the Sohanci."

Djibo nodded. "He is a good teacher. He taught me a great deal."

"I didn't know that, Djibo."

"There is much you do not know."

I drew nearer to Djibo and asked him in a low voice if we could discuss a delicate matter in the privacy of his house. He agreed.

"Something has happened, Djibo, and I need you to interpret its meaning."

"Speak."

I related the story of the _____ of a _____ chicken. I told him about the recitation of the incantation over it, and how one of Moussa's relatives had buried the chicken part under the threshold of the mean chief's house. I described for him the mean chief, Monsieur R, and what he had done to Moussa's cousin. "The mean chief was a foreigner who had little sensitivity to the way of the Songhay," I said to Djibo.

"Yes, yes, what happened to the mean chief?"

"Nothing happened to him. But his sister became ill." I repeated Moussa's account: the bizarre illness of Monsieur R's sister by which her face was paralyzed and her nose and mouth displaced to the left side of her face.

"This did not remain with her, did it?" Djibo asked.

"No. Everything returned to normal when the woman returned to Europe."

"This is good," Djibo said.

"But what would cause this kind of thing?"

"Oh, it's the Doguwa spirits which do things like that. It happens all the time if you know the correct incantations and objects to use."

"But did I do it?"

Djibo smiled and glanced at me. "Paul, you are mean."

"Mean?"

"You are mean and you are hard. You are walking along your path as a sorko."

"And the woman's paralysis was a sign of that, wasn't it?"

"In the name of God."

"But . . . ."

"But nothing, Paul! Hah. Now I will tell all of my relatives to be careful around you. It is no longer good for them to make you angry. You have strength. Meanness and hardness are in your heart."

"I've become mean and hard."

"Maybe you are not like that in America. But here you are on the path, and if you are not mean, strong, and hard, you are not prepared. And if you are not well prepared, if you do not use what you have learned, then you will die an early death. Now more than ever, you must be careful. You smell like us now."

I ran from Djibo's house, fled through the entrance of the grain warehouse and ran back to my own compound. It was dark now and the blackness of a moonless night descended upon Mehanna. I was frightened of this power as well as of the notion that sorcery was real. Up to that point I had had an academic interest in sorcery. I had never accepted the possibility of entering the Songhay world of sorcery, having considered myself a detached student of sorcery, not an engaged practitioner. Still, I needed more proof, and so I prepared to leave for Tillaberi the next day. I would attend the Thursday market at Mehanna, take a dugout back to Djomona, catch a southbound taxi and arrive at the Sohanci's compound at dusk.

The next day I entered the Sohanci's compound to find him sitting in the shade of the spirit hut. As he wove palm-frond rope, he talked with Saadu, a short squat man who wore a floppy broadbrimmed straw hat. I greeted Saadu and said hello to the Sohanci, who immediately put away his rope-weaving and stood up. He touched my arm gently and excitedly asked after my health.

"Jemma," he called to his second wife, "Paul has come. Moussa Nya," he called to his first wife, "Paul has come."

The two women emerged from their respective huts and ran toward me. They too asked after my health, my family, all the people in America. I told them that all was well with me and my family. "And the people in America thank you for asking after them."

The Sohanci asked Jemma to put my baggage in the spirit hut. He asked me if I wanted to wash.

"In a little while, Baba. First I must talk with you".

The Sohanci excused Saadu, who left the area of the spirit house to talk with the Sohanci's wives. We entered the hut and sat down on straw mats.

"What is it, my son?" the Sohanci asked.

I described to him the results of his "mean chief" medicine.

The Sohanci giggled like a child. "My son, you are mean. You are hard. Pap, pap, pap, pap. You are too mean and too hard."

His remarks confused me. "What do you mean, Baba?"

"Did you not find the ____ of a ____ chicken?"

"Yes."

"Did you not recite over it three times the incantation that I taught you?"

"Yes."

"Is the mean chief still in power?"

"No."

"Well then, you must be mean. You must be hard. Pap, pap, pap, pap. My son," he chuckled, "you have begun your walk along the path. Pap, pap, pap, pap."

"But did I make someone sick with the ____ of a ____ chicken?"

"Do you not know it, or do you not want to admit it, my son?"

I remained silent.

"The incantations I teach you, my son, are full of power. Do not think of them lightly. Be careful of yourself and hide your strength from other people. Be modest about the words and respect them. And be careful."

"I will, Baba."

I couldn't bear to consider the implications of his words. If I did my thoughts might explode. Instead I reached for my bags and pulled out the gifts I had brought from the United States. I gave the Sohanci a hardwood cane with a brass eagle's head. Thrilled by my gift, he popped out of the spirit house and called for his wives to come out and see his new cane.

"Look at this. Look at this," he said. "Paul brought this all the way from America. All the way from America."

Meanwhile, I sorted out the cloth and soap I would present to Jemma and Moussa Nya, the Sohanci's wives. Folded cloth bundled under each arm, I emerged from the hut. "Jemma and Moussa Nya," I said. "Come and accept."

Both came toward me wearing the broad smiles of great expectation. I presented each one with four yards of American cloth. Jemma skipped around the compound with her cloth. "I am thanking you, Paul. I am thanking you, Paul." She ran to the next compound to show her friends the gift. Soon ten women had come into the compound to look at the cloth which Jemma and Moussa Nya had unfolded. "It is very pretty, the cloth from America," one woman said. "Look at those bright colors," said another. "Is it no-iron cloth?" a woman asked me.

"It is," I answered.

The women oohed and ahed, and one told Jemma and Moussa Nya, "God has blessed you with a white-man son from America."

24

REPELLED BY THE COLD IN AYORU

November in the Sahel is cold and dry, and the sky is calm and blue. The air is light and clear and the mesas, trees, and bushes of the steppe stand outlined against the sapphire of the November horizon. The Harmattan races into the Sahel, blowing cold desert air which penetrates the bones of the old and frail. Wrapped in thin cotton clothing, people shiver through the cold nights. Many victims of colds or influenza hack and wheeze both day and night. Robbed of oils by the chill, a person's skin flakes and cracks. Deep cracks open in the calloused heels of children and adults.

Despite these hardships, November is normally a good time of year in Tillaberi. The granaries are filled with recently harvested millet and sorghum. The cows are fat. The sun has not yet burned the fat from the bodies of goats and sheep. There are many fish to be caught in the shallows of the Niger River. November in Tillaberi is a time for work. Young men leave the countryside in droves in search of money and adventure in Nigeria, Togo, or Ghana. The less adventurous journey to Niamey in search of wage labor. Musicians begin their tours of villages, walking long distances to perform praise-poetry, drum rhythms, or possession music. With the harvest completed, the ritual season arrives, for now people have the time and money to engage in sacred activities.

For two days the Sohanci spoke on just one subject with me or with anyone else who happened into his compound: the need to stage a possession dance. Before my arrival, four clients had asked him to stage various possession rites. One family, in fact, had asked the Sohanci to stage an initiation for their twenty-year-old son who had been nauseous for three months, a symptom of prepossession illness. "Our son is always sick," the man's mother told the Sohanci. "He was once a strong man who worked well in the fields. Now he vomits almost every day. Sometimes he is so weak he cannot get out of bed. And sometimes in the black of night, he will wake up and scream." Having had a good harvest, the family was now able to pay for their son's initiation, a ceremony which in this circumstance would last three days.

The morning of my third day at Adamu Jenitongo's compound, the Sohanci sat with a group of older men and discussed the old days. One man said that, in the old days, one never had any trouble organizing an initiation festival. "Back then," recalled another, "we had granaries filled with millet—more than we could eat, and we knew about respect. We respected and feared the spirits. We followed their path, and we were rewarded for our respect. But today—hah—today, there is little left—only the half-believers who have black hearts. We cannot even organize a simple initiation in the time of plenty after the harvest."

I thrust myself into the discussion and asked the men why they could not organize the young man's initiation. They told me that the mediums could not agree on a price for their services, that no one had accepted the responsibility of taking money from the young man's family to buy sacrificial chickens, that the local sorko had refused to participate in the rites, and that there were no gourd drummers in Tillaberi. "Without proper music," one man told me, "how can we stage a dance?"

The Sohanci looked up from his palm-frond weavings and stated: "The problem is with my son and his cronies who have gone up to Ayoru."

"What is the problem with that?" I asked.

"My son Moru," the Sohanci said, "has been in Ayoru for three weeks. He drums there every day in Howa Zima's compound."

"Howa Zima?" I echoed.

"Oh yes," one of the other men said. "Howa Zima is the great priestess of Ayoru. She is very rich. They dance every Thursday and every Sunday, the day of the market."

"Yes," the Sohanci added. "Moru is making a great deal of money in Howa's compound and he is eating well. He wastes his time chasing beautiful girls."

"Hah," one of the men snorted, "he kills his money on those young girls."

The Sohanci detached himself from the group and entered the spirit house. The other men remained seated outside, for, as they told me, no one enters the spirit house without the invitation of the Sohanci. From inside the spirit hut, the Sohanci called to me. I entered and sat next to him in the center of the hut on firm sand.

"My son," he told me, "I want you to go to Ayoru tomorrow. When you go you must attend the market and find me some korombey powder."

"Korombey powder?"

"Yes, you know it, do you not?"

"I do, Baba."

"Do you have a place to stay in Ayoru?"

"I do."

"Good. When you get there, go to Howa Zima's compound and give her my message."

"Your message?"

"Yes, tell her that I want Moru to come home so we can stage an initiation ritual in Tillaberi."

"Is that all, Baba?"

"That is all, my son, and may you travel with God's protection."

The next day I traveled by bush taxi to Ayoru. When I disembarked, a young Tuareg boy with hazel eyes walked up to me.

"Monsieur Paul, are you here to see Susan?"

"I'm going in that direction, Mohammed." I had met the boy and Susan during my first field trip. While I was in Niamey that year, I learned that Susan, an American Peace Corps volunteer, was still working in Ayoru.

"Monsieur Paul," Mohammed said, "let me take your things, please?"

I gave Mohammed my duffle bag, and we continued east toward the sound of the trucks rumbling over a rutted road. We dropped the gear in front of a green door made of corrugated tin. I clapped my hands three times and announced myself in Songhay. Susan was pleased to see me and agreed immediately to put me up for the night. She was a warm and hospitable person who housed many Europeans who were passing through Ayoru.

"Been getting many visitors?" I asked, as I carried my gear into her compound.

"All the time. Niamey people come here every market. Some people who come are just traveling through."

The compound looked like the one in which I had lived in Mehanna. Three droopy saplings broke the monotony of an otherwise empty space. Susan lived in a two-room mudbrick house which was whitewashed inside. In front of her house she had erected a canopy which was screened on three sides with mats of woven grass. Susan didn't mind these dreary surroundings; she was a person who saw the best in everything and everybody.

My arrival had interrupted Susan's lunch preparation, and Mohammed and I went to the market to make some contribution to the lunch effort. We retraced our steps and crossed the sandy space which served as the auto depot. I looked beyond the depot and the market area to the river's edge, where stood the two-storey modern tourist hotel, which featured air-conditioning, its own supply of purified water, a swimming pool, and a European restaurant. Between the hotel and the auto depot stretched the Ayoru market. Most of the stalls were empty, as it was a Saturday, the day before the fair. But toward the southern end of the market were the Hausa butchers, who worked every day. Even in Songhay towns, Hausa men from the east of Niger are the butchers; the Songhay I know consider the bloody work of the butcher to be beneath contempt but entirely suitable for a Hausa. I purchased 1,000 francs worth of roasted lamb, making sure the man gave me the best cuts of meat. From Songhay women seated in the spice section of the market, I bought dried ginger, garlic, dried red pepper, and some peanut cakes, called *kuli kuli*. Continuing along the southern edge of the market, which was lined with open dry-goods shops, I picked out my favorite shop and told Mohammed to wait for me outside. When I came out, I gave Mohammed a bag of hard candies and some gum. "Now, let's go back."

We returned to a lunch of rice and meat sauce, followed by a dessert of cookies which Susan had baked. Susan enjoyed hearing about my work, and so I told her that I was currently studying Songhay traditional medicine. I told her about some of the plants that I had seen the Sohanci use to heal people. One particular plant had proved to be quite effective for skin infections.

"Fantastic," she said. "Wouldn't it be great if lots of people could get these plants?"

I agreed with her emphatically, and then asked her about her work in fisheries. She said that the fishermen in Ayrou were a stubborn lot. They resisted learning scientific techniques of fishing. "They don't even want to learn how to preserve the fish. Nothing I say can make them change their minds."

"Must be frustrating," I said.

"It is. At least I have a lot of good friends in Ayoru."

I sensed my opportunity to ask about Howa Zima. "Is one of your friends a woman called Howa? She's a midwife and a priestess of the local possession cult. Some people call her Howa Zima."

"Oh, yeah. I know her. She lives in the next compound, as a matter of fact." Susan stood up, walked out into her compound, which faced west in the direction of the river, and pointed to the compound wall to our right. "That's Howa's compound."

"Ever been to one of her possession dances?"

"No, not even one. I'm not a believer in that stuff. Guess I'm just not interested." Susan was interested in the mechanics of social life in Ayoru but not the darker essence.

"Susan, could you introduce me to this woman, Howa?"

"No problem," she answered amicably. "She usually sits with her buddies outside her house in the late afternoon. We could go over there today."

Tired from my travels of the morning, I slept comfortably during the siesta hours. Even between two and four in the afternoon, the air remained relatively cool. One could sleep a bit and not wake with the pounding headache that made hot-season naps unthinkable. As I stretched myself alert, Mohammed appeared from nowhere to tell me that Susan had gone out on a round of errands. "She'll be back soon," he said. "She is visiting with my mother."

I opened the kerosene refrigerator and poured myself some cool water. "Good. I'll wait for her."

Susan walked in a half-hour later.

"Sleep well? Feeling better?" she wondered.

I thanked her for her concern.

"I saw Howa sitting outside her compound. Want to meet her?"

"Very much."

"Okay. Let's go."

We strolled out of Susan's compound onto the wide dusty street which leads to the market. A Fulan man, clad in a clay-brown tunic and a cone-shaped straw hat, strode past us. Behind him the clanking of bells announced the arrival of a herd of zebu cattle, longhorns with a large cartilaginous hump which rises above the shoulders. Like stick figures, four more herdsmen emerged from the cloud of dust kicked up by the cattle.

I followed Susan around the corner of her compound, up a narrow side street cut between high walls of compounds. Seated on a mat with another woman was Howa Zima. Her back was supported by the wall of her compound, and she appeared deep in thought. We approached slowly and Howa Zima did not acknowledge our presence until we were two feet away. She smiled warmly at Susan and asked after her house, her health, her family. Then she asked Susan about me, referring to me as "the stranger."

Extending my open palm, I introduced myself to Howa Zima. She was an ample woman with a thick neck, a solid chest, and an expanding belly. Her skin was café au lait, her eyes light brown. "You speak Songhay, stranger," she said to me.

"Yes, I speak a little," I replied.

She looked me over, starting with my eyes, scanning my arms, my hands, my fingers, my entire body. "Is the stranger your friend, Susan?"

"Yes, he's come to do the market tomorrow."

"Ah," Howa Zima nodded, "many strangers come to Ayoru to do the market. Are you looking for anything at the market?"

"Nothing in particular," I lied.

"There is much to see in our market."

"That is true, Howa Zima. But I do bring you a message from a man in Tillaberi."

She looked at me without blinking. "A man in Tillaberi?"

"Yes, Adamu Jenitongo."

Her face froze for an instant. "Yes, I know him. What does he say?"

"He asks if his son Moru is staying with you."

"Moru is here."

"And he says that he wants Moru to return to Tillaberi so that he can stage a possession dance."

Howa Zima raised her eyebrows and then narrowed her eyes.

"I will tell Moru and he will do what is in his heart, will he not, stranger?"

"Yes, he will."

"And what is your name, stranger?"

"My name is Paul."

"And your father's name?"

"My father's name is Stoller."

We lapsed into silence. Howa stared directly into my eyes. She did not ask us to sit down and talk. She did not tell one of her servants to brew us tea, which is the customary hospitality that Songhay offer to a traveling stranger, especially a stranger who is a friend of a friend. Sensing the tension, Susan told Howa Zima that we had to leave so that we might meet some other Europeans who would soon be arriving.

Howa Zima extended her hand to Susan. "Go in peace, and may you pass the rest of your evening in tranquillity." She did not extend her hand to me. "Stranger," she said to me, "may God guide us along the same path."

Her words struck me like pebbles from a slingshot. "Amin," I said. Inwardly shaken by Howa Zima's demeanor, I returned with Susan to her compound.

"How 'bout some reheated coffee, Paul?" she asked affably.

"That would be wonderful." Still uneasy from the encounter with Howa Zima, I lowered myself into one of the canvas deck chairs in Susan's living room. Cracks and long use had eroded the once smooth surface of the concrete floor. The ceiling, made of dried millet stalks patched together with daub, sagged badly.

Susan lit the stove. "Howa acted really weird today. Might have been sick. Maybe she was just tired."

"I guess so." I recognized that Howa did not like the message I carried. Was it a terrible affront to tell a powerful zima that she should send her drummer to another village?

After a light dinner and hours of talk about the Songhay, politics in Niger, and the international situation, we decided to turn in for the night. Susan retired to her bed in the back room of the house. Since the night air was light and cool, I took one of her sleeping bags and unrolled it on the ground outside the grass screen of the canopy.

I nestled into the sleeping bag and lay back so that I might look at the night sky. The moon had yet to rise and the sky gleamed midnight blue. The Milky Way decorated the sky. Occasionally meteors streaked across the vastness and disappeared. I could lose myself for hours in the clear Nigerien sky. Under the spell of the stars I could comprehend why the Songhay lived in awe of the universe; they acknowledged their insignificance and they respected forces, like the winds, over which they had no control. How could they think otherwise, when each night they look up to see the boundless heavens glittering above them?

Tiring though the day had been, I found it difficult to fall asleep. One of the millions of mosquitoes which lived near the river had selected me to torture. Just as I drifted into sleep, it zoomed in with its high-pitched whine and hovered close to my ear. Each time its song reached a crescendo, I slapped my ear in a vain attempt to kill the pest. But the mosquito would dodge my blow and attack again just as my eyes closed and sleep swept over my body. And so I tossed and turned thinking about sleep, thinking about how wonderful I might feel in the morning after a good night's rest.

From a distant corner of the compound came a light thump. I shined my flashlight into the obscurity and caught a cat stalking. Another cat jumped off the compound wall and thumped into the sand. It turned its head and its eyes glowed like embers in the dim light of my beam. The cats growled at one another. A third cat ran across the yard and sprang toward the other two. They growled at one another, growls as deep and guttural as the cries of a medium possessed by a Songhay spirit. The growling intensified as the cats fought. First the mosquito and now the damned cats. I wriggled out of the sleeping bag, gathered a few rocks, and threw them at the cats. They scampered over the compound wall.

I tried to go back to sleep, but the mosquito kept its holding pattern just above my head. Its steady drone deepened my frustration. The more I wanted to sleep, the more alert I became.

I heard a loud thud at the other side of Susan's grass-screened porch. Something was moving along the sand. There was a deep roar. The thing came closer and closer and roared once again. It must have been well inside Susan's grass-screened porch. I slipped out of the sleeping bag and sat on top of it next to the grass screen. The thing came closer. I heard a tongue lapping water. Another roar just the other side of the grass screen impelled me to confront the beast. I crept around the edge of the grass screen and leaped into the enclosure, my left arm outstretched, my protective rings in front of me. Tensed to do battle with some dangerous creature, I found that I was the only occupant of the tiny area. I saw nothing; I heard nothing. I found my flashlight and looked for tracks or some evidence that a creature had been in the compound. Again, nothing. Was this merely a bad dream on a bad night? I did not understand what had happened. Whatever had been roaring had not disturbed Susan, who slept peacefully in the back room. Was I the only person who had heard the roar, the loud thump?

I stood guard the rest of the night, too frightened to want to sleep. I armed myself with a large wooden club; still, I trembled. Like the Milky Way in the November sky, one thought hung like a banner in my mind: I had to get the hell out of Ayoru the next morning.

By the time Susan woke up, my bags were packed, and I was sitting on a canvas chair in the front room. Susan put a pot of water on the stove for instant coffee, not noticing my packed gear in the corner. She yawned and said hello to me.

After thanking her for her hospitality, I explained to her that something happened during the night and that I had to leave. Susan didn't understand. "Why do you have to be so mysterious?" she asked sarcastically.

I ignored her question, picked up my duffle bag, and walked to the auto depot.

25

AN INTERPRETATION

I had thirty minutes to wait before my taxi left Ayoru, just enough time to buy the korombey powder for the Sohanci. To leave Ayoru so early on the morning on market day is unheard of, so my seat in the cabin with the driver was uncontested. In a hurry to get to Tillaberi, the driver hurtled down the washboard dirt road. He did not stop until we reached the police checkpoint just north of Tillaberi. But the police were uninterested in an empty taxi and waved us through the road barrier. We rolled into Tillaberi. I got out at the north end of town, and hailed a young boy to help carry my belongings the two kilometers to the Sohanci's compound. It was late morning when we walked into the compound. The Sohanci was deep in conversation with an old man without his habitual rope-weaving occupying his hands.

The Sohanci stood up to greet me and introduced me to his visitor. "He is a Soudye," the Sohanci informed me, "from Filingue [a town 180 kilometers northeast of Niamey]."

"I am honored to meet you, sir."

The first thing I noticed about the frail-looking man from Filingue was his prominent cheekbones. His leathery skin stretched tightly over his face. He asked me about my work in Niger, about my family in America, about my health. He wondered if I had European pills in my possession.

"What is your problem?" I asked.

"I am in fine health, but I want some pills to make me strong."

"One minute," I told him. I took my bags into the grass hut that was the spirit house and looked for my bottle of multiple vitamins, the kind of pills I dispensed at this kind of request. I gave ten pills to the man and told him to take one every morning. "If they make you feel good, go to the local pharmacy and buy yourself some vitamin pills. They have them in town."

The old man nodded. "But your pills are better. I know it."

I turned my attentions to the Sohanci, who gazed east at the distant mesas. Taking the Sohanci's visitor for granted, I said: "Baba, I must talk with you in the spirit house."

"Good." The Sohanci asked the man from Fillinque to excuse us, and we entered the spirit house and sat down. The Sohanci took out his cowry shells and threw them on the sand. He studied the configurations for a moment to receive their message about my past, present, and future. He then looked up at me. "There is a nasty woman in Ayoru who dislikes me and because she dislikes me, she dislikes you."

"That is true, Baba." His statement was hardly a revelation. Surely, he knew that I had confronted Howa Zima and that she would not have been pleased with the message I brought her.

The Sohanci threw the cowries again. "The path behind you is cluttered with filth, and the path before . . . ."

"Yes?"

The Sohanci threw the shells once again and studied them. "There is another nasty woman on the path before you. Be careful, for she has great power and she will be mean to you."

The divining session troubled me. One could say that the Sohanci divined what happened to me in Ayoru, but his statements were so vague—who was to know? Perhaps that is a general principle of divining. "Will you throw the shells again, Baba?"

"That is enough for today, my son. We will try again in a few days." The Sohanci put his shells away and opened his tobacco pouch. He placed a pinch of locally grown tobacco under his lip. "Now tell me about Ayoru."

I related to the Sohanci my meeting with Howa Zima, how much her coolness had troubled me, how I had been unable to sleep the night before the market. I described the cat fight and the slow approach of the thing which vanished without any trace. I reproduced the roar that jolted me into the alertness of the hunted. "And then I leapt into the enclosure and saw nothing, not a trace of the thing."

The Sohanci shook his head. "There are bad people in the world."

"Baba, was I dreaming? Was it a bad dream?"

"No, my son. That was no dream, that was a spirit of the cold, the children of Nya Beri. Someone sent a spirit to frighten you away."

"Oh come on, Baba. How could someone send a spirit to frighten me away?"

The Sohanci's face crinkled. "Where are you today, in Ayoru or Tillaberi?

"In Tillaberi."

"Were you not frightened?"

"Very."

"Well?"

"Well . . . Baba, it was a bad dream . . . "

" . . . which brought you to my house. . . . Yes, only the spirits of the cold roar in the night, and that nasty woman has control of many spirits of the cold." The Sohanci pulled at his thin white beard. "Yes, it was good for you to leave. A good thing."

26

THE PATH TO WANZERBE

It was a cold and windy December night in Tillaberi and I could not sleep. The howling wind swept through the grass of the spirit hut, making me shiver. I was fully clothed in jeans, a shirt, and a sweater and covered by two cotton blankets. Yet I could not stay warm. Next to me, the Sohanci slept soundly, untroubled by the chill in the air. The loneliness of my wakeful nights intensified my hovering feelings of isolation and made me think of leaving the desert wastes forever. Draping a blanket around my shoulders, I left the spirit house and went out to watch the night fade. The moon had already set and the band of orange on the eastern horizon indicated imminent dawn. I stood silently and watched as the swath of light expanded in the eastern sky. Cocks crowed. I heard the murmur of early morning talk. Two women wrapped—as I was—in thin cotton blankets walked slowly into the bush, teapots in hand, in search of a private spot to defecate. I gathered as much debris as I could find in the compound and added to it some dried millet stalks. The morning fire I lit crackled and radiated comfort to my chilled limbs. I heard a grunt from inside the spirit house. Still bent from sleeping, the Sohanci emerged stiffly from the hut.

"Ah, Paul. I see you have built a fire. Good. Good. The bones of an old person are brittle and do not like the cold wind." He spread a tattered straw mat next to the fire and sat down. "Ahhh, ahhh," he said, "this is good, very good."

I put more millet stalks on the fire. Flames leaped between us. Through the flames I saw the weary face of this wise man. "How do you find the fire, Baba? Should I build it up more?"

He shook his head. "It is fine, my son. Just fine." We lapsed into silence, staring at the fire until it had burned itself out. I offered to make some instant coffee. The Sohanci insisted on sending his granddaughter to buy bean cakes. "Do you want Jemma to warm up last night's dinner?"

"No, Baba. Let's have bean cakes."

"Good." He called toward the other huts in the compound, "Kadidja! Hey, Kadidja, hey!"

A small girl wrapped in a coarse indigo shawl peered out of the center hut. "Get us a small bowl," the Sohanci told her, "and go and buy 100 francs' worth of bean cakes."

The girl took the Sohanci's money, picked up the bowl, and skipped off toward the compound where a woman made and sold bean cakes. We watched the child disappear over the dune.

"My son, it is time for you to travel."

"Travel?"

"Yes, travel . . . ."

"But I haven't been here very long, Baba. There is so much to see and so much to learn."

"That is true, my son. A man on the path never stops seeing, hearing, thinking, or learning. But you must travel."

"Where should I travel, Baba?"

"You must go to Wanzerbe."

"Wanzerbe? I've already been there. Should I go again?"

"There is a woman there. Her name is Kassey. She, too, is a sohanci. Go there and talk with her. She will have much to teach you."

"I've tried to see her once before. She refused."

"Try to see her again. It is important."

"And when should I go, Baba?"

"You must go at once. There is no time to delay." The Sohanci stood up and disappeared into Jemma's hut.

I left Tillaberi the next day. It was a Friday, the day when the Bonfebba market transformed a sleepy river-town into a frenetic center of economic activity, and a surfeit of taxis made the trip from Tillaberi to Bonfebba quick and easy. Again, I had the luxury of riding in the cabin of a Toyota minibus. The only hitch in the short trip from Tillaberi was the defective shock absorbers of the vehicle. Every time we hit a bump in the dirt road, the minibus squeaked, creaked, and vibrated terribly. The driver eased up on his suffering vehicle—and his jostled passengers—and drove more slowly than usual. It took ninety minutes to cover the sixty kilometers between the two towns.

I stepped out of the Toyota into a dusty crowded square, the auto depot of Bonfebba. I made my way to the adjacent market stalls, which ranged down on a hill overlooking the river. Scores of familiar faces said hello as I went to join the tailors, all of whom had come from Mehanna. We talked for hours as they pedaled their ancient Singers, sewing shirts, dresses, and trousers for their clients.

The muezzin's call to prayer in the early afternoon was also my signal to leave for Mehanna. I left my friends and descended to the harbor. There I found Hamidou, one of the many Mehanna boat owners who came to Bonfebba on Fridays. He wore a broad-brimmed straw hat to protect his broad face from the sun.

"When are you leaving, Hamidou?"

"In a few minutes, Paul. Get your things if you want to come."

"I do," I answered him. I ran back into the market to get my things and brought them to Hamidou's dugout, which was small in comparison to most of the vessels moored in Bonfebba harbor. Hamidou waited for me to purchase some roast mutton at the butchers' stalls, and when I returned, we shoved off up-river.

It was the usual two-hour trip to Mehanna and, as Hamidou had not patched his weathered boat in a long time, I was kept busy bailing. Within minutes of our landing in Mehanna, Idrissa was at the dugout and took my belongings to the compound. I walked up the incline toward my Mehanna house. I passed the Friday mosque and a group of men huddled around the Imam, who taught these students the fine distinctions of Koranic commentaries. In front of my door sat the round shape of Bankano.

"Ah, Monsieur Paul," she said. "We did not know that you were coming, so I do not have lunch prepared. But we shall make you a fine dinner."

"Praise be to God, my mother," I said.

"You have lost weight," she said.

"No, no."

"Maybe my dinner will help to put some fat around your middle," she said as she disappeared into her compound.

Idrissa was already inside the compound when I entered it. With short rapid strokes, he whisked garbage from the floor of my house. I asked him to stop a moment.

"Yes, Monsieur Paul?"

"Idrissa, we are going to Wanzerbe."

Idrissa beamed. "When?"

"As soon as possible, Idrissa. But I must know the easiest way to get there."

"Simple," Idrissa said without hesitation. "We go to Ayoru tomorrow on Mamadou's big dugout, and then we will cross the river on market day. Then we find a ride to Wanzerbe. Two days and Wanzerbe."

Obviously, I wanted to avoid Ayoru if I could. "What about an overland route, Idrissa?"

"Bad road. Very few taxis, Monsieur Paul. How about horses?"

"No, no, I've had enough of that." I remembered that 120-kilometer horseback ride in 1977. "We will go by way of Ayoru."

"Good," Idrissa said. "And Jitu and the marriage money?"

"You shall have what you need, Idrissa."

"Praise be to God."

In the cool moist air of dawn we waded into the murky shallows and climbed into Mamadou's 100-foot motorized dugout. Mamadou, a large beer-bellied man who had four wives living in four widely separated villages—to insure his sanity, as he put it—started his Evinrude just as the sun peeked over the horizon of the southeastern sky. As the engine hummed, he oversaw the final stages of the loading operation. He walked along the narrow ledge of the dugout's hull to make sure that the last 100-kilo sack of millet found its proper position in the bottom of the boat. Mamadou tiptoed to the boat's bow and pointed up-river, the signal for us to begin our journey. We glided out of the shallows and then pushed against the strong current at full throttle. The water was as smooth as ice, the air was cool, and the wind coming off the water made us shiver as we headed northward into the hazy gray of morning.

We discovered some thirty minutes after our departure that Mamadou had planned a local rather than an express run. We stopped at Loga, a village three kilometers north of Mehanna, where we picked up a dozen 100-kilo sacks of millet. We stopped at Mamasey, where we picked up rice, more millet, some chickens, and two goats. We stopped at four islands which were so small that they were not charted on my maps. We picked up a man on one of the islands and deposited him on another some five kilometers upstream. We stopped at Cendaaji, a large island opposite a magnificent sandstone mountain with a long flat top which dominates a bend in the river. After Cendaaji the river becomes a maze of channels and small islands. As the sun sparkled through the morning haze in this labyrinth of islands, time seemed to stop. The channels crisscrossed lush green vegetation that covered every inch of the small islands. In that verdant mass of trees, vines, and bushes, it was hard to imagine that only a short distance away lay sand dunes, desiccated millet fields, and kilometers of plains which supported only short, scraggly scrub brush.

We heard the rumble of the rapids some twenty minutes before we saw the stampeding water smashing against the rocks. Mamadou deftly threaded the big dugout through the treacherous rocks. We took on some water as we moved through the rapids, but we did not hit any rocks as we chugged into the relative calm of the easternmost branch of the Niger. We would soon be gliding into the port of Ayoru, the greatest market city along the Niger.

At Ayoru, Idrissa grabbed my things and jumped off the boat. I had more difficulty. My feet slipped in the soft sand of the Ayoru shallows. Carrying my tire-tread sandals above my head, I slogged to the shore line, only to step on a three-inch green thorn. Fortunately, the thorn did not penetrate very deeply into my skin, but my foot throbbed nonetheless. I put my sandal back on and made my way to Susan's house, where I hoped to meet up with Idrissa. In the middle of the market I came across Zakaribaba, the brother of Sorko Djibo. He had been in Ayoru for one week, the guest of Howa Zima. Howa

Zima had told him of a strange white man who had been learning about the spirits from Adamu Jenitongo. "I told Howa Zima," he said, "that the strange white man was Monsieur Paul of Mehanna and that he had also sat with me, my brother, and my father, Mounmouni Koda."

"What else did you tell her?" I asked.

"I told her everything I know about you, Monsieur Paul."

"Really. That's great, Zakaribaba. Just great."

I said goodbye and turned away. He grabbed the sleeve of my shirt. "Could you spare 500 francs for a fellow sorko? I need to buy some resins."

I gave him 300 francs and continued on to the compound of my American friend, where I hoped to find Idrissa with my belongings. As on most Saturdays in Ayoru, the streets were cluttered with travelers. Children scurried through the streets adding dust to air already thick from the arrival of herds of cattle and goats. Mohammed noticed me as I approached Susan's compound. He ran up to me and grabbed my right hand. We walked into the compound. Susan was entertaining three women whose bulk hid the straw mats on which they sat. Their bottoms were too large, no doubt, for Susan's chairs. Susan cheerfully introduced me to the ladies, who talked of babies and other ladies. I disappeared into her house and noticed my things stacked neatly in a corner. I settled into a chair to wait until the guests had left.

Eventually, Susan came in and sat in one of her canvas chairs. She restated her belief that a Songhay spirit world did not exist. "I don't believe in all these stories about witches, sorcerers, and spirits. It's all superstition, you know."

Not knowing what to say, I remained silent.

Susan continued. "Strange things happened here right after you left." She described to me noises that sounded like the cat's growl, but were deeper and louder—like a roar.

My heart thumped.

"I was scared shitless, Paul."

"Tell me. Tell me," I said nervously.

Susan had heard these roars in her compound in the middle of the night. "I'd go outside with my flashlight, and everything was quiet. In the morning I looked for tracks. . . . Nothing, Nothing."

"Did it last a long time?" I asked. "Two nights?"

"That's right! How did you know? It was the two nights after you left."

"Jesus!" I felt terrible. Had I exposed this woman to danger? I told

Susan that someone had created the noises to scare me away. They had obviously succeeded. Susan remembered the tightness in my face the morning of my departure two weeks earlier. In my haste it had not occurred to me to bury a charm under Susan's threshold to protect her from attack. When I left, her household remained vulnerable. "You see, when a Songhay sorcerer casts a spell to frighten someone, it usually spans three days. The noises scared the hell out of me the first night, and you the following two nights, and then they stopped. Right?"

Susan frowned. "I can't believe all of this. This is all crazy!"

"May I bury something in front of your threshold to protect this house?"

"Why not?" Susan shrugged.

I suggested that I spend the night elsewhere in town. Susan insisted that I stay in her compound, certain as she was that the noises could be explained in a rational manner. I buried under Susan's threshold a piece of slag the Sohanci had given me for protection. The slag, a waste product of ancient iron production in the region, could be found in large heaps throughout Songhay country and was accorded magical power. "Bury this under the threshold of a house," the Sohanci advised, "and it will be protected from all witchcraft and sorcery." No noises startled us in the middle of that night.

The next day I scoured the market for supplies for the trip to Wanzerbe. Idrissa, who had spent the night with his relatives, went into the market to buy 50-kilo sacks of rice. Knowing that Wanzerbe had little in the way of cooking spices, I purchased garlic, dried ginger, red peppers, locust beans, nutmeg, and anise. I also found millet couscous.

In late December the market teemed with activity as swarms of European tourists joined the local trade. One could count on the tourists to stop in their tracks when they spotted the flies which rested on butchered meat like a black blanket. Generally, the tourists kept their distance from the fish- and meat-stalls, preferring to roam about the handicrafts area where they might bargain for a camel saddle or a bright cotton blanket. I caught bursts of English, French, and German as local entrepreneurs offered to sell this or that.

Idrissa found me sitting under a tree on the river bank. He told me that a man would be leaving for Dolsul on the west bank of the river. I got to my feet. "Good. Get the rice and we'll go."

We saw Dolsul in the golden light of late afternoon. Three vehicles had been parked close to the river bank. One appeared to be an antique truck; the other two were Land Rovers. Next to the vehicles lounged a police officer with a rifle slung over his shoulder. Further up the sandy hill there were five or six mudbrick houses. "That's all of Dolsul," Idrissa informed me. Porters carried our goods and placed them next to the empty vehicles. The policeman motioned for me to present myself. He asked me in French whether I had papers. I showed him my presidential research authorization and then said hello to him in Songhay. He invited me to sit down and called to a young man inside his one-room mudbrick office to prepare some tea. I asked the policeman when one might expect to leave.

"Oh, sometime soon," he said, looking at the sinking sun.

"Good." I did not relish the idea of spending an evening in Dolsul.

The young man, who was lame, brought out a tea service consisting of a metal tray painted in blurred flowers, three shot glasses, and a small blue enamel teapot. He then brought out a brazier, fanned the hot coals in it, and put the teapot on them. He brewed the tea and we drank it. Time passed. Daylight faded into twilight. Dugouts coming from Ayoru coasted through the shallows and landed at Dolsul. Young men waded into the water to unload goods which were placed next to the three vehicles.

"Where are the drivers?" I asked.

"They haven't come yet," the policeman told me. "They should be here soon."

The driver of the ancient truck did arrive on the next dugout. A Mossi from Upper Volta, he was squat with the unusual facial features of heavy brow ridges and large, wide-set eyes.

I asked whether I could ride in the front of the truck with him. That spot had been taken, he informed me. "There are places in the back of the truck."

Even as I tried to book a seat, young men finished stuffing the carrier of the truck with goods: mattresses, bed frames, sacks of grain. I watched people clamber up the sides of the truck to seat themselves atop this mountain of goods. Knowing that the road from Dolsul to Wanzerbe consisted entirely of the deep tracks cut by previous vehicles, I told the Mossi driver that I would wait for the next truck.

"Suit yourself," he said

A crowd of people covered the hill of goods like sauce on a mound of boiled rice. An apprentice found the crank and inserted it into the front of the truck. The irony of the operation amused me—I had come halfway around the world to witness a marvel of bygone technology that my father was too young too remember. The apprentice turned the crank once, twice. Finally the engine turned over and the truck chugged away, disappearing over the dune.

Djibril, the driver of one of the Land Rovers, arrived at sunset. Pressed for time, he told us to get in. The cabin seats had already been booked, so Idrissa and I squeezed into the enclosed carrier among chickens, goats, and sacks of grain—including ours, of course. When we reached the top of the dune, darkness had descended over the countryside.

27

A TEST OF HARDNESS

We did not arrive at Wanzerbe until the middle of the night, thanks to having been stuck in the sand twice during the trip. On the first occasion, we freed ourselves easily. The second time proved to be more difficult; it took all of the passengers more than an hour to dislodge the tires of the Land Rover from the soft dune sand.

Djibril dropped us off at the center of Wanzerbe. The space was deserted but for one man who sat in front of his dry-goods store. Idrissa called to him. "Hassane, come."

Hassane's shaved head gleamed in the full moonlight. He carried one of the two sacks of rice to the compound of Idrissa's family in Karia, one of the two quartiers of Wanzerbe. Idrissa carried the other one. Trudging through the thick sand of the path, we were soon at the compound, in which no person stirred. The compound, an ellipse of thirty mudbrick houses, looked the same as it had during my last visit. Idrissa knocked on the door of his father's house. "Baba, it's Idrissa."

Koundiababa, Idrissa's father, opened the door. He squinted at us. "Idrissa?"

Idrissa asked his father for lodging. He gave us the house next to his own, since its usual occupant, Mamadou, was away in the Ivory Coast earning money to supplement the family's income. Idrissa found some blankets, and we bedded down for the night.

The next morning Idrissa's family welcomed us to Wanzerbe. Some of them brought chickens; others made us gifts of butter oil. A young boy appeared carrying a side of mutton on his head. His father had slaughtered a sheep in honor of our arrival in Wanzerbe.

Idrissa and I hauled out the two 50-kilo sacks of rice and opened them, for we intended to distribute rice in equal portions to the members of his family. Women came by in the morning with small sacks which we filled. Rice was a rare commodity in Wanzerbe. People generally drank millet porridge and ate millet paste with either sesame or gumbo sauce. People in Wanzerbe rarely ate meat, fowl, or fish.

In the midst of the morning's activities, I asked Idrissa whether I might meet with Kassey. Idrissa explained that, the day before our arrival, Kassey had gone off to Markoy, a town thirty kilometers to the west in Upper Volta. On my first visit to Wanzerbe Kassey had gone off to Markoy!

"Off to Markoy?" I echoed.

"There's a boy. He's spirit-possessed," Idrissa mumbled.

"When will she be back?" I asked.

"Three weeks, maybe four."

"Three weeks," I muttered. "Idrissa, I do not know whether we can remain here for three weeks."

"Kassey's friend, you can see her," he ventured. She's called Dunguri."

"Who is she?"

"She's a zima. She's very strong, Monsieur Paul."

What choice did I have? Having come all this way, I felt I had to see someone. Would I ever get to see Kassey? Was her leaving before my arrival again a refusal to see me? "When can I see this woman, Dunguri?"

"After late afternoon prayer, Monsieur Paul."

We walked down a sandy embankment toward a road that separated the two neighborhoods of Wanzerbe. The space between the two neighborhoods contained empty market stalls. Just beyond them stood the minareted Friday mosque. We plodded along sandy paths between the low walls of compounds. We greeted women who were pounding millet in their mortars. Once in the quarter of Sohanci, we encountered many of Idrissa's people from his mother's side. They greeted us and asked after our health. Next to the small neighborhood mosque in the center of Sohanci was a clearing with a free-standing thatched canopy in the center. A dozen older men reclined in the shade of that roof. We greeted them and asked them not to get up to shake our hands. They did not. Finally, we reached Dunguri's compound, which had no walls. Dunguri's house was squeezed between two large granaries and a mudbrick corral for calves.

A Powerful Woman in Wanzerbe

Idrissa clapped three times outside the door of the woman's house. She came out and hugged him. As she greeted Idrissa, she glanced at me. "Who is this stranger?" she asked Idrissa.

"This stranger," I interjected in Songhay, "is Paul from America. I am Idrissa's friend."

"Idrissa, come into my house. We should talk. You, too can come in, stranger."

We stepped down into Dunguri's house. Bright cotton blankets covered her whitewashed walls. She had draped a score of additional blankets over two beds which had been placed at either end of the rectangular room. She gave us metal folding-chairs to sit on. She, too, sat down on a hardbacked chair, but eschewed its support as she leaned forward with her hands on her knees.

Idrissa and Dunguri discussed the health and sickness of the people they knew. So-and-so's son was in Niamey serving in the army. So-and-so's daughter had married and was living in a neighboring village. Amadu had not been well lately. He had gone off to Tera for medical attention, but the Guinea worm still made him suffer. And an older man had recently died from liver disease. Idrissa asked Dunguri about the harvest.

"It was good, Idrissa. My husband worked hard and brought in three hundred bundles of millet."

"Our harvest in Mehanna," Idrissa told her, "was not good."

Dunguri nodded. "Some years we are blessed and in other years we are cursed. A town like Tegey only ten kilometers from here— Tegey might have a good harvest while we here may not harvest one bundle of millet."

During the conversation Dunguri ignored me: she did not look at me even once. Coming from someone else I would have deemed the behavior rude; from a Songhay it was most peculiar. In most circumstances Songhay are hospitable, and they are curious about the ways of strangers—not so this woman Dunguri. I sat impatiently as they conversed, taking the opportunity to study her face. I would have never guessed that this small plump woman was a zima. Her puffy face did not look particularly intelligent, nor did her gaze seem forceful. Suddenly I heard the word "stranger." Dunguri was asking Idrissa about me. This woman had the audacity to ask Idrissa about my work when I was present in the room. I remained silent, though, as Idrissa crudely outlined my work in Mehanna and Tillaberi. He told her I was writing a book.

"He will not be using a machine to shoot film, will he?"

Idrissa assured her I had no interest in film.

She turned toward me. "Stranger, where did you get your rings? They are very beautiful."

The Sohanci had warned me never to reveal to anyone the true nature of the rings that he had given me for protection. "Thank you," I said to Dunguri. "I just bought these rings in Ayoru. I like Tuareg rings very much."

Dunguri addressed Idrissa. "Show the stranger my granaries and animals. I have no more time to talk with him today." She stood up, stepped out of her house, and walked into her compound.

Idrissa and I looked at one another. Never had I been treated so ungraciously by a Songhay host. Idrissa frowned and muttered something about Dunguri's recent sufferings and suggested we look at her granaries and animals. When we stepped into the compound, we saw no one. The granary was filled with millet, and Dunguri, unlike most of her neighbors in Sohanci, possessed a small herd of cows and calves, a sign of wealth.

"She lives better than the others, does she not, Idrissa?"

"Yes," he agreed. "She is a zima and a powerful magician. She is well paid for her services."

That evening Idrissa and I sat in his absent brother's house and shared a meal of rice topped by a thin green gumbo sauce. In addition a child brought us a plate of roast mutton. The sour sauce diminished my appetite. We ate slowly before an uninvited audience of small boys who had come into our house hoping for our leftovers. The sun set and the temperature plummeted. I put on a wool sweater. Idrissa draped himself in an old raincoat he had purchased in the used-clothing section of some market.

We went out into the compound to sit with some of Idrissa's relatives who were warming themselves around glowing coals in braziers. We talked about the weather, about America, about increasingly bad harvests, about all the young men who left Niger in the cool season to seek their fortunes in Togo and in the Ivory Coast. One young man, Siidi, would leave for Nigeria in two days. Another, Karimoun, had left two weeks earlier for Togo. Without their monthly checks from the coast, most people would not be able to live in Wanzerbe. How could one survive without good harvests if it were not for the money young men sent from Togo? With the money, Wanzerbe people could buy the millet they could not grow to fill their granaries. In this way the five-hundred-year tradition of the village might continue.

Idrissa asked me to accompany him back to our house. He

confided that he had once again asked for Jitu's hand in marriage and asked me for brideprice money.

I gave him the 5,000 francs and wished him good luck.

"All is well, now, Monsieur Paul," he said. "I will go now and see you in the morning."

Tired and frustrated, I prepared for bed. What was the sense of my coming to Wanzerbe? I couldn't wait three weeks for the elusive Kassey. And why had the woman Dunguri been so abrupt with me? I longed to return to Tillaberi or to Niamey. I longed for home. But I had to remain in Wanzerbe for at least one week, because there were no trucks going to Ayoru until Saturday, the day before the market. My kerosene lantern flickered out, I reconciled myself to spending some time in that God-forsaken place, and I slipped into sleep.

Sometime later I awoke to the tattoo of steps on the roof of the house. Was there a donkey on my roof? I did not move, and I heard nothing more. Suddenly I had the strong impression that something had entered the house. I felt its presence and I was frightened. Set to abandon the house to whatever hovered in the darkness, I started to roll off my mat. But my lower body did not budge. I pinched my leaden thighs and felt nothing. My heart raced. I couldn't flee. What could I do to save myself? Like a sorko benya, I began to recite the genji how, for Adamu Jenitongo had told me that if I ever felt danger I should recite this incantation until I had conquered my fear. And so I recited and recited and recited and continued to recite it until I began to feel a slight tingling in my hips. Encouraged, I continued to recite the incantation, and the tingling spread down my thighs to my legs. My voice cracked, but I continued to recite. Slowly, the tingling spread from my legs to my feet. I pinched my thigh—it hurt—and tested my response along the length of my legs. Gingerly, I rolled off the mat and stood up. The presence had left the room. Exhausted, I lay back on my straw mat and fell into a deep sleep. The next morning Idrissa woke me. I got up slowly and told Idrissa that I was going to visit Dunguri.

"I'll come with you."

"No, Idrissa. I must go alone."

I can't explain why I felt obliged to confront Dunguri, for I was certain that it was she who had precipitated the paralysis in my legs. The previous night I had reacted to my crisis like a sorcerer and, having weathered the crisis, I had to continue to behave like a Songhay sorcerer. And so I slowly walked out of my compound in Karia. The sun was still low in the eastern sky and the air cool and dry. But I was tired and my heart pounded against my chest and I wondered what might happen when I confronted Dunguri. I walked past the compound of Kassey and saw no one inside. I climbed up the small dune upon which was situated the quartier of Sohanci. An old man in a tattered white robe greeted me in Songhay but, seeing my eyes, told me to continue. As I neared the top of the dune I saw Dunguri's compound ahead. The air was still, and I froze to the spot. Then I remembered what Adamu Jenitongo once told me: "When a man on the path reaches the fork in the road, he must make his choice of direction and continue forward." And so I did. With trembling arms and wobbling knees I entered Dunguri's compound and stood in its center, waiting. After what seemed to me a very long time, Dunguri emerged from her house. She stared at me, and I tried to conceal my nervousness. But then she smiled at me and approached, her pace quickening. I was fixed in place by my own apprehension. As she closed the distance between us, I saw that she was beaming. Stopping a few feet from me, she said: "Now I know that you are a man with a pure heart." She took my left hand and placed it in hers. "You are ready. Come into my house and we shall begin to learn."

III · 1981

28

RITES OF CLAIRVOYANCE

I returned to the Republic of Niger in the summer of 1981 to continue my apprenticeship with Adamu Jenitongo in Tillaberi. Three hours after leaving Niamey and government officialdom behind, I led a tiny procession to the Sohanci's compound, which, like the compounds of most great healers among the Songhay, was at the edge of town, a good two kilometers from the Tillaberi depot. The Sohanci had recently moved his lodgings even further from town to make room for a new primary school built to serve the increasing population of an expanding town. My companions were two enterprising boys whom I had hired to carry my belongings. As we plodded over the dunes, my mind drifted back to my last visit to Niger in 1979. Wanzerbe had turned my world upside down. Before my paralysis, I *knew* there were scientific explanations of Songhay sorcery. After Wanzerbe my unwavering faith in science vanished. Nothing that I had learned in academe had prepared me for Dunguri. In Wanzerbe, I had crossed an invisible threshold into the Songhay world of sorcery. Now I knew the fear of facing my own mortality. Now I knew the exaltation of repelling the power of a great sorceress. I could no longer be a dispassionate observer of Songhay society; I had become more deeply involved in things Songhay than I could have ever imagined. Had Dunguri propelled me into darkness? What would happen to me this year? Why had I returned to Tillaberi? Oh, I knew the answer all right. Yes, I said to myself, I had power and knew how to use it. No matter the dangers, no matter the counsel of my colleagues, at home, I had to continue my apprenticeship. I was drawn inexorably to the power, the people, and the mystery of the world of Songhay sorcery. How I longed to be like them!

We arrived and I found the Sohanci napping in the shade.

Jemma woke him as soon as she saw me. He grunted as he got up. I advanced to greet him.

"Baba, how is your health? How is the health of your compound?"

"Praise be to God. And how is your health? How is the health of your family? How is the health of all the people in your land?"

"They are thanking God."

The Sohanci called Moru, who had been in Jemma's hut. "Get Paul's things and put them in the spirit house."

I followed Moru into the spirit house and emerged with the gifts I had brought: a snake cane (Damballa) from Haiti for the Sohanci and "Dutch Wax" cloth I had bought in the city for his wives. Soon the neighbors came to greet me and ask after my health.

After a seemingly endless round of greetings, the Sohanci took me back into the spirit house. "We have much to learn. How much time do you have?"

"I've got three weeks here in Tillaberi and one week in Mehanna."

"Good. I will teach you sorcery, but first you must have vision and protection."

I remained silent.

"Yes, I will give you vision. I will give you vision this afternoon."

Although it was early June, the rains had not yet come to Tillaberi. Rains had fallen in villages three kilometers south and five kilometers north of Tillaberi. There, farmers had already planted their millet and sorghum fields. The fields around Tillaberi were parched from the nine-month-long dry season. The day of my arrival was another day of fiery heat, and I passed the afternoon with the Sohanci's family—Moru, Jemma, Moussa Nya, Adamu Jenitongo—under the thatched canopy, swatting at flies and drinking mug after mug of water. At last, when the sun's rays no longer blistered unprotected skin, the Sohanci asked me into the spirit house.

"It is time for you to gain your sight."

Again, I remained silent.

He took a small clay jug that hung on a short cord from one of the hut's rafters. Then he poured some water into the jug and placed into it three red cola nuts. "You see this, my son?" he asked rhetorically. "This is an offering to Wambata."

"Nya Beri?"

"Yes. She controls vision. She sees in the past. She sees in the future. She sees the good and bad in people."

The Sohanci put the forefinger of his left hand on the rim of the jug and recited a series of incantations unknown to me. At the end of each incantation he spat three times into the jug.

"There," he said, wiping sweat from his brow. "The work is finished, and I am tired."

"What were those words, Baba?"

"You will learn them when your time comes, my son."

"I must be patient."

The Sohanci nodded. He put a flat basketry cover over the jug. "We must wait three days."

During those three days a steady stream of clients flowed into the Sohanci's compound. Two secondary-school students consulted him the next morning. Because their families were not from Tillaberi, they boarded with townspeople. At the end of every school year the government gave these students $75 to pay their hosts. One of the two boys who came to visit, however, had lost his money. The Sohanci threw cowries to divine what had happened to it. He told the young men that a fellow student had stolen it. He described the thief and suggested that they confront the culprit.

A woman struggled into the compound that afternoon. She had a wound on her chest that was swollen and oozing pus. I asked the woman whether she had been to the clinic in Tillaberi. She had not. The Sohanci asked her how she had been hurt. She said that her husband had shot her with an arrow in a fit of rage. The arrow had merely torn her flesh, but she could not prevent an infection. When the infection became serious, she left her village and walked ten kilometers to Tillaberi to see the Sohanci.

The Sohanci took out a large leather satchel from which he pulled a handful of small cloth pouches. He rummaged through them and opened one to extract a pinch of light green powder to sprinkle on the tip of the woman's forefinger. He seized her hand and stuck the coated finger into the wound. The woman cried out in pain.

"That is all," he said to the woman. "Stay in Tillaberi for a little while. Come back tomorrow and the next day."

From under her faded indigo wraparound, the woman pulled a cloth pouch of her own. She offered the Sohanci a 500-franc note.

He gently pushed her hand away. "Only when your wound heals will I accept your money."

She bid us good-day and left.

The students returned to the Sohanci's compound at dusk with the news they had found the missing money. The had confronted the fellow student whom the Sohanci had described. The boy admitted the theft and returned the stolen money. The students gave the Sohanci 500 francs.

"Praise be to God," the Sohanci proclaimed.

"We thank you, Baba," the students muttered.

After they left, the Sohanci turned to me. "Every year it is the same thing. The students get paid and they either lose the money or someone steals it. These students are horrible. The world has passed us by."

The next morning a tall and angular Fulan woman came to call on the Sohanci. She wore a faded blue indigo tunic made of coarse locally spun cotton and covered her head with a bright red and white checked kerchief.

"How is your health, Baba?"

"It is fine. And how is yours, my child?"

The woman spoke of her son, who had been working in his field when sudden illness grabbed him. Not knowing who or where he was, he threw himself on the back of his donkey, which wandered back to the woman's compound. "When I saw my son, I knew I must come to see you, Baba."

"Where is your son now?"

"On the donkey, just outside your compound, Baba." The Sohanci asked Moru, who had joined in this consultation, to bring the still unconscious man into the spirit house, where the Sohanci examined him. "Go into town," he told the Fulan woman, "and bring me a black sheep and 5,000 francs."

The woman returned later in the day with a black sheep and a 5,000-franc note.

"Good," the Sohanci said. He asked Moru and me to secure the sheep. As we held the animal, the Sohanci carefully slit its throat. He observed the flow of the flood. "If the blood flows from the head of the sheep toward its hind legs, it is a good sign. If the blood flows in the other direction, it is very bad."

In this case the blood flowed toward the hind legs of the sheep; the spirits had accepted the sacrifice. The Sohanci turned to the Fulan woman. "Your son will get better."

The Sohanci invited the Fulan woman, Moru, and me into the spirit house. The patient was sitting up and he greeted his mother with some confusion.

"How did I get here, my mother?" he asked.

"A spirit in our field attacked you," she explained. "Baba took care of you."

"God is great," the Sohanci proclaimed. "God is great."

"So he is," the Fulan woman agreed.

The woman with the infected chest-wound returned the morning of the third day. Her wound was healing.

"How is your health, my child?" the Sohanci asked.

"I'm thanking God," the woman responded.

"How is your body?"

"No problems," she responded. "No problems at all."

"Wonderful. Wonderful."

The woman again offered the Sohanci a 500-franc note. "Here, Baba, this is for you."

"May God be thanked for his grace!"

The Sohanci and I ate a lunch of rice smothered with a viscous green gumbo sauce. Jemma's cooking did not rival that of Bankano, my cook in Mehanna. We ate quickly, drank water, burped, then stood up and headed for the thatched canopy. There we lay down on straw mats in the shade. The Sohanci fell asleep a few minutes before I dozed off.

After our nap the Sohanci asked me into the spirit house, where he uncovered the clay jug.

"It is ready, my son. Soon you will have vision."

He removed the three red kola nuts from the jug and directed me to hold two of them over my eyes. I held them there for what seemed like five minutes.

"Give me the kolas."

I did.

"What do I do now, Baba?"

"Hold that last kola over each eye for a while."

I did as he instructed.

"Give me the last kola."

I gave it to him.

"Close your eyes."

He gently touched my eyes three times. "Open your eyes."

I opened them.

"Now you have vision."

I confessed that I didn't notice any difference.

"But you *are* different, my son."

"Do you mean that if I throw cowries now, I'll be able to see the past and future?"

"No. Your vision is like that of a baby's; it must grow. In time you will find a path to develop it."

29

SOHANCI BUSINESS

I lived in the Sohanci's compound for two more weeks that June. Each day clients came and spoke to us about their misfortunes, their physical pains, their mental anguish, their fears of the spirits. Each day the Sohanci spoke to his clients and soothed their pain, extinguished their fear.

Between clients, meals, conversations, and naps, the Sohanci taught me about "fixing" things. "If you do not 'fix' a situation," he instructed, "you will be forever unprotected and your work is bound to fail. For almost everything you do, you must protect yourself from your enemies, from the whims of the spirits."

"Everything?"

"Yes. In this world, you take nothing for granted, my son. Nothing!"

I nodded.

"Listen carefully. This is how you fix a field for planting."

"I'm listening, Baba."

"When I was young, I went to Aribinda. I went there to circumcise and to look for millet power. You see, in Aribinda the Korumba have great millet power. Even in bad years, they have good harvests. And so my father asked me to find some special millet. I met an old Korumba woman who owned the special millet. I worked many weeks for her, but we did not talk with one another. One day when I had finished hauling water for her, she spoke:

" 'What is it that you want for all of your work?'

" 'I want to know how to protect my millet fields.'

"The old woman took out a long, rusty nail and recited three incantations over it.

" 'Take this nail to the center of your millet field,' she said, 'and there dig a hole. Put the nail at the bottom of the hole. Then take a rock and put it on top of the nail. Then close the hole and stand on it. Without moving, recite to the east, to the west, to the north, and to the south an incantation of protection.'

"I returned home with the nail and buried it in the center of my field. I buried other nails in my father's field, in my father's brother's field, in my mother's brother's field. That year our fields yielded more millet than ever before."

"What was the text you recited, Baba?"

"That I cannot tell you. The time is not right."

"Do you still fix fields?"

"Do you remember the Bella man who came here yesterday?"

"Yes."

"I gave him three nails to bury in his millet fields. If the rains come, he will harvest much millet this year."

"If the rains come?"

"The nails protect the fields from the rats, birds, and worms. If there is no rain, there are no millet plants."

One morning later in the week, a tall slender young man dressed in a khaki shirt and matching trousers came into the Sohanci's compound. He bowed to the Sohanci and greeted me in French.

"I am fine," I answered him in Songhay.

"You speak Songhay?" he asked.

"My son speaks good Songhay for such a young man," the Sohanci interjected on my behalf.

"If you speak Songhay, you are Songhay," the visitor declared.

"No, no," I insisted. "A floating log is never a crocodile."

"My God! You know proverbs, too."

"A few, but that doesn't make me a Songhay."

"Your words ring true." He turned to the Sohanci. "Baba, I have come to talk."

"Very well, my son, come into the spirit house."

I remained seated on a mat in the shade of Jemma's hut. At the entrance of the spirit hut, the Sohanci turned to me. "Are you coming?"

I stood up and walked toward the spirit hut. Still uneasy about listening to the deeply personal problems of perfect strangers, I asked: "Does he mind my presence?"

"Come and listen." the Sohanci commanded.

The man had been married for two happy years during which his wife had given birth to a son. In recent months, however, his wife had become quarrelsome. "Buy me something better." "This is not good enough for me." "So-and-so wears much better cloth than I." Finally, the woman took their son and ran away with a wealthy man. "When she arrived in Niamey, she sent me a message."

"Yes. What was the message?" the Sohanci asked.

"She said she will never return to me."

"Divorce this woman," the Sohanci suggested.

"I want her back, Baba. I don't want to divorce the mother of my son."

"Very well. Come back after the late afternoon prayer. We will fix your marriage."

"Do you want money, Baba?"

The Sohanci laughed. "And who in this world does not want money, my son?"

"How much?"

"I do not take money from anyone unless the work is good. Bring money when your wife returns. Good work is not about money, it is about respect and love."

The young husband returned late in the afternoon and waited for us under the thatched canopy. Earlier the Sohanci had sent me to a road separating two millet fields to collect some sand. When I returned, the preparations for the rite were almost complete.

The Sohanci opened his powder satchel and took out three pouches. "My son," he said looking at me, "give me that cup near the center post [of the hut]."

I gave it to him.

"Good." He took three pinches of powder from each pouch and put them in the open cup.

"What are those powders, Baba?"

He smiled at me. "I cannot tell you today."

The Sohanci added other powders to the cup, sprinkling three measures of a burr-like plant, *feeji dano*, and three measures of *koma subu*, a wild grass, into the cup. "Where is the sand that you gathered, my son?"

I gave it to him.

He took three pinches of sand, put them in the cup. "My son, we are ready." He stood up and called to his wife, Jemma. "Bring us a brazier with hot coals."

We emerged from the spirit house and saw the young man waiting.

"Young man," the Sohanci called to him, "we must go behind the village. Come."

Jemma gave me the brazier with hot coals and we walked beyond the wall of the Sohanci's compound until we reached a fork in the road. "Put the brazier down at the crossroads," the Sohanci ordered.

The Sohanci recited the genji how and a second incantation that I did not know. He poured the ingredients of the cup onto the hot coals. White smoke streamed from the brazier. "Young man, kneel before this brazier and breathe this smoke. Rub the smoke into your forehead, your arms, your arm-pits, your elbows, your belly, your knees, and your ankles. Stay here until there is no more smoke.

When you finish, bring the brazier back to my compound and go home."

"Yes, Baba."

"You understand?"

"Yes, Baba."

"One more thing, young man. When you leave, do not look back at the fork in the road.

"Why, Baba?"

"Do as I say!"

"Yes, Baba."

One week later the young man returned to the Sohanci's compound. He gleefully told us that his wife and son had returned. He gave the Sohanci 5,000 francs, four chickens, a sheep and a goat.

"Praise be to God," the Sohanci proclaimed.

30

JOURNEY UNDER THE RIVER

The morning of my departure I made coffee for the Sohanci, Moru, and myself. As I waited for the water to boil I wondered how a simple rite like burning those powders at the crossroads could reunite an irreconcilably estranged couple. What power, I marveled. What power!

I was leaving that day because the Sohanci had thrown cowries to see my future path. He told me to leave Tillaberi at once. "Go to Mehanna. On the other side of the river there is someone who has much to tell you."

I arrived in Mehanna at dusk that day after having survived the rigors of public transport in Niger: the overstuffed carriers of bush taxis, the thick dust of the road, the overzealousness of the police at roadblocks, the endless wait in Bonfebba market for a Mehanna-bound dugout, and the relentless pounding of the Nigerien sun during a two-hour canoe ride upstream. After hours of the noise and crush of crowds large and small, it was a pleasure to wade through the shallows and climb the bank to the friendly, sandy wastes of Mehanna. No sooner was I on level ground than children swarmed me chanting:

"Paul ka. Paul ka." (Paul has come. Paul has come.)

Elders joined the crowd and welcomed me. One man sent a child to search for Idrissa. "Tell Idrissa that his older brother has returned to Mehanna."

I broke away to my compound and collapsed on a canvas deck chair in my house. What a wonderful feeling it was to be greeted as if I were a native son of Mehanna. But I wasn't. I suspected their motives. Perhaps my motives—unexamined as they were—were not pure either.

I heard Idrissa calling me.

"In here, Idrissa."

Idrissa entered the house. In less than two years, he had aged appreciably. Deep lines cut across his forehead, and there were puffy bags under his eyes.

"God has brought you back to Mehanna, Monsieur Paul. You are a fine man, and I give thanks. Jitu gives thanks. My daughter Harijitu gives thanks."

"And how is your compound, Idrissa?"

"We give thanks for our health and prosperity."

The compound, however, was in disarray. Despite Idrissa's attempts to plant trees, only the ever-present acacia seemed to have survived heat, drought, and poor soil. The north wall of the compound had washed away during a particularly violent rainstorm. The roof of my house had caved in during another rainstorm. And Idrissa hadn't the money to make repairs.

"A long time in Mehanna?" Idrissa asked nervously.

"Perhaps one week, Idrissa. My time is not long this year."

"And Wanzerbe?"

"Not this year. There's no time," I lied. I was afraid to go to Wanzerbe.

Idrissa didn't seem terribly disappointed. "Tonight, you eat well. Bankano will bring dinner, and Jitu will make your lunches."

"That is good."

"I'll get water for washing," Idrissa called as he walked out of the house.

"Oh Idrissa?"

He came back and stood at the threshold.

"Is Djibo in town?"

"Yes," he grunted. "You better not see him. He's only after your money. He can't be trusted. Stay away from him. He'll betray you."

"Thank you, Idrissa." Some things would never change in Mehanna.

That night, after a fine meal of millet paste and peanut sauce, I walked to the grain warehouse to see Djibo. The bright light of the full moon illuminated the night sky. Merchants sat talking in front of their shops. Young men sat at tables sipping café au lait. The local deaf-mutes huddled around a table signing vigorously at one another. One of them stood up and greeted me. He insulted my mother, my father, and my mother's brother. I insulted his grandmother and his grandfather. Our laughter shook the night air.

I entered the grain warehouse. Djibo sat on a metal folding chair in the middle of the compound.

"Hello, Djibo, hello. I am greeting you. I am greeting you."

Djibo remained seated. "And I am greeting you, Paul. How is your health? And the health of your parents?"

"They are thanking God, Djibo. And how is your house?"

"All is well. I have many, many clients. People know that I have become a great sorko."

Adamu Jenitongo had taught me to be wary of the sorcerer who is boastful. Perhaps people distrusted Djibo's boastfulness. "So I have heard," I murmured. "What news have you, Djibo?"

Djibo motioned for me to sit down on the other folding chair in the compound. The air was hot, humid, and stagnant. "My cousin Moussa has left."

"I heard. Idrissa told me in a letter."

"My cousin, Karimoun . . . ."

"Yes?"

"He died."

"What!" I cried. "How and when?"

"In a car accident last year. An overloaded bush taxi went over a cliff. Everyone died."

"How horrible!"

"It is our path, Paul," Djibo said sadly. "We all end up in the same place, don't we?"

"It's our path," I repeated.

We glanced at each other for a moment. "I have a new wife. You will meet her tomorrow."

"Wonderful. What other news have you, Djibo?"

Djibo told me that since my last visit he had gone to a sacred place and, like his father, Mounmouni Koda, had walked under the water until he had reached the village of Harakoy Dikko, the river goddess.

"Your time came?"

"Yes," Djibo affirmed. "It came."

Djibo invited me inside his house and lit a kerosene lantern. He unrolled two straw mats so that we might sit facing each other.

"Seven months ago, the king of the sky came to me in a dream. He said my time had come. He said that I must now enter the river and walk to Harakoy's village.

"I left Mehanna on a Thursday evening and walked north all night along the edge of the river. I approached Ayoru, where the river is wide and deep. This is where the spirits have their village under the water. I was looking for a smooth black boulder, because the boulder marks the spot where the sorko enters the river. Just before sunrise I found the boulder and I entered the river.

"I went into the river, but I did not become wet. I followed a path of smooth white sand. The more I walked, the whiter the sand became. I walked on. To my right and left I saw the river. I saw crocodiles and fishes, but whirlpools kept us separated.

"When the sand changed from white to a dark gray, I saw three large jugs in a line. Sadyara, the large black snake with a horn on its head, was coiled next to the first jug. Frightened, I recited the praise-poetry of the Tooru spirits. Sadyara opened his mouth, hissed, and flicked his forked tongue. Harakoy Dikko sat to the other side of the first jug, swaying back and forth, back and forth, back and forth. Her eyes were covered with long white hair that touched the ground. She brushed her hair back and motioned for me to approach.

"I sang more Tooru praise-songs and came closer to the jugs. I saw a sacred tree and a sacred vine growing out of the dark gray ground. I removed some bark and broke off part of the vine. With these plants, I could save people whom lightning had struck. Behind the first jug, I saw the sacred kobe tree. If I could get some of its bark, I could enter the river any time. I took out my knife, but before I could get beyond the first jug, a force knocked me down. A voice said: 'You cannot yet cut away the bark of the kobe tree.'

"The first jug was filled with fresh milk, which I drank. It was sweet. I moved ten feet to the second jug, which was filled with special sorko medicines: *sah nya*, *dugu nya*, *wali belinga*. I put a little bit of each powder in cloth pouches and put them in my pockets. The third jug was filled with blood. There was a special vine floating on the surface. I recited an incantation and took it.

"I sat down on the ground of the spirit village and scooped into my pockets some of the dark gray soil of the spirit village. I stood up to leave, but I could not find the white sandy path leading to our world. And so I recited the Tooru praise-poems again. The Tooru surrounded me. I screamed. They gave me a powder I had never seen and made the white sandy path reappear. A wind caught me from behind and pushed me away from the village of the spirits. Soon, I emerged from the river completely dry. A voice told me that I could return next year, but not before."

Djibo's story provided me a wealth of data, but I wanted to know more. "How can a person walk into the river and not get wet?" I wondered.

"I knew you would ask, Paul. I have something to show you." Djibo opened a pouch, revealing a dark gray powder. "Do you see that small jug over there?" He pointed in the direction of his bed.

"Yes?"

"Give it to me."

He took it, and filled it with water, and put it on the sand between us. With his right hand, he scooped a small amount of the powder and molded a small pile of it on a flat stone; it looked like an eroding mountain. He submerged the stone and powder into the water. "Look at it, Paul. Look at it. Shine your flashlight on it."

The powder had maintained its shape under the water, taking on a metallic glow as if it had developed a protective outer shell. "What is going on?" I asked.

"Wait! Wait!" he said excitedly. Carefully he removed the stone and powder from the jug. It was completely dry. "Touch it!" Djibo cried.

It was completely dry. I had never seen such a thing. "What is this powder?"

"Because I like you, Paul, and because you are a sorko, I will tell you. But you can never reveal the name to anyone." He told me the name.

"But that is not a Songhay word, is it?"

"That is the word that my father revealed to me on his deathbed."

I was troubled. "But you shouldn't be telling me this, Djibo. If your father only told you about this powder on his deathbed, how can you reveal it to me, a foreigner?"

Djibo ignored my protest. "I want you to take this powder back to the United States. I want you to show it to people, so they will know the power of the sorko. I want you to eat this powder."

"Eat it?"

"Yes. When you eat this powder you can enter the river and not get wet. With this powder, the sorko can remain under the river, like my father Mounmouni Koda, days, weeks, even years."

"I can't take this from you. It's too precious."

"You must take it, Paul. I can get more of it."

Blood rushed to my head. "I don't want to take it. I don't want to eat it."

"You must, Paul. You must. One day, you, too, will journey under the river to the village of spirits."

He closed the pouch and thrust it into my hands. I took it, stood up, and left Djibo without saying good-bye.

31

AMADU ZIMA

I did not return to the grain warehouse. I kept my pouch of gray powder hidden in my gear. I didn't want to see Djibo again. He wanted to see me, however. On several occasions following his revelation he came over to my compound. I was out each time he came to visit, and Idrissa relayed a message to me.

"Djibo Sorko came here, Paul. He wants to see you. He will come again."

"I won't be here."

"Good. He's a bad man. He'll harm you. He'll take your money. He'll tell you lies."

Those weren't the reasons I didn't want to see Djibo. Djibo had told a great secret to a stranger, a young one at that. This act violated a sacred trust among Songhay sorcerers. No matter my transitory feelings of triumph and power, the words of Adamu Jenitongo haunted me. "You must grow old," he had told me, "before you can learn the great secrets." How mercurial I had become. At one moment I would say that because I wasn't a sorko it was unethical for me to learn great secrets. And then Djibo would tell me that I was a sorko and that I had to accept a powder that his father had given him as he lay dying. One minute I swelled with the thrill and confidence of power, and the next I shrank into the indecision and melancholy of guilt. And I didn't want to see Djibo; I wanted to avoid him. Djibo was my first teacher, but I could not accept him. Even when he was teaching me sorko incantations, I realized that his father, Mounmouni Koda, was the source of sorko power in Mehanna. Djibo taught me a great deal, but I never respected him.

From the beginning I had been wary of Djibo and he had been wary of me. We were age-mates—natural competitors. He possessed something that I wanted—firsthand knowledge of the world of sorcery. I possessed something he wanted—firsthand knowledge of the European world with its prestige and money. I manipulated him for his knowledge of *sorkotarey* ("sorko work"), and he manipulated me for my knowledge of things western and, of course, money. I found myself supplying him with birth-control pills from a sympathetic American doctor—but for his girl friend, not his wife. He mined my awareness of world events to fuel his conversation in evening get-togethers around a radio with other young men. The money, however, was absorbed silently, and I never saw a trace of it.

The elders considered him a braggart. Through demonstrations he had tried to impress them with his knowledge of sorko sorcery. He had succeeded only in earning their unabashed contempt. He had tried to impress me, and succeeded only in increasing my uneasiness. The driving force of Djibo's personality, I realized, was his unrestrained competitiveness. He competed with the elders. He competed with me. He competed with Adamu Jenitongo, a man of whose power, prestige, and knowledge I stood in awe. Adamu Jenitongo was the wise father; Djibo was the rival sibling who pestered me for attention of all kinds.

Djibo finally caught up with me along the river bank. I was watching women wash their pots and pans in the river. Children splashed water at one another. Their wraparound skirts rolled up, the women bent over their pots in the shallows and scrubbed them with sand.

Djibo grabbed my arm. "You don't want to see me?"

"Not true, Djibo," I lied.

"You do not like Djibo, but Djibo likes you. How is that?"

"Not true, Djibo."

"What is more important than sorko business?"

I remained silent.

"Paul, I like you. I want to tell you many things."

"I *know* that Djibo."

"Good. Then you will come to the grain warehouse tonight."

"Tonight?"

"Djibo has had a hard, hot season. His children are hungry, Paul. He needs a new hat. His new wife needs new clothing. Djibo is suffering, Paul. And he suffers even more when you do not come to visit him."

"Djibo, this is money business you are talking. I don't like money business, and you know it! Adamu Jenitongo never speaks to me of money. This is not the way men on the path act."

Djibo ignored my rebuttal. "There is so much for you to learn. I can give you power, Paul. Power!"

I kicked the sand and walked away from the river toward the empty market stalls. A group of men sat under a thatched canopy playing *dillo*, the Songhay version of checkers played with dune-palm pits. I greeted them.

I walked up to l'Hotel de Mehanna, a one-room mudbrick restaurant where one could buy an omelette for 50 francs. A bowl of rice and sauce cost 50 francs, and a glass of coffee 25. Above the doorway of l'Hotel was a sun-bleached magazine photo of a Dogon horseman sculpted in wood. Mounkaila, who was standing in the doorway of l'Hotel that day, had been the cook at the restaurant since its opening in 1979. He was tall and lean with a broad face and splotchy skin. The right side of his nose rested almost flat against his cheek; when he was a child, a horse had kicked him. "How about a cup of coffee, Monsieur Paul?"

I consistently refused Mounkaila's terrible coffee. How could I drink coffee that consisted of Lipton tea (Mounkaila, for some unfathomable reason, added Lipton tea bags to his boiling water), Nescafe instant coffee, and thick, sweet evaporated milk. Mounkaila never took offense. "No thanks, Mounkaila. I've got to go."

I was headed to Alfaggah Abdoulaye's. I often consulted this kind and wise Islamic cleric. When the people had lied to me about their linguistic abilities in 1976, Alfaggah Abdoulaye suggested that I learn as the Songhay learn—by listening and participating in the discussion groups of men and women. Now, confused and troubled by my quest for power, I hoped the cleric could give me direction.

There was only one compound along the path to Alfaggah Abdoulaye's that did not have a high mudbrick wall. Each time I passed this compound I greeted the old man, Amadu, who lived in it. Amadu never left his compound. On market days he sent his wife to buy goods.

In his youth Amadu must have been an imposing figure, for despite a bent posture, he was tall and broad-shouldered. The whites of his eyes had yellowed from both age and constant exposure to dust and dirt. His wardrobe, as far as I knew, was limited to two pairs of trousers and one faded blue robe that was frayed around the neck.

When he greeted me in his soft voice, he always touched my hand lightly. Over the five years of my many visits to Mehanna I had

A Street in Mehanna

greeted this man often as I walked by his desolate compound. "How is your wife? How are your wife's people? How are the people of your compound? How is your health?" He always responded that all was well and asked after my health. Until that day in 1981, I knew nothing else about Amadu.

"I am glad to learn that you are in good health," he said to me that morning.

"That I am, Baba." Out of respect I called all Songhay elders "Baba."

"For five years you have greeted me."

"That's true."

"And you have asked nothing of me."

"That's true, also."

"For five years I have watched you. Today you will know me." He beckoned me. "Come into my house. I want to tell you the story of my life."

I wondered what he would tell me. It was dark inside the thatched hut. A ritual altar rested against one side of the hut: orderly rows of perfume vials, old coffee tins filled with powders, and larger containers which probably contained medicinal and sorcery powders. We sat on frayed and soiled straw mats and faced each other.

"I am a zima. I have been one for fifty years."

"I didn't know, Baba." My voice registered surprise.

"We Songhay do not reveal ourselves to anyone. We must know people first. We must trust people as I trust you." He touched my hand. "I have seen into your heart, my son. And I have heard the truth of your voice. I want you to know me." He paused. "Go and get your machine [tape-recorder]. You must open it and learn my story."

I rushed out of Amadu Zima's hut, ran to my compound, found my tape-recorder, and slung it over my shoulder. I had been on my way to visit a different wise old man, but that mission had lost its urgency as I prepared to return to Amadu's house. I put on a full shirt—a petit "boubou"—to conceal the machine. I didn't want to arouse the curiosity of the neighbors.

Before beginning, Amadu Zima waited till I had settled myself.

"I am opening my heart to you, Paul. In my heart there is only truth. I was born an orphan on the island of Sinder in the country of the Wogo [a Songhay-speaking ethnic group which lives on the islands in the Niger River]. My father died before I was born and my mother died when she gave birth to me. My father had no brothers in Sinder, and my mother's family lived far away. The noble families of Sinder cared for me as the Songhay master cares for his captive. I was fed, clothed, and housed, but my masters made me work. As a child I worked in the village. As I grew older, I learned to farm millet and rice.

"As the years passed by, I grew into a tall and strong young man. Working in the fields, I never tired. But I wanted to travel. And so one day I left my village and walked to the west. I stopped in one village and worked as a farmhand for a few months. Then I left that village and found another. Then I came to the village of Aribinda.

"In Aribinda I met a man who had a large field. Since he was too old to farm it, and his sons had deserted him, he needed a strong young man like myself to farm for him. I worked hard for him that first planting season. In God's name, I harvested more bundles of millet than the old man had ever seen. He asked me to remain with him. 'I like you,' he told me. 'I want you to stay with me, help me farm.' I remained with this old man. Two years later, I learned from others in the village, that the old man was a great sorcerer.

"The people of Aribinda, you see, are Korumba. They are great farming sorcerers who have special knowledge to produce great millet harvests."

"I've heard of Aribinda and its millet charms," I interjected.

Amadu Zima continued. "Since my young mind was sharp, I learned the Korumba language quickly. The man and I became like father and son. I asked nothing of him. I was happy to be with a great man of knowledge who treated me like a son.

"Seven years passed. The great sorcerer asked me if I would marry his daughter. She was beautiful, but I did not want to marry her.

" 'Then what do you want, my son?' he asked me.

" 'The only thing I want, Baba, is sorcery.'

"The old sorcerer told me to take a saber to the large termite hill in the center of his field. 'When you see the termite hill, cut it away from the earth.' I cut it away. The termite hill gave way to a large hole in the earth. I heard something coming up from under the earth. Great God! It was a python, a python that was very long! With my saber, I killed the python and cut it into seven sections. I put the python pieces in the sack and returned to the old man's house. He smiled at me and told me cook one piece of the python each day for seven days. For seven days, I roasted the python for my noon meal. 'With python in your belly,' my master told me, 'you can now learn our magic. Without python in your belly, the words I teach you would be without power.' The old man taught me everything he knew and then told me to move along my path.

"I walked south to the Borgu [northern Togo and Benin]. Amid the trees and the grasses, I found another master. I farmed for him. He housed me, and clothed me. He asked nothing of my past and nothing of my future. He said that he liked me; he wanted me to stay with him. After seven years in the Borgu I announced my plan to return to Niger. 'What would you like from me, my son?' he asked me. 'Nothing,' I said. He insisted on giving me a gift. 'Tell me what you want.' 'Sorcery is what I want.' The old Borgu man taught me about plants. From him, I learned to heal people of village and bush [spirit] sicknesses. From him, I learned to know the many plants of our country.

"I returned to Niger, but I had no home and no family. I went to Sangara, where I lived for one year with a great Sohanci who was also a zima. He said that he liked me a great deal. He said that my heart was ready to receive powerful knowledge. This man taught me about the Songhay spirits. He taught me how to see spirit sickness. He taught me to heal spirit sickness. I memorized the praise-poems of the spirits. After one year he wanted me to stay in Sangara and work with him. But I felt like a stranger. I left Sangara and walked to Mehanna.

"In Mehanna I became the zima of the community. Every year, I sacrificed a bull to the spirits on the dune behind the village. Every year, I blessed the fields. Every year, I organized the rain dances and the dance for the black spirits. The granaries filled with millet. I had many followers. The people of Mehanna welcomed me. I was given this compound and built this house. I married my first wife, who gave birth to my only child, a daughter. Finally I had a family. People respected me. People relied on me. I wanted a son, but my seed did not again sprout in my wife's belly. I was very sad.

"I continued to serve the people of Mehanna year after year. Then my first wife died. Then I was struck with illness—my back. Moslem clerics came to town and told the people that the old ways of the spirits were evil. I lost followers. My illness made me weak. And so I remained in my compound. Some people still came to me to treat their burning stomachs or their throbbing heads. Some people came to me for spirit power to ensure their success in the world. Owners of wealth paid me for my work. In time, I had enough money to marry again, but my second wife was barren. I have not divorced her. She takes good care of me.

"Few people visit me today. If people come, they never sit down and talk; they come for sorcery, for a blessing, for medicinal herbs. I am a lonely old man."

Amadu Zima and I talked hour after hour during my stay in Mehanna. "I would not tell my life to anyone," he frequently asserted. "But I tell my life and secrets to you, Paul, because I like you. And you like me. You ask questions. You want to learn my ways. You are like the son I never had."

Somehow I held back my tears, thinking that I was not worthy of such heartfelt affection. Thoughts of the ethical contradictions of my apprenticeship sank to the recesses of my consciousness. Why think of Djibo when such a wonderful man had taken me into his confidence?

Amadu Zima presented me his version of Songhay sorcery. He spoke at length about the spirits and taught me new praise-poems and incantations. And then he told me about *horso* (slave) power.

"You know about the horso?"

"They were slaves."

"Correct. I, too, am a horso. Men like me are masters of the word, possessors of power. But our power and our words are different from those of the sohanci and sorko. We have two powers."

"Yes?"

"We can make a village disappear and we can make a man irresistible to his fellows."

Amadu Zima explained that during the precolonial period, the horso protected their villages from marauding Tuaregs. The horso burned resins and recited the appropriate incantations. "When the Tuareg warriors came, they passed our villages. They could not see them."

"They couldn't see them?"

"In God's name, it is true." In the past, Amadu Zima explained, the horso also prepared resins for young nobles. If a particular noble inhaled the smoke of these resins, he could not be denied the chieftaincy. "Even today, some of the young men who work for the government come here for these resins." He fumbled for a moment among his things and then handed me a small pouch. "Open it," he said.

The pouch contained a brown mixture.

"Burn this over hot coals, Paul, and breathe the smoke."

"And?"

"You will walk forward without fear."

"Every day?"

"No, no, no. Only for big occasions. If you must speak before many people, or just before you travel to a distant land. I give you this because I like you very much, very much."

I stared at the sandy floor of the hut, not knowing what to say. Like a fool, I reached for my pocket.

"Put your money back in your pocket," he said softly. "You are my son, and that is worth more than any amount of money."

32

AN INVITATION FROM KASSEY

In the heat of late June the market crowds did not swell to the size they reached in the coolness of mid-February. Still, my friends from Loga came bearing rice. Bella from Lugi, Seruum, and Mamasey brought millet and firewood. The Hausa-speaking *sorkowa* (fisherman), the proprietors of motorized dugouts, came to market toting bundles of freshly caught fish. Sitting majestically atop their camels, the Tuaregs, dressed in long robes and tall indigo turbans, came to market with intricate leather handicrafts: tooled knife sheaths, tooled and dyed camel saddles and pouches. These they would exchange for tea and cloth.

Smoke rose from fires over which the Hausa butchers roasted freshly slaughtered sheep and goats. By mid-morning the market was awash with people. I bought deep-fried bean and flour cakes—my favorite snack—and brought them into my house. As I sat munching on the cakes, Idrissa clapped at my door.

"Yes, Idrissa?"

"Monsieur Paul, a man is here from Wanzerbe."

"From Wanzerbe? All the way from Wanzerbe?"

"What for?"

"For you," Idrissa said.

The man was short and very thin, and, like Idrissa, he had a scar stretching from the just under the corner of his left eye to the center of his left cheek—the mark of the Songhay.

"Wanzerbe people send you their greetings, Monsieur Paul," the man proclaimed.

"Praise be to God," I cried.

Idrissa interjected. "He has something for you."

"Yes," the man agreed, taking from his pocket a small cloth pouch.

I looked at the pouch. "Open it," I said.

The man opened it to reveal a green powder. "Kassey sent me here to give this to you. She said that if I did not find you here, I must return the powder to her."

I was astounded, for I had not written Kassey to inform her of my itinerary that year. "How did she know that I would be in Mehanna today?" I wondered aloud.

"Kassey knows much," Idrissa smiled.

"Yes she does," I admitted.

"Monsieur Paul," the man broke in. "Kassey knows you very well. I think she's met you. And I think she's seen you."

I remained silent.

"Kassey said you must eat the powder. You put the powder in millet porridge, coffee, or tea."

"Is that all?" I asked, wondering what this sudden generosity meant.

"No. Kassey says that you must not eat it until you return to your land. Kassey says that this is a very special powder. Strangers pay her more than 75,000 francs [$300] for it. She said she was giving this powder to you because you are a good man who respects our way, a man who speaks our language. Kassey also said that this powder protects you from guns, bullets, accidents, and evil people. May God be praised."

"I'm thanking God for Kassey's gift. And may God protect you on your journey back to Wanzerbe." I turned to Idrissa. "How long does it take to walk from here to Wanzerbe?"

"Two days. We walk at night. Too much sun in the day."

The next day I said goodbye to Idrissa, Jitu, and to Alfaggah Abdoulaye. Djibo did not come to say goodbye. I was relieved—no more questions, no more lies, no more arguments, no more malaise. I didn't know what to think of Kassey's gift. Why had this woman, whom I had never met, sent me a pouch filled with green powder? Why did she burden that poor man with a 120-kilometer delivery—on foot! The powder might be poison, I reasoned. It might be hallucinogenic. I didn't want to eat it without getting an opinion from Adamu Jenitongo. After my paralysis in Wanzerbe, I refused to ingest anything that had been sent to me under mysterious circumstances. I boarded the dugout, and the current of the great Niger caught us and swept us downstream toward Tillaberi.

I reached the Sohanci's compound at midday. After greeting his wives and the people in his compound, I asked him for a consultation in the spirit house.

"What is it, my son" he demanded eagerly.

I took out the Wanzerbe pouch and opened it. The Sohanci peered at the powder. He stuck his forefinger into the pouch and tasted it.

"Where did you get this?"

"Why do you ask, Baba?"

"This is *our* powder. This is sohanci powder. Only a few people know of it; it is very hard to get." He tasted it again, and put a pinch of it in his mouth. "It is our powder, our powder. Where did you get it?"

I told him.

"Kassey of Wanzerbe sent this to you?"

"Yes, she said that I should eat it when I return home. But I wanted you to see it first."

Without asking, the Sohanci took out an empty can and put a portion of my powder in it. "This is for me. The rest you must eat when you return to America. It will protect you from guns, bullets, and accidents."

I asked him for the name of the powder.

"Pa, pa, pa, pap. I can't tell you. But it will make you strong. It will carry you forward. It will protect your body and your shadow."

I was still perplexed. "But why did Kassey send me such a potent powder?"

"You do not know?"

"No, I don't."

"You do not know why she sent the powder?" the Sohanci repeated, uncomprehending.

"No."

"Ta, ta, ta. Kassey wants to see you the next time you visit Niger."

"The powder is Kassey's way of saying that next year we will meet one another?"

"That, my son, is the white truth."

IV · 1982–83

33

A FATHER AND HIS SON

The cold season. The millet farmers filled their granaries. The rice farmers cut their rice. People streamed to markets with their grain surpluses. Merchants smiled, for the farmers now had money to buy cloth, kola, and tea. Those who had particularly good farming years might even buy a few goats and sheep. People left their isolated farms and went to visit their relatives in distant villages. Young men left the countryside to journey to Niamey, to Lagos, to Lome, or to Abidjan in search of money and adventure.

Adamu Jenitongo, however, isolated himself from these seasonal changes. For him, the cold season translated into increased suffering. The cold morning and night winds penetrated his frail body. From morning to night, his joints ached. From morning to night, he shivered from the cold. He dreaded the fine dust of the ever-present Harmattan which clogged his lungs and made him cough. He dreaded catching a cold that might become a bronchial infection and result in his death. Each day, he rose in the morning and built a fire fueled by twigs and garbage. Each day, he sat next to the fire waiting for the sun to rise higher in the sky, waiting for the heat of the sun's rays to sooth his beleaguered body.

When I returned to Niger in 1982–83, I learned that the millet harvest had been good. Most people would have enough to eat that year. As usual, I applied for and received all the necessary papers for my short mission. Without papers from the Ministries of Higher Education and Interior, the researcher in the field is summarily expelled from Niger. Burdened with all of my field provisions, I left for Tillaberi one week after my arrival in Niger. Being a veteran of bush-taxi travel, I picked a no-nonsense driver for my trip to Tillaberi. We arrived in Tillaberi a mere two hours after our departure—record time. As soon as I stepped off the taxi, I heard some children proclaiming:

"Anasara zima ka. [The European priest has come.] Anasara zima ka."

I did not acknowledge these welcomes, but I smiled inside. Whatever its validity, my reputation had grown in western Niger. That year in Niamey strangers knew my name. Knowing that I had been to Wanzerbe twice, the students at the University of Niamey asked

179

me to verify my alleged status as a sorcerer. I told them I was simply an anthropologist. They smiled and said they understood. Understood what? Did they understand that a person on the path must deny his status to strangers? My private smile turned into a frown. To deny my identity as a "little" sorcerer was to deny the triumph of my apprenticeship. But to deny my identity as an anthropologist was to deny my existence—to engage in what Sartre called "bad faith" (*mauvaise foi*). One step onto the sands of Tillaberi meant one step into a field of unresolved ethical contradictions.

Saadu, the alcoholic dispatcher, greeted me in slurred French. Standing next to him was a large soldier in green fatigues from whose smooth fat face gleamed beady eyes. His huge head sat directly on his massive shoulders, and his enormous belly extended beyond his barrel chest. This was Djingarey. Known in town as *Sodje*, he was a sorko who often officiated at Tillaberi possession dances. We had met years before at a possession dance staged in Adamu Jenitongo's compound. Djingarey welcomed me to Tillaberi; he didn't ask for my papers.

"Are you staying with the *albora*?"

"Yes, I am." I told him. In Songhay one never addresses a powerful elder by name. In some cases, such as my own, one can address such a man as "Baba." In other cases one addresses him as "Albora," which translates to "the old man."

Djingarey took my gear, put it into his battered Citroen, and drove me to Adamu Jenitongo's compound. A few minutes later, I jumped out of the car.

"Paul has come. Paul has come," Jemma called.

Moru burst from his straw hut. Jemma ran toward me, as did Moussa Nya. The Sohanci was still inside one of his huts.

"Did you not hear?" Jemma called again. "Your son has arrived. Paul has come back to Tillaberi."

"Paul! May God be praised." The old man came forward, his arms outstretched.

"How is your health, my son? How are your people in America?

"May God be praised, Baba. They are thanking God for their health. And how is your compound?"

"We praise God for his mercy. We are blessed with health and tranquillity. The harvest has been good. Moru cut much millet this year. Our hearts are light this year."

"May God continue to bring your compound health and happiness, Baba."

Moru took my things and put them in the spirit house.

"Jemma," the Sohanci summoned his wife. "Prepare food for lunch. Make it black sauce over rice." He gave her money for the spices. "And buy some meat for the sauce."

"You can't buy meat and sauce with sand," she retorted sarcastically.

The Sohanci gave her more money.

From the time I arrived at the compound, I noticed a young Fulan girl, Djebo. She was visibly pregnant, and I wondered why this young woman wasn't home with her mother.

"It is a long story," the Sohanci told me as we stood in front of the spirit house.

"It's disgusting," Moussa Nya added from the vantage of her hut. Like Jemma, Moussa Nya registered her distaste through sarcasm.

"What's going on?"

Djebo, the Sohanci explained, was hardheaded and quarrelsome. When she lived at home her battling with her mother had the result of denying her domestic training. The battling had compelled Djebo to leave home and move in with Moru—shameless behavior for a never-married girl. Still considered too young for marriage—most Songhay men do not marry until they are thirty—Moru was a musician whose earnings were erratic. When he did have money it flew from his hands, which were always open to his "friends." Moru and Djebo brought much shame to the Sohanci's compound. Although first time-brides are not expected to be virgins, they are expected to avoid shaming their families. The Sohanci could have asked Djebo to leave, but he did not. How ironic, I thought. Although the Sohanci was powerful in the world of others, he seemed powerless in his own compound.

"It is bad enough that Moru has not married the young woman he lives with," the Sohanci lamented, "but this woman is a stranger, a Fulan—a stubborn Fulan at that!"

Eventually, Djebo became pregnant. Now, all the neighbors could see that Moru and Djebo had been living in sin. What to do? One option was abortion, a long-standing though unpopular Songhay practice. Another option was to send Djebo home to have her "fatherless" child, the usual Songhay practice. The last option was, of course, marriage. No one wanted an abortion. Moru wanted to marry his love. The Sohanci, Moussa Nya, and Jemma wanted the pregnant girl to return to her mother's compound.

"My son, what would you do with her?"

"You're asking me?" I was in the middle of Songhay Peyton Place.

"Moru should marry a Songhay woman," the Sohanci stated. "He should marry one of the girls from our home near Simiri. If he marries one of our people, everyone will be happy. Do you not agree?"

"Yes," I said, concealing my uneasiness.

Moru, who had been inside his hut, must have overheard our discussion, for he ran out to confront us.

"And what about me, Baba? Doesn't anyone ask me, Moru, about my feelings? I want Djebo. I want to marry her. I want her to have my child."

The Sohanci scoffed at Moru. "Marry her! First you bring this Fulan woman into my compound. Then you make her pregnant, and now you want to marry the worthless bitch." The Sohanci turned to me. "Paul, what is the world coming to? The young people have no respect." He turned now to Moru. "You live in my household, you eat my food, you learn from me our heritage, but you have no heart and no mind. You are still a child."

"No, no, Baba." Moru turned toward me. "Paul, can't you talk some sense into the old man's head? Tell him how a young man's heart can ache for a woman. Tell him!"

"What do you want me to tell him, Moru?"

"Tell him that I'm right, that I should marry Djebo."

Feeling much like the proverbial rabbi, I told Moru and the Sohanci that they were both right. What else could I do? I could neither deny tradition nor ignore the realities of contemporary Niger.

Moru stormed off to his hut, fuming. Jemma returned with meat and spices. Moussa Nya, her co-wife, informed her of the most recent confrontation in the compound. She looked at me.

"Paul, don't you think it is wrong for that worthless Fulan woman to be here? Look at her," she said loudly, waving her arms at the girl who was sitting on the threshold of Moru's hut. "She's pregnant, but she's here with us. Pregnant women must live with their mothers so that they give birth to healthy babies. Does that worthless Fulan do this? No! She sits here. She follows Moru to possession dances. Sometimes she walks for hours—she and the baby in her belly."

"Is this bad?" I asked Jemma.

"They say that a mother who wanders with a baby in her belly will produce a monster child. That worthless Fulan is breeding a monster. I am certain of it."

"She should be with her mother," Moussa Nya reiterated.

"What do you think?" Jemma asked me, catching my eye with a cold stare.

"Yes," I agreed. "Djebo should be with her mother."

The next morning, my second day in the Sohanci's compound, I awoke at dawn. The morning cold had slipped through the heavy wool sweater I had worn to bed, and I shivered as I lay on my straw mat. From bed, I saw the Sohanci bending over his straw mat on the other side of the hut. He had a thick wooden club in his right hand. Noticing that I was awake, he put his forefinger to his pursed lips. "Shh."

"What's going on?"

"Shh." Slowly, he lifted one end of the straw mat to reveal a sleeping snake. Quickly, he smashed its head with the club. "Finished. I have killed it," he said proudly.

"Snake?"

"Yes. A snake. We call it 'millet pain' [a viper]. Its bite can kill a child and cause a man great pain. Sometimes it can kill a man."

"Oh yeah?"

"But I have medicine for it. The medicine works very well."

"That's good."

"No need to worry." He sat on the mat. "You know, that snake was under my mat the entire night. Early this morning I felt something move under me. I thought it might be a snake," he chuckled, "and in God's name, it was." He picked up the dead snake. "Look at it. Just look at it."

"I am. I am."

"Pa, pa, pa, pa, pap. Another snake, Paul. Another snake."

"How often do snakes come here, Baba?"

"All the time. Vipers, cobras. But the worst snakes, like the *gezema* [Boa senegelensis], remain in the bush. There are some bad people in the world, Paul. You must always be prepared for bad people. I find snakes under my mat three, four times a year. This is no accident, my son."

"Then it must be sorcery."

"That is it. There are people who wish me ill and who control the movements of some snakes. But I have too much power for them."

"Who are these people, Baba?"

"Some of them say that they are my friends, but I know their hearts. They will pay the consequences."

By that time I knew much about the consequences people pay for their actions. The sohanci's comment reminded me of the seriousness and potential danger of my apprenticeship. I had overcome fear in Ayoru and paralysis in Wanzerbe, but I had only begun to walk my path. One had to be aware of his or her enemies all the time. Someone might send a viper to bite me? At that moment all of my vague notions of power coalesced and I saw in sharp focus the perilous situation of the sorcerer. He is both the hunter and the hunted in a world of power seekers, of individuals who enjoy vanquishing their competitors no matter the costs of their victories. What a terrible world it was, and I had become part of it. But I was just beginning my apprenticeship.

Moru took the dead viper away. We sat on a mat next to the spirit house warming ourselves in the sun. The Sohanci announced that he would make kusu for me the next day. He wanted me to walk my path with power.

"But I have already eaten kusu, Baba."

"When?"

I described to him the special food Djibo and his father, Mounmouni Koda, had prepared for me in 1977.

"That is only sorko kusu," said the Sohanci. "To walk your path, my son, you need sohanci kusu, Sonni Ali Ber's food."

The next morning the Sohanci and I sat in the spirit house.

"Sit, watch, and listen," he commanded.

The Sohanci etched a five-pointed star in the smooth sand floor of his house. He turned around for a moment and fumbled among his ritual things, finally producing a small black clay pot, which he placed in the center of the five-pointed star. From one of the clay water jugs behind him, the Sohanci filled a tin cannister, and he poured the water into the black pot.

"We will now begin our work."

From his satchel he took out seven cloth pouches and opened them. With his thumb and middle finger, he took three pinches of each powder and sprinkled each one onto the surface of the water.

"Pa, pa, pa, pa, pap. This will be good, my son. It will carry you far, very far."

"Praise be to God," I said.

Placing the forefinger of his left hand on the edge of the black pot, he recited his incantations. I recognized a praise-poem to Nya Beri, an incantation to Dongo, deity of thunder, and the powerful genji how, but that was all.

"The work is finished, my son. You wait here until your kusu is ready to eat." He picked up the pot and took it to Jemma's hut, where he cooked the paste of power. From my vantage near the opening of the spirit house, I watched the Sohanci prepare my kusu. While I hoped that eating this kusu would increase my personal power, I avoided considering what it could contribute to my research. Even if I knew all its ingredients, which I didn't, my sense of ethics required that I keep secret the recipe. During my apprenticeship I had stepped over the boundary of professional ethics time and time again. Adamu Jenitongo had prepared for me, a relatively inconsequential person in my own society, a feast of power, and I had yet to develop the will to resist his tempting offerings to make me powerful. And then I considered the mysterious kusu itself. Would I feel a jolt of energy when I ate it? Would the kusu thrust me into another dimension, another world? Could this kusu be another test? Could a person die from eating it?

The Sohanci returned to the hut with the black bowl and a wooden spoon. "Eat all of it, and may God be praised."

In the bowl there was a glob of the green paste. It was difficult to swallow. After three spoonfuls, I was full. My belly distended. The Sohanci watched me eat and smiled.

"Continue. Eat, my son. Eat," he insisted.

I ate and ate, not knowing how I could finish the kusu. I coughed and bent over to vomit.

"You must not vomit. Let the kusu sink to your belly. That is where it will soon sleep."

When I finished the kusu, I couldn't move. I couldn't suck in my stomach. "I feel awful," I complained to the Sohanci. "I want to vomit."

"You cannot vomit, my son. Put your head against the pole of the hut and rest. I will return later."

The Sohanci left and I leaned against the center pole of the spirit house. Jemma came by to look in on me.

"Look at my stomach. Look at it. This is terrible."

"No," Jemma disagreed, "it's good. The kusu always makes the stomach swell. If the stomach doesn't swell, then the kusu is no good. Be patient, Paul. When the kusu goes to sleep, your stomach will be flat again."

Jemma left me to my misery. At lunch time the Sohanci brought a large pot of rice and gumbo sauce and put it in front of me.

"Are you hungry, my son?"

"Hungry! In the name of God, are you kidding?"

"Pa, pa, pa, pa, pap. A young man must eat."

"Look at my stomach; it has trapped too much wind."

The Sohanci looked at my stomach. "So it has, my son. So it has. This is good, very good."

Easy for him to say, I thought. "Take it away, Baba. I can't eat."

He took the pot of rice away.

I fell asleep, only to awake to stomach rumblings. From the texture of the light, I guessed it was late afternoon. More stomach rumblings. Oh no, I thought to myself. First it was the nausea and distended stomach, and now the runs, which in Africa are better characterized as the sprints. I stood up, squeezed out of the spirit house, and ran toward the bush, looking for a large enough tree to afford me a small measure of privacy. As my gastric explosions splattered the sand below, I heard laughter from the compound. Was my distress so funny?

It was indeed, for back in the compound the Sohanci, Jemma, Moussa Nya, and Moru greeted me with laughter. "Did you have a nice trip behind the village, Paul? How long did it take you to find the right spot?"

"What's this all about?" I asked.

"Don't you know, Paul?" Moru responded.

"Know what?"

"Don't you know that everyone who eats our kusu will run to the bush? Everyone," Moru emphasized.

That night I sprinted to the bush seven times. The next day, I ran to the bush eight times. The third day, I began to feel better. The fourth day, my appetite returned. I heartily ate two meals of rice and sauce. My diarrhea, however, returned with a vengeance, and continued the fifth day, the sixth day. Seven days after eating the kusu, my digestion returned to normal.

"Wonderful, my son," the Sohanci told me. "The kusu has taken. It now sleeps in your belly, and there it shall remain for the rest of your life. From now until you die, you will always be a hard man."

34

FATOUMA

After one week in Tillaberi, I traveled to Mehanna. My arrival was met with a trickle of visitors which soon gushed to flood proportions. A young girl with a shriveled polio leg led her blind mother into the compound. I gave them a gift. A man whose left foot was so swollen with disease that it looked like an anvil hobbled into the compound on a crutch. I gave him a gift and told him to use the money to go to Niamey so his elephantiasis might be treated. A mother brought her skeletal three-year-old into the compound. The mother had tried to feed her child, but the child refused to eat. I gave her some money and suggested that she see the nurse at the local dispensary. My fictive relatives came to greet me. Some of my "mothers" brought pots of steaming food so that their weary "son" might recover from the rigors of his journey. I gave them cloth and soap. My fictive "fathers" came and greeted me with praise-poetry. I gave them cheap digital watches and money. The procession seemed as though it would never end. In his own interest, Idrissa chased away the remaining people and closed the door of the compound. We ate with gusto.

"Idrissa, we go to Wanzerbe this year."

"Praise be to God."

"We'll go to Ayoru on Saturday, do the market on Sunday, and take a truck to Wanzerbe Sunday afternoon."

"In the name of God, I give thanks, Monsieur Paul. My child is in Wanzerbe with her grandmother. I haven't seen her in eight months."

The next day I eagerly watched the market build. Early in the morning one of the Islamic clerics, Mamadu, slaughtered scores of animals: cows, sheep, and goats. The butchers skinned the animals, cutting the cows into large pieces. They hired young men to carry the pieces to the butchers' stalls. Skinned goats and sheep were carried whole to the stalls on the backs of young boys.

As the market filled with dust, smoke, noise, and people, I took a stroll to buy some bean cakes and visit the shopkeepers. Women showed me palm-frond mats. Men asked me to buy sugar and candy. Refusing them politely, I walked south toward the condiments section of the market, where I found Fatouma, seated behind her wares, dried okra and vegetables. Her large eyes brightened when she saw me.

"Hello, Fatouma. How is your health? How is the health of your family?"

"We are all thanking God. And you, Paul?"

"God is big. He looks after my people in America."

I met Fatouma in 1976, my first year in Mehanna. She lived with other women in a compound in the Zerma section of Mehanna. When I visited, Fatouma often recounted the horrors of her four marriages. Her husbands had been cruel. The first one beat her regularly; the second burned her with cigarettes as she slept; the third belittled her in public; and the fourth refused to give her food. Why Fatouma told me these horrors I do not know. She talked and I listened.

"How much for the squash?" I asked her.

"Twenty-five francs each."

I gave her a 50-franc piece.

She searched for change among the coins on her straw mat.

"Keep it, Fatouma. Buy some extra condiments at the market today."

Fatouma motioned me to draw nearer. "Ever since I've known you, you've looked out for me. When I talked, you listened. When you had money, you gave me some." She paused for a moment. "Can you do one more thing for me today?"

"Name it."

"Buy a vial of perfume and bring it to my compound late this afternoon."

"What for?" I asked.

"Don't ask what for, just bring the perfume."

That afternoon I bought a vial of Bint al Hadash and brought it to Fatouma's compound. Fatouma sat on a frayed straw mat in the shade of her straw hut. We greeted one another.

"Did you bring the perfume?" she asked.

I gave her the vial.

"You brought the wrong perfume!"

"What?"

"You brought the wrong perfume. You should have brought Bint al Sudan, not Bint al Hadash."

"What do I know about perfumes?"

"Not much," she conceded, holding the perfume in her hand. "I don't know if he'll be pleased with this perfume."

"He?"

"I don't know whether I should put this perfume in my baata."

"You have a baata!"

"I do. I make offerings to it all the time."

"I didn't know that you were a sorceress. I've known you for seven years and you told me nothing about your baata."

She laughed. "We Songhay don't like to tell people about ourselves. We talked a lot, you and I, but I said little. You were kind, and you asked nothing of me. Today the moment is right to reveal myself. I am a sorceress, as you say, and I read cowry shells. My father gave me the gift of reading shells."

"In the name of God!"

Fatouma stood and walked toward the hut. "Follow me, Paul. Come into the hut." I followed her inside. Towers of painted metal casseroles rose from a crudely made wooden table. Opposite the table was Fatouma's iron-springed bed. From under the bed, she took out a long rectangular tin—her baata. The sweet fragrance of perfume quickly filled the room, as she opened the lid of the tin. She put the vial of perfume I had brought among the others in the tin—it was the only one of its kind—closed the lid and placed the container on the sand next to the center post of her hut. Then we sat down outside the hut.

Fatouma frowned. "I don't like the Bint al Hadash in his container."

"Whose container?" I asked.

Fatouma pointed skyward.

"Do you mean Dongo's container?"

"Yes, that's his container." Fatouma kept looking back into her hut. "I don't like it."

We returned to the hut. We kneeled and Fatouma slowly opened the baata.

"Oh! Oh!"

She showed me the container. The vial I brought was broken—smashed to bits. And strangely, I didn't smell the perfume.

"Didn't I tell you, Paul. He didn't accept your offering. Go get some Bint al Sudan."

I rushed back to the market area, bought a vial of Bint al Sudan at Larabu's shop, and dashed back to Fatouma's compound. The late afternoon light cast a deep orange glow on the mudbrick compound walls. I found myself in a cloud of dust raised by cows trotting past me to their homes. Fatouma was waiting in the shade on her straw mat.

"Show me," she commanded.

I showed the vial to her.

"This is good." She reenacted our earlier scene in the hut and sat down on the straw mat outside. She took out her cowry shells. Shaking them in her cupped hands, she recited an incantation under her breath. She inhaled deeply. "Do you smell it?"

"Smell it?"

"Take a deep breath."

I did and was nearly overwhelmed by the sickly sweet fumes of Bint al Sudan that had suddenly filled the air.

"He has accepted your offer," Fatouma said, smiling. She threw the seven cowry shells on the sand. "You see," she pointed at the configuration, "he has accepted you and he has commanded me to teach you to read the shells."

A year and a half before, when the Sohanci had given me the power to see, he said: "You will find a way to read the shells." And now I marveled at how Fatouma had revealed herself to me, a white man! I couldn't believe my good fortune. I could hardly contain myself.

"This is wonderful, Fatouma," I said.

"No it's not," she insisted. "Reading shells is serious and dangerous. It's a burden to tell a person that he will die."

I agreed with her.

"We won't begin now, Paul."

"Why not?"

"Because the time isn't right."

"When will we begin, then?"

"I'll show you a few things tomorrow, but we'll truly begin to learn when you come back to Mehanna next year."

"Next year?"

"Yes, I've seen in the shells that you will be back next year. We'll begin to study the shells then."

35

KASSEY

Idrissa woke me early in the morning. We had arrived in Wanzerbe the previous night after two days of travel and had bedded down in Idrissa's house. Siidi, Idrissa's half-brother, was still in the Ivory Coast after two years, selling watches on the streets of Abidjan.

"Is Kassey in town?" I asked Idrissa.

"She is, Monsieur Paul. She wants to meet you."

"At last," I sighed.

Idrissa's neighbors came by to greet us. Among the greeters was a child, the son of Mossi Sirfi, the local guunu (circumciser). The young boy told us that his father, who was Idrissa's uncle, wanted some coffee.

"Tell him," I said, "that I will send some to him in a moment."

I put a pot of water on my Camping Gaz burner and added the

Nescafé. People continued to stop by and greet us. I gave a mug of coffee to Mossi Sirfi's son.

A child brought us a plate of fried millet cakes, which we ate with gusto. "When are we going to see Kassey?" I asked Idrissa.

"Let's go."

I slung my tape-recorder over my shoulder.

"Leave that. No machine."

I put the tape-recorder away, and we left the compound, following the narrow paths that separated the walled compounds of the quartier called Karia. We shuffled down a sandy hill to the empty market area and passed the Friday mosque, which stood in the shade of a seventy-five-foot Gao tree. We came to the intersection of two roads, marked by truck tracks in the sand. The tracks to the west led to Markoye in Upper Volta as it was then called. The tracks to the southwest led to Dolbel on the Niger–Upper Volta border. Dunguri's compound was just up the dune, but heeding Idrissa's caution, I wouldn't visit her this trip. Kassey's compound was at the corner of the intersection. I turned toward Kassey's house, but Idrissa restrained me.

"She's not in her compound," he said.

"Where is she then?"

Idrissa pointed left to a short plump woman who was spreading manure to dry in the sun.

"Is that the notorious Kassey?" I asked.

"That's my mother."

We approached this old woman, who stood no taller than five feet. Frozen in his tracks, Idrissa greeted her from a distance. She stood up straight and stared at me as I walked toward her. Idrissa sang praises to her greatness. After Kassey wiped her right hand on her faded print skirt, I shook her hand, bowing to show my respect.

"My mother, I greet you and ask after your health," I said.

"My son, I greet you and pray for your health and prosperity."

"My mother, I have tried for seven years to meet you," I continued.

"I know my son, and you have been patient. Those who are patient in life are rewarded, is it not so?"

"Indeed, it is," I said.

"Good." She looked back at the manure she had spread. "I have work to do in my garden. Come to my house tonight. Then we will talk."

We left her to her work. In a society governed by men, Kassey was a powerful, independent woman. In sorcery she had no equal, for as the Songhay say: When a woman succeeds in sorcery, her path is much more powerful than that of a man. For charms and amulets, Kassey might charge a person $100, a sum that often surpassed the person's yearly income. No one, of course, challenged her price, and no one refused to pay, for fear of the consequences. But sorcery did not complete Kassey's world. She was an avid commercial gardener who sold her produce at local markets. Like many other women in Wanzerbe, she planted carrots, radishes, lettuce, manioc, cucumbers, and potatoes. But hers was by far the largest garden plot. From November to early March, she left her house early each morning to work all day in her garden. She did not work the large garden alone, however. Her sons worked for her. And there was always one or more strangers who worked in exchange for a few of her secrets—an incantation, knowledge of plants. Fishing was another of Kassey's passions. She had an iron-hulled canoe that lay on the dry, sandy bottom of a Garuol river, which flowed only during the rainy season. Conditions permitting, she sometimes traveled in her boat to other villages along the river. Her sons and workers used the boat to fish. From her gardening, fishing, and sorcery, Kassey became a prosperous women in a society where men controlled marriage and the marketplace.

We returned to Karia to visit Mossi Sirfi. He told us he was sixty-five years old. He looked his age. Large bags hung like empty millet sacks under his eyes. Deep wrinkles crisscrossed his forehead and face. We sat and chatted under the thatched porch of his two-room mudbrick house.

"Do you know what that is, Paul?" Mossi Sirfi indicated a calabash filled with reddish-brown powder.

I knew what it was but I didn't want to interrupt.

"It's *kosorey*. I use it in my work."

"What for?" I asked.

"When I cut a boy's foreskin, I use the kosorey to heal the wound."

He looked behind him for an instant. "Sofi," he called to his wife, who had been in the back room of the house. "Bring me my little bottle."

She brought the bottle. It was Mercurochrome! "The nurse told me I should also use this to heal the wounds," Mossi said.

"I know that medicine," I said. "I've used it myself."

"I will be leaving soon," Mossi Sirfi announced.

"Leaving?"

"Yes. When I get a truck, I go to Abidjan. Every cold season I go to Abidjan to do circumcisions."

"But aren't there people in Abidjan who do circumcisions?"

"Yes, but when they see the man from Wanzerbe, they let me cut. They know me," he said proudly. "They fear the men of Wanzerbe. They know and fear Wanzerbe all over West Africa. But you know that from your books, don't you?"

I admitted that I had read about Wanzerbe. "May God grant you health and prosperity on your trip," I said.

Carrying my tape-recorder, we went to Kassey's house that evening. Dressed to receive guests in a fresh wraparound skirt, top, and head wrap of the same Dutch-Wax cotton fabric, Kassey sat on a mat in her front room. She asked us to sit down.

"My back is very, very sore," she said. "I am getting old, and when I bend over all day in my garden, it hurts my back."

"When I come back next year, I'll bring paste that will help your back," I promised.

"Good," she responded. "I will thank God for that day."

Kassey asked us whether we had eaten. Regrettably, we had. With the proper ingredients, Kassey's daughter, Mumay, was a cook without equal in Songhay country—better even than Bankano!

"Then what are we to do?" she asked.

I had been waiting for this opportunity and I began my oration. "My mother, I have heard about you for years. You know a great deal about the Songhay, about charms, about the universe. I have come all the way from America to learn from you. For seven years I have tried to meet you, and now, finally, we are sitting face-to-face."

"My son," she replied, "I know that you have been trying to meet me for seven years. Seven years ago, I knew you were coming to see me, but I did not know you then. I *never* talk to strangers. Three years ago you came to Wanzerbe to see me. I knew of your plans, but you had not proven yourself to me. So I made sure to leave Wanzerbe before you arrived. Last year, I sent a man to see you in Mehanna. He saw you and gave you our special Sohanci powder. You took it and ate it. That was my word for you to come and see me. And now you are here."

"Yes, I am here."

"You are here because you are a patient man with a pure heart. This we have seen in Wanzerbe. You met my sons and daughters and treated them with respect and kindness. You and my son Idrissa are brothers. Instead of selling your horse seven years ago, you gave it to Idrissa. Idrissa sold the horse and built a house for himself. Three years ago, you gave Idrissa money so he could marry our daughter, Jitu. Idrissa is now married and has children."

"All true, my mother," Idrissa chimed in. "Monsieur Paul is a pure man."

"Paul," Kassey continued, "you have been among our people for many years. You have been kind, and we have told you about ourselves. You have respected our ways of living and learning. You have earned our respect. You have lived among us as we live, and you speak our language. How can I refuse to talk with you?"

"I am thanking God for your thoughts and feelings, my mother," I said.

"There is more. You and Idrissa are close. Since you are brothers, I can open my heart to you. My heart has been silent for more than thirty years. A long time ago, the Anasara wanted me to talk with him, but I refused because I did not know him. Others have come here seeking my knowledge. I have refused them, too, for they were impatient. The people of Niamey want me to go there to talk. I have refused, for I do not know the people of Niamey; they, too, are impatient. I am opening my heart to you, Paul, because of your patience, because your heart is pure."

I was speechless, but Kassey didn't wait for me to ask questions; rather, she told me to open my machine. She talked for more than three hours that night. She recounted myths concerning the Songhay kings who ruled long before Sonni Ali Ber. She told of the founding of Wanzerbe, the origin of the magical lake, Youmboum. She talked of her heritage, the woman's path of sorcery, the man's path of sorcery.

I was awestruck by her memory, her intelligence, the complexity of her discourse, her pride in the past. She talked, and I mused about her and all the other people among the Songhay who had been so forthcoming with me. We anthropologists travel thousands of miles to visit people like Kassey. Most of us seek information from others. But how many of us have ever opened our hearts to a Kassey, to an Adamu Jenitongo? I decided to open my heart to Kassey.

"My mother," I began after the three hours of tape had been exhausted. "People like me always come to visit people like you. We ask for information. We ask about your family, about your heritage."

"That is true, my son."

"But people like me never open our hearts to people like you."

"That, too, is true," she acknowledged

"You have opened your heart to me. Now I open my heart to you."

"This is sweet to me, very sweet," Kassey said.

I told Kassey that my people were Jews from Russia. My earliest ancestors, I explained, were sheepherders from Misra (in and around Egypt) and that Ibrahim was our great ancestor. Just as Gao, the imperial Songhay capital, "cracked," so Jerusalem fell and our ancestors fled to every corner of the world. I described the persecution of the Jews and recounted the horrors of the pogroms in Russia, explaining that my paternal great-grandfather had to leave his village to save himself from the Cossacks, murderous warriors not unlike the Tuaregs of past generations. Most of my mother's family, I told her, remained in Europe. When World War II came, Hitler, whom I described as the ultimate mean chief, killed six million Jewish people, including most of my maternal kin.

"You have suffered, Paul, but these bitter memories make you a harder person," Kassey said when I finished.

Kassey yawned. It had been a long, emotionally exhausting night. "Come back tomorrow night," she urged. "We shall continue."

V · 1984

A Dust Storm Approaching Tillaberi

36

POWER IN THE COMPOUND

The midmorning sun baked the countryside, sapping the last drops of moisture from dying millet plants. Between Niamey and Sansane-Hausa the millet stood no more than one foot above the sandy earth. North of Sansane-Hausa, farmers sat at the edge of the road, staring at their barren fields.

In 1984 I was working with my wife, Cheryl Olkes, a sociologist and a veteran of Songhay country. A specialist in research methods and design, Cheryl was to design interviews on the therapeutic uses of medicinal plants, the subject of the research proposal that brought us to Niger that summer. Once we had gathered information, Cheryl would categorize and analyze the data. But there were two other reasons for Cheryl's presence that year. As a fellow social scientist she would add a measure of objectivity to my admittedly subjective approach to the Songhay; she could observe me as I interacted with sorcerers. As my wife, Cheryl's presence legitimized me as a normal person in Songhay eyes. In 1976–77 Cheryl had conducted research in Niamey, and on a number of occasions she met friends in Tillaberi and Mehanna. On subsequent trips people asked: "Where is Cheryl?" "When will you bring her to Tillaberi?" "It is not normal for a man to be away from his woman for so many months." I would tell my friends that Cheryl was in America, and that one day she would return to Niger. When Kassey heard me talk about Cheryl, she said: "Don't return without her!"

And so we both traveled to Niger in 1984 and I wondered whether her presence would add a new dimension to the research. Would it change things? Our trip from Niamey had been a long one, for police had already halted our taxi four times. Just south of Tillaberi, we came to another police stop.

A corporal ordered everyone out. "Let's see all the baggage."

The driver's apprentice clambered up to the roof of the taxi and untied the baggage. He passed down the luggage piece by piece. The corporal interested himself in our luggage. He waved to me.

"Open it, Monsieur."

"Yes, sir," I said respectfully. I had learned over the years how to interact successfully with petty officials. One always spoke to them in French, using *vous*, the formal pronoun for "you." One always addressed these people as "sir" and used the conditional mode, a marker of respect in French.

"Come on. Open it!"

I managed to open our two pieces of luggage. The corporal looked at our old clothes and equipment.

"Take it all out."

I tried to suppress my hostility. Cheryl cursed in English. "Do you want to see my papers?" I asked him.

"Give them to me."

I gave him our research authorizations. He read them and quickly gave them back to me.

"Are they in order?" Cheryl asked sarcastically in French.

"Remove the rest of your things," he ordered.

A crowd gathered. No one liked the police, especially when they rifled through a person's belongings.

I removed everything, including an assortment of dried plants, vines, and tree barks that I had bought in Niamey for the Sohanci.

"What are these? Drugs?"

It was time for me to switch into Songhay. I explained to the corporal that I was bringing the plants to the Sohanci. "It's medicine, not drugs," I insisted.

"You use black man's medicine?" he laughed, trying to ridicule me in front of the crowd.

"Sometimes. But my Baba is too old to walk to the bush to get the plants he needs."

He pointed to a bundle of dried vines. "What's that?"

"That is *dosari*," I explained.

"What's it used for?"

"You use it to kill intestinal worms." I lied to him, for dosari is used in sorcery.

"And this?" he pointed to the tree bark.

"That is kobe, which is used as a tonic for children and adults," I said, telling him another lie.

"And this?"

"That is *ferrey*."

"It's a very good medicine. May I take some?"

"Of course," I said smiling, concealing my anger.

He took one small piece of the bark and flashed me a nervous smile. "What's your name?"

"My name is Paul. My father's name is Stoller." He was, of course, uninterested in Cheryl's identity.

"We call him Anasara Zima," someone from the crowd said.

"Anasara Zima," the corporal repeated.

The corporal and I shook hands. Like the other disgusted passengers, Cheryl and I threw our clothes back into our suitcases and handed the luggage to the taxi apprentice. Finally we arrived at Tillaberi auto depot.

Sadou, the taxi dispatcher, sat on a wooden bench, filling out receipts. A group of children gathered around our taxi.

"Anasara Zima has returned," one of the children said.

Cheryl and I got down from the taxi.

"How far to the Sohanci's compound?" she asked.

"About two kilometers. We'll need porters." Two young men presented themselves.

Under a blistering sun, we began our two-kilometer trek over the sand dunes. Sweat streamed from my body and plastered Cheryl's hair to her forehead. As we approached the Sohanci's compound, Moru ran up to us, offering his aid. He took Cheryl's water jug and my tape-recorder. A torrent of greetings flowed from him. Jemma and Moussa Nya greeted us, asking excitedly after our health and the health of our people in America. When we finally entered the compound, the Sohanci greeted us.

Moussa, Moru's older brother, greeted us. He had not been in Tillaberi during my previous visits. In 1981, he had worked as a laborer on an irrigation project. In 1982–83, he was in jail, having been arrested on drug-possession charges. Although Moussa maintained he had been framed, he nevertheless spent eighteen months in prison. Now earning a living as a tailor, Moussa had saved enough money to build himself a small two-room mudbrick house.

"Paul, we are happy to see you and Cheryl. Use my house while you are here."

We thanked Moussa for his generosity.

A child no more than a year and a half old waddled over to us. Laterite dust powdered her body. Mucus had caked on her upper lip.

"That's my daughter, Jamilla," Moru proclaimed.

Jamilla burst into tears when Cheryl approached her.

"She's not used to white people," Jemma opined.

"She's a monster child," Moussa Nya declared.

The term "monster child" swept me back to my previous visit and the discussions that had raged about women who wander when they are pregnant. Had the prediction come true?

"And no wonder," said Jemma caustically, "with a mother who wandered the countryside with a child in her belly."

Paul Stoller and Cheryl Olkes in Adamu Jenitongo's Compound

Moru told me that he and Djebo were married shortly after my departure the previous year.

"And you didn't write?" I joked.

Moru shrugged. Djebo pounded millet next to the compound's second mudbrick house, which Moru had built for his family. "Djebo," Moru called to his wife, "prepare a fine meal for Paul and Cheryl. They are tired from their trip, and we must honor them."

The Sohanci gave Djebo money and told her to go to the market and buy good spices and a good cut of meat. Djebo took the money and frowned. When she had left, Moussa, Jemma, and the Sohanci complained about her. She was lazy. She was quarrelsome. They didn't trust her. She didn't know how to cook—an ironic exception to the legendary subtlety of Fulan cuisine. When she prepared meat it was so tough that even Moru couldn't chew it. The sauces were tasteless even though the Sohanci gave her money to buy the best spices. But no one did anything to change the domestic situation.

"Why don't you teach her how to cook?" Cheryl asked.

"Hah!" Jemma snorted. "She doesn't want to learn."

"Why don't you show her the right spices to buy?"

"She doesn't care, Cheryl. She doesn't care," Jemma answered.

Cheryl and I excused ourselves to unpack our things.

"Isn't it strange," Cheryl remarked, "that they are unwilling to do anything to change a situation that is a problem for all of them. Why don't they do something?"

"One reason might be that Djebo is the junior woman in the compound, and the junior woman cooks, cleans, and fetches water, while Jemma and Moussa Nya sit in the shade of their huts."

"They would rather sit and suffer than change things in the compound?"

"Precisely. Their social position in the compound is more important than whether they're getting a good meal."

Cheryl was troubled. "And so Djebo is getting even by pocketing the money the Sohanci is giving her."

"I bet she is, Cheryl."

"Isn't it ironic. Here is Djebo, a young mother with no personal or supernatural power."

"Yeah?"

"And she has the nerve to defy the Sohanci. He is such a powerful man, but he is powerless in his own compound."

37

A LECTURE ON MEDICINE

During our stay in Tillaberi we had a series of sessions with the Sohanci on medicinal plants. In the late afternoon of the day before our departure, a Thursday, the Sohanci asked me to sit next to him on his stick bed in front of Jemma's hut. The heat of the nights did not afford any of us the luxury of sleeping inside.

"Tell me," he began. "In your country, there are many people who treat the sick, people we call here Lokotoro [Doctor]."

"Yes, Baba. There are many doctors in my country."

"Do they all do the same thing?"

"No. They do different things. Some doctors cut the body and remove sickness from inside the person. Some take care of women. Others take pictures that see inside the body. Some doctors take care of adults and others treat children."

"Is that all?"

"No. There are doctors who treat the mind. They work with people who talk to themselves, who shake from fright. You know, people who are lost."

"Those lokotoro are like me, then," the Sohanci said. "I help people who are lost, who shake from fright. There are many suffering people who come to me. When they come here, they don't know their front side from their back side. It is the spirits that frighten people so."

"But Baba," I interjected, "you also treat people for skin problems and people who have worms in their intestines. You help children who suffer from village [physiological] and bush [supernatural] illnesses."

"Your words have truth, my son."

"You are many different kinds of doctors."

The notion of being a specialist in a number of medical areas pleased the Sohanci. "Yes. Yes." He peered at me intently. "Our talk about plants has pleased me greatly. From now on, Paul, you must study plants. You must become a knower of plants. That, my son, is your path."

The Sohanci sensed that I had reached a turning point in my apprenticeship. We both knew that I couldn't stomach the ongoing battles the sorcerer-warrior must fight in the Songhay world of war.

We both knew that my hunger for power was not great enough to lead a life in which one is continuously protecting oneself from the death-inducing spells of others. The Sohanci's solution would resolve my brooding conflicts.

"Yes, Baba. I want to learn about plants."

The Sohanci reached into one of the deep side-pockets of his white tunic and pulled out three cloth pouches. He opened the first bag. "This is *follo kadji*," he said. "You sniff a small measure of it and it clears your blocked nose. After a few moments, it makes your body relax." He opened the second pouch.

"That's *godji deli*," I volunteered. "You put the leaves in a brazier with hot coals and breathe the smoke. It makes you relax."

"Pa, pa, pa, pa, pap. How did you know that? Full of surprises, you are." He opened the third pouch. "This one is very rare. It is very, very strong medicine, my son. Take this to America with you and eat it with rice or millet paste."

"What is it, Baba?"

"It is a mixture of *hanza kasi* [a rare moss found on the tops of hanza trees], *zeban bundu* [the grasses of the vulture's nest], and the nail of the vulture's claw."

By now I had grown accustomed to the unappetizing nature of kusu.

"It will make your path a long one. With it in your belly, you will move forward without fear."

"Thank you, Baba."

"There is more, Paul." From his other pocket he removed a large brass ring similar to the ring he wore on his thumb. "This is for you, my son. I have spoken into this ring from my heart. Wear it always. As long as you wear the ring, Baba will be with you, even if you are far away in America. I will know where you are. I will know what you are doing. Through the ring, I will look after you today, tomorrow, and even when I am no longer on earth." He paused a moment. "Yes. Yes. Wear the ring and you will feel me. Wear it. Never take it off."

At dusk Cheryl dragged into the compound. The Sohanci and I were still seated on his stick bed.

"You look tired, my daughter."

"I spent the afternoon at the market," she panted.

I showed Cheryl what the Sohanci had given me.

She turned to the Sohanci. "What you have given to Paul is what a father gives to his son, Baba."

"True words, daughter. True words."

Adamu Jenitongo Reciting an Incantation

The Sohanci then took out the leather pouch in which he kept his cowry shells. He felt for something inside and produced two small, perfectly round stones, one white and one brown. "My father gave me these stones sixty years ago. Paul, you take the white one. Cheryl, you take the brown one. They will be good for you. Keep them always."

We thanked Baba from our hearts and went into Moussa's house to prepare for our trip to Mehanna.

38

MEHANNA REVISITED

We left the Sohanci's compound early in the morning. Moru, Moussa, and two of their friends helped us to carry our things the two kilometers to the auto depot, where we easily found a ride to Bonfebba. Cheryl "tipped" the driver to let her sit in the cabin. I squeezed myself into the back of the pickup truck where I was sandwiched between a fat woman and a skeletal man whose deep cough sounded tubercular. Overloaded, we sputtered out of Tillaberi only to be stopped by the police two kilometers out of town.

A tall policeman with seven scars on each side of his face strolled over to the taxi. He strutted around the taxi, asking people for their identity papers. He saw me.

"Anasara, get out of the taxi!"

I got out. So did Cheryl.

"Your papers," he demanded.

We gave him our authorizations, which he couldn't read.

"Baggage!"

I pointed to the roof of the taxi.

"We need to see your luggage. You're not special, Anasara."

He rifled through the contents of our suitcases. He opened my dop kit to discover a Ziploc bag that contained one of the powders the Sohanci had given us.

"What is this!" he thundered.

"It's medicine," I pleaded.

"No medicine. Drugs! Wait here."

He ran into the police office, a 10′ x 10′ mudbrick room. Cheryl and I cursed in English. Minutes passed. He emerged at last with his supervisor, the same corporal who had previously harassed us. They walked over to us. The corporal greeted me respectfully and returned the Ziploc bag. I wasn't surprised, but the tall policeman was open-mouthed. Although our business in Tillaberi that year was plants, for etiquette's sake we had attended the possession ceremony held the second day of our stay. And who had walked in, clad in kelly-green mufti, but the corporal? He greeted me then, and subsequently, so cordially. "No problem, Monsieur Paul. Have a safe journey to Mehanna."

Maybe the Sohanci's advice about studying plants had been his way of saying that he would teach me no more about sorcery. Besides, I had yet to tap into the reservoir of Wanzerbe sorcery. I felt the brass ring that I wore on a string around my neck. I would seek more power in Wanzerbe. I would become Kassey's apprentice.

One hour later we arrived in Bonfebba to discover a market much reduced since my last trip. The stalls were occupied by merchants with few goods to sell. But people had little money to spend—lack of rain cheated the nomads of profitable livestock, and the farmers were in the midst of an especially lean belt-tightening season. Even without money to buy, erstwhile customers arrived for the festive change the market provided. Our friends from Mehanna took our baggage and arranged for us to cross the river. As for everything else in Niger, however, we had to wait hours to leave Bonfebba. We found a shady spot under a cluster of thorn trees and sat on the bumper of a Toyota Land Cruiser, the vehicle that would take us across the river. The Toyota was not amphibious. The river had simply dried up. When the muezzin called the faithful to prayer, we watched men from Faba, the island facing Bonfebba, walk across the empty bed in their Friday best.

Soon thereafter, Mahamane, our driver, asked us to get into the cabin. We were finally leaving hot, dusty Bonfebba.

We drove out into the dry riverbed. We crossed vast plains of cracked clay that had once been rice fields, crept up dusty banks that had once harbored fleets of dugout canoes, bounced over boulders that had once produced dangerous rapids. Appalled, we watched this panorama of despair through the dirty windshield of the little pickup. We looked at one another not knowing what to expect in Mehanna, where, we had heard, cholera and meningitis had killed many people. In front of Mehanna the mighty Niger was reduced to a stagnant waterhole in which children, animals, and women were bathing.

The Toyota crawled up a sandy enbankment, leaving the dry

riverbed behind. A path between desiccated gardens led us into town and we came to a stop in front of the green door of my compound. My former cook, Bankano, leaned against the wall of her house and smiled weakly at us. Idrissa's daughter Harijitu ran up to me and held my hand.

"Greetings to you, Baba. Greetings."

Idrissa's wife, Jitu, gave us a cold greeting. A delegation from the neighborhood followed us into the compound. We greeted them all and asked after their health. There were fewer deaths than we expected in Mehanna because the government had installed new small-bore wells. The people who died had preferred the taste of Niger River water to that of the new wells. Idrissa arrived and praised God for our safe return.

"We are happy to see you both," Idrissa said.

We walked inside the larger house. Cheryl noticed that Idrissa had nailed our pictures and letters to the wall. Exhausted from our trip, we fell into chairs made from sticks fastened with rawhide.

"How long this year, Paul?" Idrissa asked.

"One week," Cheryl told him. "Then, we would like to go to Wanzerbe."

Idrissa beamed. "Wanzerbe! Wonderful. I've not seen my people in a very long time."

"Listen, Idrissa," I directed. "You must see if we can get an overland ride to Wanzerbe. I don't want to travel to Ayoru and then wait all day for a taxi to Wanzerbe. Let's try to find a ride there a week from Saturday—on Wanzerbe market day."

"We'll get a ride," Idrissa answered us excitedly. "Many taxis go there on Saturday."

Idrissa left to investigate the Mehanna-Wanzerbe transport situation. Cheryl and I gladly washed away the grime of hours of travel in 120-degree heat.

39

THE WAY OF THE COWRY

We spent most of the next morning and afternoon inside the the house, protecting ourselves from the heat. Normally by mid-July the heat would have broken. Without rain, however, the hot season continued relentlessly. It was only after the second afternoon prayer—around 4:30—that we left the compound to visit Fatouma, the diviner. We walked through the market area, greeting people. We pushed forward over the soft and shifting path which gave way to dune sands by the time we reached Fatouma's compound. Like the compound of Amadu Zima, Fatouma's enclosure had no wall, only a fence of thorn bushes. Fatouma was in her yard feeding a large black goat that had a bell around its neck. During my previous visit that goat resided in Djibo's compound. The goat, Djibo had explained, was Dongo's familiar, a sacred animal that was given special care. Why was this goat living in Fatouma's compound? I was condemned to an unscratched itch; Fatouma wouldn't volunteer the information, and it was indiscreet for me to ask.

We saw each other simultaneously.

She clapped her hands in delight. "My family people have come! My family people have come! My family people have come!"

Her elation was contagious. "Your family people have returned, indeed," I said. "May God be praised."

"I am thanking God for your return. I am thanking God for Cheryl's safe arrival." She waved us into the compound. "Come in. Come into my house," indicating to the small mudbrick structure that had replaced her straw hut.

"When did you build it, Fatouma?" Cheryl asked.

"Four months ago."

"Wonderful," I said. "Wonderful."

We took off our sandals and stepped onto the cool clean sand floor. She unrolled two new palm-frond mats and we sat down in the center of the room. "Well, Paul. Are we ready to begin?" She smiled at me.

"Your shells or mine, Fatouma?"

"The chief of the sky told me to retire my shells; they were too hot. I haven't been throwing shells much this year. Seeing so much death makes me sad, and I get headaches when I throw too much."

"Then why are you going to throw shells with me?" I asked.

"Because the chief of the sky told me so." She pointed to the white cloth pouch I had taken from my shirt pocket.

"Show me your shells."

I emptied my twenty-one cowries onto the sand.

"Do they see?" Fatouma asked.

"Yes," I answered. The Sohanci had given me fourteen of his shells in 1981. And just the week before he gave me seven additional shells that had been imbued with the force of Nya Beri, the spirit that gives the gift of clairvoyance. In Tillaberi Cheryl had observed closely the Sohanci's divining method. He placed any number of shells on the sand. He looked at his client for a moment and then spoke about his or her past, present, and future. Then the Sohanci moved the shells as if to illustrate his vision. Cheryl suggested that he was a visionary who used cowries as legitimating props. Fatouma, however, threw seven shells at a time and interpreted their configurations.

Just as in 1982–83, Fatouma picked seven shells and shook them in her cupped hands as she murmured an incantation. She threw the shells.

"Oooo! Luck is on both of your sides. When you and Cheryl travel to the United States, your path is clear."

This prediction sounded much like others in scores of cowry arrays read by the Sohanci. He would finger the shells and say: "You will make a great deal of money"; "You will receive a letter in Niamey carrying good news"; "There is a man in America who is jealous of your work. He wants to prevent you from moving forward"; and "There is health and happiness on your path." He did pinpoint some of Cheryl's frustrations, but as she argued, his conclusions could be drawn by any perceptive acquaintance. I suspected that the Sohanci's telepathic methods worked well for those culturally proximate to Songhay, but not nearly so well for people like Cheryl and myself.

Fatouma threw the shells and looked at Cheryl. "There are two women in America who are jealous of you. For many years they have blocked your path. They are your enemies." The Sohanci had made a similar interpretation.

On the third throw, the shells revealed aspects of my past. During the previous year the two enemies who blocked my path had been repelled. Again the enemies! Fatouma's view of my life, like the Sohanci's, was devoid of chance. Any barriers I encountered, they "saw," were caused by people working against me. And Cheryl, too, had similar villains in her life whose jealousy blocked her progress. I had underestimated the danger my Songhay teachers believed lurked in everyone's way—not just in the way of those on the path of sorcery. If this was the Songhay world of war, then even noninitiates had to "protect" themselves as warriors did.

Fatouma was still studying the configuration of the third throw. She said that my path was now full of health and happiness. She saw an altar in my house. "Before you left for Niger this year, you made an offering to protect your house. You also have a spirit that shadows your movements." Fatouma was correct about the altar and the offering. The existence of the benevolent spirit was not so readily confirmed.

She threw the shells once more. "Paul, you must give candy to children and small amounts of money to the poor. Also, give a white chicken or a white sheep to a blind man. Do this and the spirits will look after you."

We adjourned till the next day. Cheryl went to the market festivities of the day, and I prepared to meet with Djibo.

40

SHOWDOWN WITH DJIBO

Djibo and his brother Zakaribaba lived in the same Mehanna compound. Over the years they had built four small mudbrick houses for their relatives. The two brothers, however, preferred to live in grass huts, finding them cooler in the hot season. I had not seen Djibo during my previous visit in 1982–83. He had taken a second wife and spent much of his time with her in Namarigungu, a town on the east bank of the Niger some twenty kilometers south of Mehanna. How relieved I had been to learn that Djibo was not in town. In 1984 Djibo made sure that he and I would be in Mehanna at the same time.

When I walked into the compound, the children landed on me like hungry flies. Djibo's first wife, Maymuna, emerged from her hut, an infant in her arms. Other women I didn't know joined the crowd.

"Another one?" I asked Maymuna.

"Um hum," she responded.

"It's ugly. It has no ears," I proclaimed.

"The ears will grow, won't they?" Maymuna protested.

"Paul, you speak Songhay better than we do," one of the other women told me. "You are a true Songhay."

"The floating log," I retorted, "never becomes the crocodile."

"Great God!" the woman cried. "Great God!"

Djibo was not in the compound. "Is Zakaribaba here?" I asked Maymuna.

"He's lying down in his hut with a bad headache."

I had known Zakaribaba for more than eight years, but I had not studied with him. As Djibo's younger brother, I reasoned, he had not been privy to his father's deep secrets; he had little to teach me. I clapped and entered his hut, which was dark, cool, and roomy inside. Zakaribaba's house was unusual in that it had been built with deliberation. It was round, like a traditional grass hut, but larger. Indeed, from the outside it appeared to be an ordinary grass structure. But once inside I could see the difference. The floor and the lower portion of the walls were baked mud. At once cool and clean, as he told me proudly. He used the advantages of mudbrick without losing the fresh air of the grass design.

Zakaribaba was seated on a straw mat. He didn't look well and he greeted me dully. He offered me a short stool.

"How long will you be in Mehanna?" he asked.

"One week. Then off to Wanzerbe."

"You are looking for Djibo?"

"Yes. I want to study with him tomorrow."

"He'll be here," he said.

"Tell him I'll be coming early in the morning." Wouldn't it be terrific if I could avoid seeing Djibo until the next day?

"Studying what?" Zakaribaba asked. "Sorko chants?"

"No. Plants."

Zakaribaba's face lit up. "That's what I know, Paul. I know about plants. May I come too?"

"Of course," I answered without hesitation. I hadn't expected Zakaribaba to be an expert on plants, but after eight years of casual acquaintance I barely knew him. I could only be happily surprised. Besides, Djibo would have to restrain himself in the presence of his brother and Cheryl. Suddenly, I felt better about the upcoming confrontation with Djibo.

Zakaribaba rummaged through a cardboard box and presented me with a dried brown root. "This root," he stated, "opens a closed heart."

"Asthma?"

"Yes. Closed heart," he repeated. "You put the powder of this root, *boowre*, into boiling water and count to a hundred. Then the person drinks it."

"And then?"

"He can breathe again."

How fantastic! "We'll talk about it tomorrow," I suggested. How much knowledge dwelled in the modest architect of such a house!

Zakaribaba put his hand on his forehead.

"Your headache?" I wondered.

"Yes. I haven't had my tea today. That's why my head aches."

I gave him 500 francs for tea and left the hut. As I was preparing to leave, Djibo strutted into the compound. He beckoned me to his hut. Oh shit, I thought, here we go again. His altar was in place: a small table on which was arranged a semicircle of perfume vials. Five hatchets with small bells nailed into their heads (Dongo's hatchets) had been wedged into the joints of the beams supporting the roof. I sat on Djibo's bed.

"I heard you came yesterday," he said softly. "Why didn't you tell me you were coming?"

"I wrote you, Djibo," I lied. "Didn't you receive my letters?"

"Not one," he barked. "I wrote you for money, but I received nothing."

"The letters must have been lost," I lied again.

"When I heard that Paul Sorko had come to Mehanna, I left my rice fields to come and see you. I can stay only until tomorrow."

What a relief, I thought. What if he had decided to stay for a week! "Can we meet tomorrow morning?" I asked.

"How about tonight?"

"I can't tonight, Djibo."

"I have many secrets to reveal. Great secrets. Come tonight. You must learn these things to become a great sorko."

I knew that he was after money. He called me a sorko, knowing full well that I was a stranger. Djibo had always wanted to profit from our relationship, and he was too arrogant to realize that his importunities had undermined our friendship. "I'll never be a great sorko, Djibo. And I can't come tonight."

Djibo shrugged. "Very well. Come tomorrow." He paused as if to ponder his strategy. "Djibo has sacrificed much to come to see Paul. My workers are hungry. And the secrets are very dear."

My face reddened. "Djibo, don't you know that I hate money talk? Is that all you want? Did you come for my money?"

"No. No. My talk is not money talk. It is sorko talk, Paul. You can become a great sorko."

"Sure, Djibo. Sure," I muttered in disgust. What to do now? I could buy Djibo off. I would give him so much money and ask so little of him that he would be flabbergasted and leave me alone. Yes, I would beat him at his own game. I took out a 10,000 franc note. "Here Djibo. Take this money. It should pay you for your lost time."

He folded the note and put it in his pocket. "Come tonight, Paul. Come tonight."

"No. I'll be back in the morning. Cheryl and Zakaribaba will join us."

"Both of them?"

"Yes, Djibo. We'll be talking about plants."

The next morning Cheryl and I carried our tape-recorder over the dune to Djibo's compound, which was several tons of sand beyond Fatouma's. We went to Djibo's hut to find him sitting on his bed. I asked one of the children to find Zakaribaba.

"How is your house, Djibo?" Cheryl asked.

"We are thanking God for our health and happiness," Djibo answered. "And your house?"

"There are no problems in my house," Cheryl stated.

Moments later Zakaribaba popped in. In the morning sun I was struck by how much he resembled his father, Mounmouni Koda.

We were all ready to start. Djibo brought tension to the hut with his opening sentence. "Paul," he said. "You are a sorko. Do you have an altar in your house?"

"I do, Djibo," I answered, barely controlling my anger. "But I am not a sorko."

Djibo ignored my assertion. He picked up one of his baatas. It was a tin box that had been wound with black thread. "Do you have one of these, Paul?" Djibo asked.

"I do."

Djibo showed me a leather amulet meant to be worn around the biceps. "And this, do you have this?"

"No, I don't."

"You should have it," Djibo insisted. "This is strong medicine."

My mind boiled with fury, but I remained visibly calm. "I have enough strong medicine, Djibo. I don't need it. Keep it for yourself."

My answer did not deter him. Djibo searched through his things and showed me a reddish-brown substance. "Do you have this?" he asked.

"That is kobe, Djibo. Sure, I've got a lot of it."

"And what about this?"

I looked at the light-green powder. "Oh, I have plenty of wata gay gaya."

Zakaribaba fidgeted in the corner as Djibo reached for another specimen. The next words were not Djibo's, however, but a woman's "Good morning." It was Fatouma. She poked her head into the hut and took in the situation. "I was just passing by and stopped to say hello. Sorry to interrupt. See you later." With that she was gone.

Djibo resumed his challenge game, holding up a blackish root. "Do you know this one?"

I admitted that I did not.

"Of course you don't," Djibo said smugly. "Last night I went into the bush just for you. It is dangerous to dig this up because you find cobras in the same place you find this."

"What do you call it?" Cheryl broke in, watching Djibo's face.

"It is called komni tunda."

I had seen the root in Niamey, but I did not know its uses.

"It's used to make people disappear," Djibo stated.

"You also use it," Zakaribaba added, "to kill intestinal worms. It works quickly. You put the root in water and let it soak from morning to noon. Then the person drinks the water."

Djibo frowned and continued to rummage through his ritual objects.

I told Djibo that the Sohanci had given me many things. I showed him my brass ring.

"That is only a sohanci charm," Djibo scoffed. "I will give you sorko things."

I had to put an end to Djibo's exhibition. "Our work this year," I declared, "is not with sorcery; it is with plants. I will name a plant, and I want both of you to tell me the uses of its leaves, stems, bark, or roots."

"Is that *all* you want, Paul?" Djibo asked incredulously.

"That is our path this year," Cheryl informed him.

I started to recite the names of plants. It soon became apparent that Zakaribaba knew much more about medicinal plants than his brother. During the interview he often contradicted his brother's statements. Several times, he provided detailed information on plants that were unknown to Djibo. Djibo had been upstaged, and I had discovered a fellow traveler on the path of plants.

I finished running through my list. Cheryl clicked "off" the tape-recorder. The interview was over. Djibo's eyes flashed toward his brother. Perhaps he realized that one working relationship had ended and another had begun. We all went out in the midmorning sun. Zakaribaba returned to his own hut. In the bright light Djibo seemed smaller, contracted. He asked me huskily, "Is this all?" I cut him off, saying we had other people to see that day. I wished Djibo a safe trip back to his rice field, which in the past year had supplied enough food to feed his entire family.

Cheryl, who had watched my apprehension build in anticipation of the session that had just ended, complimented me on my victory. "You controlled the situation," she said. "Djibo was beside himself. I observed him during the interview. After each question, he was looking for his opening, his chance to seize the initative. If he were a boxer he would have been jabbing. But you didn't let him land a punch."

Yes, I had behaved like a hard man and I was beginning to understand what that really meant.

41

LAST STAND IN WANZERBE

As soon as we arrived in Wanzerbe, I wanted to turn around and return to Mehanna. It didn't matter that we had suffered for four hours in the stifling cabin of a Toyota Land Cruiser. It didn't matter that Wanzerbe was the much striven-for destination of our research mission that year, where I would reap the rewards of years of patience. It didn't matter that I could increase my powers to unimaginable magnitude in Wanzerbe. None of this mattered as I slumped against the open window of the Toyota.

People gathered around the truck, but I didn't respond to to their greetings; rather, I looked back at the road that had brought us to Wanzerbe that day: vast moonscapes of laterite, boulders and carcasses where nothing grew and nothing grazed; farmers sitting in their barren fields, gazing at the cloudless eastern sky; herders driving scrawny cattle over dunes where grass once grew tall and thick. The drought had sapped the vitality of Songhay country.

Cheryl grabbed my arm and shook me. I felt the pressure of her ring on my arm—a circle of twisted copper wire that Fatouma insisted she wear for "protection." "The soldiers want to see us, Paul." She pointed to my right.

The driver had halted opposite a shady area that served as a small military outpost—ten cots under the trees and a mudbrick field office. I swallowed my reservations and climbed out of the cabin of the Toyota. Cheryl followed. We greeted the soldiers in French and gave them our papers. While we waited for the sergeant to pass on our authorizations, Hassane, one of Kassey's sons, welcomed us to Wanzerbe.

"Is your mother in town?" I asked.

"Oh, yes. She'll be at the market later," he answered.

Hassane nudged me just out of earshot of the others. "My mother is old and stubborn. She won't tell her secrets even to her favorite son, Larabu."

"Larabu?"

Hassane explained that Larabu had been a student in Tera. During his last year of secondary school, he was caught stealing from his teachers and had spent a year in jail. He was now a sergeant in the Nigerien army.

Hassane's talk of Larabu jolted my memory. I had been his teacher. He had stolen from me, among others. And I was one of the people who filed a complaint against him. In other words, I was responsible for sending him to jail. I masked my uneasiness. "Perhaps the time is not right," I suggested.

"Maybe so," Hassane allowed. "Maybe we'll learn something after the harvest."

I watched him go and wondered whether there would be a harvest in Wanzerbe. It was late July and still no millet grew in the Wanzerbe fields. And it was hot. Even the air burned my skin.

Cheryl waved to catch my attention. Our papers were in order. "Where and how long are you staying?" the sergeant asked.

I told him we planned to spend one week in Karia, but that we might leave earlier. With that, Mahamane drove us to Idrissa's compound, where we unloaded our gear and the food we had brought for his family amid the excited crowd of his relatives. We put our things in Idrissa's Wanzerbe house.

At midday Cheryl and I went to the most pitiful market that we had seen in our years in Niger. Local Tuaregs offered us faded and cracked leather bags. Women sold shriveled onions and small amounts of sesame flour. Songhay merchants sat behind piles of exposed dry dates that attracted clouds of flies. No one seemed to be selling livestock, and only the merchants from Mehanna and Tera had come to sell rice to the people of this famine zone. Their own stores of millet long ago exhausted, people of the famine zone paid twice what the price for rice had been at the Bonfebba market a week earlier.

We walked around the market, a single line of traders' stations—not even a dozen could properly be called "stalls"—that snaked over half of the allotted market space. The carnival gaiety of rural markets was missing here. Several people we met confessed that they had been eating mush made from the pounded stumps of the previous year's millet stalks—something even the hungry cows refused to eat. Their children had been eating one meal every two days.

We didn't see Kassey at the market, but I did bump into Dunguri, who was dressed in expensive imported cloth. She greeted me effusively and glared at Cheryl. Given my mood, her effusiveness and mean stare aroused my suspicions. In 1982, I had given her two meters of expensive cloth. She liked the cloth, but she had wanted money as well. I refused to give her any, and she had been furious with me. Now I wondered what her "fish-eye" had in store for me or for Cheryl.

The afternoon sun pulsed in the cloudless sky. I tasted the salt that had gathered in my mustache and felt a heat headache coming on—a slow but persistent throbbing in my left temple. I suggested to Cheryl that we return to Karia to eat the lunch I knew Idrissa's cousins were preparing for us. On the way back to our compound, we came upon a Toyota pickup truck from Tera, the regional administrative center. The driver sat in the carrier talking to his cronies.

"Want a ride to Tera?" he asked me in Songhay.

"What for?"

"You don't want to stay here, do you?"

"Yes," I said half-heartedly.

"Crazy. Crazy."

"Why?"

"No one wants to stay in Wanzerbe," he said, switching momentarily into French. "No food, and the people are dangerous."

"I know all about it," I replied. "We're going to stay four days. Maybe a week."

The driver shook his head. "I'm leaving at 4:00. There's a place for you if you want it."

"Thanks," I said. "When will you be coming back?"

"Not until next market. You won't see any trucks at all until the next market."

To escape Wanzerbe! How I wanted to get on that truck and go to Tera. But I knew I couldn't. And so we walked away from the market and the trucks and ate lunch in Idrissa's house. In the distance, I heard the drone of engines as the trucks left us trapped in Wanzerbe.

That evening we visited Kassey. The previous year, she had welcomed me into her house warmly. In 1984, she was distant and formal. Even the six meters of lavender eyelet cloth that we had brought for her from America failed to warm her mood. Although she joked about how Cheryl and I were trying to make her into a young woman again, I could see that something had changed. She was bitter. Was it the lack of rain? This, she said, was in the hands of

God and the spirits. Was it the government's neglect of the Wanzerbe region? Perhaps, for she had nothing good to say about the empty promises of local officials. Somehow, however, I sensed that my presence had inspired this bitterness.

It was a black night and stars abounded in the clear sky. We sat on canvas chairs in Kassey's courtyard. She sat next to her daughter, Mumay, on the edge of a wide stick-bed. We talked idly about gardens, possession dances, and the hunger of children.

There was a clap outside Kassey's gate.

"Enter," Kassey commanded.

A man in a white turban and robe came through the gate. Kassey stood up.

"Ah," she said, walking toward the man. "Come with me. We will talk."

By this time Hassane, Kassey's son, had joined us. He explained that the man was Kassey's client. Six months ago, Hassane said, the man asked Kassey to perform a rite that would resolve his marital difficulties. This she had done to perfection, for within the next month the man's wife returned to his house after a one-year absence. Four months ago the man told Kassey of his good fortune. Pleased with herself, Kassey charged the man 25,000 francs ($100), a sum that the man couldn't pay. Claiming that he was broke, the man begged Kassey to lower her fee. Kassey refused, suggesting that the man borrow money to pay her. Two months passed and the man made his first payment—10,000 francs. During the two months between the first payment and the present, the man had failed to make a second and final payment. He had come to explain to Kassey his financial difficulties.

The man spoke softly. Kassey spoke loudly and clearly, so that everyone could hear what she was saying.

"Now listen," she told him. "You came to me seeking a powerful charm. I gave it to you. If the charm didn't work, it would be like we had never seen one another, like we had never talked. But the charm did work, did it not?"

"That's the truth."

"And when the charm works, one pays for it, doesn't one?"

"Yes."

"And your wife is living in your house, is she not?"

"Yes."

"Then, what is there to discuss?"

"For two months," the man stammered, "I have tried to borrow the money. El Hadj X refused me because I haven't yet repaid him for the first loan. I have talked to El Hadj Y. He'll give me the money when his business is better."

"I see," Kassey said curtly. "But all of us are suffering the consequences of these difficult times."

She rose abruptly and maneuvered the man to the entrance of her compound.

"Please," the man pleaded. "Please, would you reduce the fee?"

"No."

"Then please, please, give me more time to pay you," he begged.

"More time?" she asked menacingly.

"Please, a few more weeks."

Kassey relented. "I have no problem with that."

We heard the man's sigh.

"Please send my greetings to your mother. And give my greetings to your wife and wife's mother who are related to me through my mother's people."

"I will," the man rasped as he disappeared into the night.

Kassey reclaimed her seat, chuckling. "He will pay me soon because he fears the consequences."

The word "consequences" opened the cage door of my private fears. Kassey was the epitome of hardness. She *would* hurt a man who was married to her maternal kin. She reveled in his terror. After witnessing that encounter, I did not doubt that she would do anything to enhance her reputation for power. The chill in her demeanor made me shiver when I reflected on my involvement with her favorite son, Larabu. In 1969–70, I had been Larabu's English teacher. As the laziest student, Larabou failed my course. He wasn't the only student to flunk, but his lack of application had—for me—a novel twist. He had contended that he didn't need to study, because his mother was a great sorcerer who'd give him charms to ensure academic achievement. I didn't expect trouble on that account; I knew that Kassey regarded his miserable school record as his own fault. But Larabou had been involved in a much more serious incident in the spring of 1970. He had stolen from the faculty—from me and from the other teachers, who were French, at the school—helping himself to our cooperative household funds. We pressed charges and Larabu spent a year in prison. Despite his unmistakable guilt, he vowed vengeance. We could have dropped the charges, but we didn't. And so I was partly responsible for sending Kassey's youngest son to jail. Kassey had no doubt deduced my true identity—as I had her son's. Would she seek revenge? I didn't believe that all the "protection" I carried in and on my body could fend off an angry attack, and I knew that Cheryl was vulnerable.

Kassey invited us back early the next morning so that we might work together. We took our leave. Cheryl was full of expectation. I was full of fear.

After a restless night, we ate a hurried breakfast of coffee and fried millet cakes and rushed off to Kassey's compound. Kassey greeted us coldly and told us to sit down on some stools under the thatched canopy that fronted her mudbrick house. "I have a few chores to do," she told us "Rest. I will soon be with you."

Cheryl looked at me. "Why does she need to do house chores when she has workers to do them and guests waiting?"

No Songhay I knew had ever behaved this rudely to me. Cheryl and I had scrambled to comply with Kassey's request that we arrive early and now she was pounding millet and cleaning house. Kassey's behavior reminded us of the unwilling hostess who says she is busy with food preparation so that she can avoid interacting with the guests. Two hours passed. Three hours. The sun rose higher in the sky, heating the air to skin-burning temperatures. Finally, Kassey appeared.

"Let me bathe and then we can sit and talk."

One hour later we entered her house. Idrissa appeared, having spent the morning hours visiting his maternal relatives.

"Make yourselves comfortable," Kassey told us. "I will be back in a little while."

"She's really sticking it to us, Paul," Cheryl stated.

"No kidding," I said. I turned to Idrissa. "What is it? We come early in the morning to work and she makes us wait until noon. We came all the way from America to see her."

Idrissa seemed nervous. "She'll talk. She'll talk."

"Good," I said. "What's going on in town?"

Idrissa ignored my question. "I hear that a truck will be leaving here on Wednesday."

"Really!" Cheryl exclaimed.

I turned to Cheryl. "Can we complete our work here in four days?"

"Certainly the plant stuff and the architectural photos. The rest, no. But we didn't come all this way to cut our visit short, did we?"

"I think it best that we leave here as soon as possible."

Idrissa didn't disagree. "I'll look for a ride. Maybe we'll find something sooner."

Kassey brought in our lunch. She had killed three chickens in our honor and Mumay had prepared a sesame sauce—my favorite. "Eat, we'll talk later," she commanded as she once again popped out the door.

I stared at the steaming casseroles Kassey had set before us. Dared we eat this food? Given her knowledge of plants and her irascible temperament, she could easily poison us, and the only available chickens were stewing in the sauce.

"Idrissa," I said. "Come and eat."

Idrissa shook his head. "You eat first."

Cheryl and I picked up our spoons and ate the rice, sauce, and chicken.

"It's delicious," Cheryl proclaimed.

"Sure is," I agreed. "Mumay is the best cook in these parts if she has the proper spices."

We satisfied our hunger in short order and passed the casseroles over to Idrissa, who ate with abandon. When Idrissa finished, he took the casseroles outside and called to Kassey. Gracefully, she entered her house, unrolled a new palm-frond mat and sat down to our left.

"What is your project?" she asked me.

"My mother," I began, attempting to duplicate my oration of the previous year, "from America Cheryl and I have come to visit and talk with you. This year we have two projects. First, we would like to talk to you about the plants that people use in healing. Second, we would like to produce *your* book."

"My book?" Kassey echoed.

"Yes. You tell us of your life. We record it in the machine. Then we take your words from the machine and put them on paper. In this way, people from Niger to America will know your words and know your wisdom."

"Good. Very good," Idrissa nodded.

Kassey arched her back and grunted. "This is good," she said gruffly. "Begin with the plants."

I explained the method. I would recite the name of the plant and she would indicate its use in healing or sorcery. As we went down the list, I recognized that Kassey was holding back. We discussed kobe, for example. The Sohanci had taught me about the numerous uses of kobe in charms. But Kassey identified it only as a powder used by her ancestors; she did not specify its variety of uses. And so it continued. She provided detailed descriptions of the medicinal uses of plants, but she refrained from discussing their use for super-

natural purposes. For several powders with only supernatural application, she said curtly, "We work with that." How disappointed and
troubled I was. I had returned this year under the impression that
this difficult woman had accepted me as her apprentice. She hadn't
at all. She treated me with the suspicion and reserve that Songhay
used to maintain distance between themselves and strangers. We
had come to Wanzerbe enmeshed in a web of false hopes, and now
we were caught here in a web of real fear. By the time we had run
through the protocol, everyone was drained—squeezed by the heat
and the weight of apprehension. We thanked Kassey profusely for
her time, and asked whether we might return that evening to work
on *her* book.

She accompanied us to the entrance of her compound and wished
us a peaceful and tranquil afternoon. She said something to Idrissa.
When we were well along the way to Karia, Idrissa informed us that
Kassey did not want to see us that evening.

"Why the hell not?" I demanded.

"Other business," Idrissa answered.

In the language of sorcery, "other business" meant that she would
be performing some secret rite that night. For whom? To whom?

That afternoon the heat of the summer sun fused with the humidity of approaching rain. For hours, we sat and sweated in Idrissa's
house—some of the longest hours of my life. Idrissa was in and out
as he continued his familial visits. Each time he stuck his head in, he
assured us that he would find us a ride to Tera by Wednesday or
Thursday. "Maybe sooner. Maybe sooner."

"He wants to leave just as much as you do, Paul," Cheryl observed.

"Yeah," I sighed. "I wonder if he knows something that we don't."

It was too stuffy to talk. I walked outside and saw lightning in the
distance. The oldest woman in the compound pointed to the east.
"It's raining in Tegey."

"May God bring rain to Wanzerbe, my mother," I said.

"Amin."

Together we watched the expanding band of red-brown dust
creep toward us. We smelled rain in the air. Expecting a storm, people tethered their animals and shuttered their windows. A howling
wind threw a blanket of dust over the sun. The temperature plummeted. And then a drop, two, three, followed by sheets of water. The
compound quickly became a shallow lake. The pounding rain
abated and in the distance we heard screams; the rain deities had
possessed their mediums and were strutting, crawling, or rolling

their way to the compound of the local zima. We emerged from Idrissa's house. The air was clean and cool. People smiled. Kundia-baba, Idrissa's father, thanked me for bringing the rain to Wanzerbe. I said that my prayers for rain were no stronger than his.

He shrugged off my disclaimer. "Tomorrow," he told me. "We go to our fields to plant."

"May God grant you a bountiful harvest," I told him. We both knew it was too late to plant millet.

The evening was cool and humid. We ate a tasteless dinner of rice and gumbo sauce and then sat in the little court outside Idrissa's house. People stopped by to visit, but I didn't feel much like talking. What I did feel was vaguely but increasingly sick. Fever. Pain in my side when I breathed. General uneasiness. What caused my discomfort? Our water came from an artesian well. The food? True, others—unseen—had prepared it. But Cheryl seemed untroubled. Perhaps it was the silent killer— sorcery. We had brought food and money to Kassey's and Idrissa's people. We had brought nothing to Dunguri or to Halidu, the local zima, himself a sohanci of great reputation. I knew Wanzerbe to be a place of spiteful people. I knew that if people felt that they were slighted—Kassey included, to be sure—they would seek retribution; they would make someone pay the consequences. What text was Dunguri reciting over her altar? What was Halidu saying to the spirits that he controlled? My mind was churning with my stomach. I had to get out to preserve my sanity.

At nightfall I grew progressively weaker, but I resisted sleep. To sleep, I reasoned, was to place us in mortal danger. No, instead of sleeping I recited the genji how. By the time the cocks crowed, I was as bone-weary as the night watchman that I was. Cheryl slept peacefully. Had I once again fought off the spells of my spiteful attackers?

Idrissa came by at daybreak and greeted me glumly. He too had foregone sleep, having spent the night in a deathwatch as his two-year-old nephew slipped away. Our grieving neighbors wailed at the loss of such a young life.

"Paul," Idrissa said meekly. "They don't have money for the funeral shroud."

The death of this child in the next compound unnerved me completely. I gave Idrissa the money and expressed my heartfelt sympathy. Then came the other news: Idrissa's maternal uncle had also died. The storm had caught him in his field. He had taken refuge in his straw granary, and died of a heart attack there during the night. One night and two deaths. What had I done, I agonized. People had sent death to my house and in warding it off I had diverted it elsewhere. The world of sorcery was too much with me. Dread swept over me. Suspicion flooded my mind. And then I felt the intestinal rumblings. I ran to the hole Idrissa had dug for us behind the houses. What emerged shocked even me, a person accustomed to the indelicacies of diarrhea in Africa.

I returned to the house and said nothing to Cheryl, who was on her way to the hole. When she returned, worry lined her face. Her stool had been similar to mine.

"We've got to get the fuck out of here!" I screamed.

Cheryl tried to calm me. "It's nothing serious."

"Oh yeah! It's fucking serious!" I shouted. "Fucking serious!"

Idrissa appeared. "There's a truck that's leaving in about thirty minutes."

"Where is it?"

Idrissa pointed just beyond the compound. Sure enough, there was a Berliet stopped along the road. The driver was repairing something.

"Run and tell him that we're coming. Run!"

Idrissa ran off. "Cheryl, let's pack up our stuff and get the fuck out of here."

"Come on, Paul. You're hysterical. You can last another day."

"No!" I yelled. "I know my limit and I've reached it. Let's pack."

We rushed into the house and began to pack up our things. People from the compound wondered why we were leaving so suddenly. I patted my belly. They accepted my lie—or did they understand?

Idrissa brought the driver to the house. He, too, was in a rush to leave. We were so nervous that we couldn't roll up our bed gear. Kundiababa interrupted us.

"I am sorry you must leave so soon. Today we go to the fields to plant." He presented three chickens to me. "Some meat for you and Cheryl—a token of the honor of having you as our guests. When you are far away in America, you will be in our thoughts."

His warmth softened me. This man's sincerity and affection reminded me that there were good people in Wanzerbe. Still, I had to escape.

A procession of well-wishers escorted us to the truck. Idrissa and Harijetu, his daughter, climbed onto the truck's carrier.

"I'm glad we're leaving, Paul," he told me. "I wanted to leave when we arrived."

Cheryl and I looked at one another. "You know, Paul, I had the same feeling. When we arrived on Saturday, I fought the impulse to leave immediately."

"No shit."

We climbed into the cab of the truck and the driver started the engine. We chugged up Surgumey, the magic mountain, and I relaxed a bit, having fled a world in which "bad faith" had almost destroyed me.

EPILOGUE: IN SORCERY'S SHADOW

Time has healed the confusion and terror I felt on my last day in Wanzerbe. My fright did not disappear when our truck descended the east slope of Surgumey and Wanzerbe disappeared from sight. I was vaguely ill for many weeks, convinced that someone had tried to "fix" me as I had once "fixed" a mean chief. The "illness" lingered but eventually disappeared after I returned to the United States.

During the past seventeen years I have taken many trips to Songhay country. On each of those trips I played a different role: a wide-eyed English teacher; a theory-testing incipient anthropologist; a skeptical apprentice to a sorcerer; an accomplice in an attack of sorcery; a metaphysical adventurer following an existential path; a victim of an attack of sorcery.

How could such a rich experience end so abruptly that day in Wanzerbe? It didn't. Songhay is more than a fond memory to me; it is part of me. My teachers invited me to share fully their world; I accepted their invitation. My teachers revealed many of their secrets to me; I will always live with them. My teachers showed me how to carry myself in the world of sorcery; I have used those lessons in my daily life.

In my case anthropology has become something more than the gathering and presentation of data. The Songhay world challenged the basic premises of my scientific training. Living in Songhay forced me to confront the limitations of the Western philosophical tradition. My seventeen-year association with Songhay reflects the slow evolution of my thought, a thought profoundly influenced by Songhay categories and Songhay wisdom. When I began to write anthropological texts, I followed the conventions of my training. I "gathered data," and once the "data" were arranged in neat piles, I "wrote them up." In one case I reduced Songhay insults to a series of logical formulas. In other cases I used data "collected" among the

Songhay to write about metaphor, social theory, and social change. There is nothing wrong with this kind of writing. Anthropologists use it to create a corpus of knowledge that can be assessed critically and corrected. Through this truly scientific process, our knowledge of social phenomena grows. And as our knowledge of social phenomena grows, so does our authority in the world.

But is that what we are all about? I hope not. Anthropology is a scientific discipline; but it is also a profoundly human experience. Early in my experience I considered Adamu Jenitongo to be my principal informant, a knowledgeable person who supplied me with information. When we shared food from the same bowl and slept in the spirit hut, our relationship was transformed; we became father and son. He could no longer be my informant; I could no longer be a stranger. And he taught me many things—things he had not yet revealed to his actual sons.

Profound ethnographic experience is both possible and desirable in anthropology. I will never become a Songhay, but I have nonetheless penetrated a world that few Songhay know directly. How did I enter the world of Songhay sorcery? Two birds did mark me for Sorko Djibo Mounmouni, birds that, Adamu Jenitongo later told me, embodied the deities Dongo and Harakoy Dikko. One can only speculate about why that occurred. But bird marksmanship is not the answer; rather, the answer lies in our conception of fieldwork. If my fieldwork had been limited to one, two, or perhaps three trips, I might have stepped into the world of Songhay sorcery, but I would have never understood it well—from a Songhay perspective. In 1979–80 I discovered my interpretive errors of 1976–77. In 1981, I discovered that "X," my trusted friend and "informant," had lied to me. In 1982–83, I discovered more interpretive errors made in 1976–77, 1979–80, and 1981. In 1984 the famine forced me to reassess everything I had learned about Songhay.

Long-term field study, while valued by anthropologists, does not guarantee profound experience. For that one must also be able to speak the field language. Using an interpreter should be an interim—perhaps emergency—tactic. An interpreter is like a life jacket: it keeps one afloat—even saves one from drowning— but it inhibits immersion and prohibits deep exploration. Although it is easy to make misinterpretations even if one speaks the field language well, it is much much easier to do so if one relies upon field assistants and other interpreters.

Long-term fieldwork and field-language fluency are two important ingredients in the recipe I am compiling. But the most important ingredient, I am convinced, is deep respect for other knowledge, other worlds, and other people. As anthropologists we must respect the people among whom we work. We have long been concerned that our studies not produce difficulties for the people we have studied. For me, respect means accepting fully beliefs and phenomena which our system of knowledge often holds preposterous. I took my teachers seriously. They *knew* that I used divination in my personal life. They *knew* that I had eaten powders to protect myself. They *knew* I wore objects to demonstrate my respect for the spirits. They *knew* I had an altar in my house over which I recited incantations. They liked the way I carried my knowledge and power and taught me more and more. . . .

But ethnographers can go too far. They can pursue the other's reality too hotly, crossing a line that brings them face to face with a violent reality that is no mere epistemological exercise. If they know too much they must swear an oath of silence. If they reveal what they shouldn't, they may be murdered. I sauntered across that line in Wanzerbe in 1984. Kassey *knew* what I knew and demonstrated her unequivocal disapproval. Terrified by the force of her disapproval, I turned and ran. To have walked further down that unknown path would have prevented me from telling my story.

My experience in a world of sorcery is not unique. My skill as a fieldworker is not extraordinary. The genre of this book—the fieldwork account—is now commonplace. There is no longer the need to justify ethnographic memoirs that feature vivid descriptions, dialogue, dusk-dreams, humor, and irony. If I have discovered anything from my experience of Songhay sorcery, it is that sorcery is a metaphor for the chaos that constitutes social relations—Songhay and otherwise. We all suffer *zamba*, a good friend's betrayal. Things crumble and are reconstituted in all societies; we are *all* in sorcery's shadow.

I left the people of Wanzerbe abruptly that day in 1984, but I have not divorced myself from them or from the other people I met in Niger. No matter how terrifying or commonplace, one cannot easily ignore the events, people, and places that one has encountered on life's path. Anthropologists leave their field sites, but life continues for the others. People in Tillaberi, Mehanna, and Wanzerbe suffered in 1984–85. There was no rain and no harvest. Food was scarce. There was disease and many people died. The Niger River reached its lowest level in recorded history. But the Songhay people I know are a gritty bunch. In Tillaberi Adamu Jenitongo's family came through the famine. In a fit of rage the Sohanci's grand-daughter, Fodie, threw a stone at one of her uncles. The stone missed its target and struck Adamu Jenitongo in the left eye. The eye's major blood vessel burst and his "eye died." He is gradually losing sight in his other eye. Jemma and Moussa Nya continue to carp at Djebo, who is still married to Moru. The monster child, Djamilla, died in the summer of 1985. Wandering after a downpour, she fell into a water-filled garbage pit and drowned. Meanwhile, Djebo gave birth to a son. Moussa continues to make clothing for his clients and saves the little money he makes so that he can marry his girlfriend.

Sorko Djibo is spending more and more time away from Mehanna. He rents a number of irrigated rice fields in Narmari-gungu on the Niger's east bank. Although he did not harvest a bumper crop in 1984–85, his fields yielded enough rice to feed his family in Mehanna. When he is in Mehanna, he walks with his head down and mumbles to himself. Djibo's brother Zakaribaba has be-come a respected herbalist in the Mehanna region. From great dis-tances people travel to Mehanna to seek Zakaribaba's medicines. Fa-touma, the market woman and diviner, has quietly taken on more burdens as a spiritual guardian of her community. In January of 1986 she was initiated as Dongo's medium—the most important medium in a Songhay possession troupe.

The five-hundred-year tradition of Wanzerbe has weathered yet another drought and famine. Koundiababa went to his field in Au-gust of 1984 to plant millet for the third time that year. But the crop failed. Many people left the region in 1984, walking for days to the nearest food distribution center. But Kundiababa remained in Wan-zerbe, eating infrequently and waiting for a telegram indicating that one of his sons had sent him money from Lagos, Lome, Abidjan, America. Kassey, too, remained in Wanzerbe, jealously keeping her secrets and her vast knowledge to her herself while ridding Wan-zerbe of its impurities.

The rains came back to the Sahel in the summer of 1985. The farmers returned to their fields. The fishermen returned to a Niger River full of water and fish. Rice cultivators returned to their flooded paddies. The rain brought people back to their rural villages to reas-sume their independence as competent subsistence farmers.

I also returned to Songhay in 1985–86. Idrissa had a new daughter, born in Mehanna in May of 1985, the hottest and most trying time of the famine. In five years of marriage, Jitu had given birth to three children. In my time with Idrissa, Jitu had never hidden her antipathy toward me. No matter, Idrissa was my "younger brother." He trusted me and I trusted him. In 1984, he even gave me his initiation ring. I had not known that he was a spirit medium.

But in December of 1985, Idrissa stole 25,000 CFA ($100) from me. I was crushed. The loss of money didn't bother me; theft is a fact of life in every society. But Idrissa was not just another informant, not just another Songhay. We had shared many trying moments. I considered him as I had considered Adamu Jenitongo and Adamu Zima—as men more interested in seeking the light of close friendship than the shadow of material gain. For the Songhay, *zamba* is always a danger on the path they walk. I was no exception. Not realizing that I had discovered the theft, Idrissa visited me in January 1986 at Adamu Jenitongo's compound in Tillaberi. Apparently, I had left one of my shirts in Mehanna, and Idrissa took it upon himself to bring it to me—a wonderful gesture. I was surprised to see him, but no more so than the Sohanci.

The Sohanci looked long and hard at Idrissa and pulled me aside.

"I know that man."

Twenty years earlier Idrissa had come to Tillaberi on a market day. When the market was crowded, Idrissa placed a pestle on the ground and danced on it—a sorcerer's dance that inspired such fear in the people at the market that they gave him money to protect themselves from his power. Someone summoned the Sohanci and, when he arrived, Idrissa fled for his life, for only the most powerful sorcerers in a community can perform such a dance. If another sorcerer dances, as Idrissa did, he could be killed, especially if he misrepresents himself.

"I decided to let him run off," Adamu Jenitongo told me. "He was so young." He looked at Idrissa again. "Paul, I never forget a face. This boy is the same one who came here long ago. He is the one who took your money, isn't he?"

"Yes, Baba."

"His character hasn't changed, has it?"

Idrissa spent the night, and the next morning he asked me for transport money.

I gave him 1,000 CFA ($4).

Then he told me that the spirit Cirey had taken Kassey's body in Wanzerbe three nights earlier. Through Kassey the spirit said that Paul should buy him a new costume.

"How much did Cirey ask for?" I mumbled.

"50,000 CFA [$200]," Idrissa said.

My heart cracked. I knew that spirits like Cirey never possessed their mediums after sunset, especially on days other than Thursday—the day of the spirits. Idrissa was lying and would no doubt pocket the money himself.

"Let the people of Wanzerbe write me about Cirey's costume, and then I'll send *them* the money."

"Are you sure you don't want to give me Cirey's money?" Idrissa persisted.

"I am."

Disappointed, Idrissa walked off toward the west, his small body casting a long shadow on the sand.

I, too, was about to leave Tillaberi. I was organizing my gear when the Sohanci called me to his mat.

"Your heart is spoiled, is it not?"

"Yes, Baba."

"Zamba is hard on a person's heart. But there is more than zamba on your path."

"I know."

"Baba is on your path. Paul is on Baba's path. Just remember that. Remember that."

"I will, Baba."

Moru popped out of his house and grabbed one of my bags.

"Paul, we must go if you're to catch your truck."

"Okay."

We stood up and the three of us walked to the edge of the compound. "Paul," the Sohanci said, "you must come next year to see Baba."

"God willing," I said.

"May God agree to it," the Sohanci responded.

Feeling the warmth of the Sohanci's gaze in the crisp dry air, Moru and I marched off to the truck depot at the western end of town. We bumped bags and I glanced down to see our shadows dancing ahead of us.

GLOSSARY OF TERMS

Amiru: the chief of a village. From the Arabic, *emir.*

anasara: European. From the Arabic, *insara,* i.e. Christian.

Aribinda: a village of the Kurumba peoples in Borkino Faso, renowned for farming magic.

Atakurma: the first people, who were short and fat.

baata: a sorcerer's sacrificial container.

baba: father. From the Arabic. The term is also used to denote respect for old men among the Songhay.

Bella: the former slaves of the Tuareg who now supply Songhay markets with firewood and surplus millet.

Bint al Hadash: a perfume used to attract Songhay spirits.

Bint al Sudan: a perfume used to attract Songhay spirits.

boowre: an unidentified plant used in the treatment of asthma.

boro bi: black man or black people.

boubou: a loose-fitting robe worn by men.

chef de poste: the title of a district administrator who reports to a regional adminstration.

ceeyndi: an unidentified resin that is burned to attract the spirits.

cimikoy: possessor of the truth (lit.) A sorcerer who scrupulously obeys the traditions of his or her ancestors.

diggi: a name of a paste eaten by sorko to increase their supernatural strength.

doguwa: the name of a Songhay spirit family of Hausa origin.

dosari: Tephrosia linearis, a plant used in sohanci sorcery.

duo: the husk of the millet seed. Witches hide the souls of their victims in piles of millet husk.

El Hadj: a Moslem who has completed the pilgrimage to Mecca.

Faran Maka Bote: the legendary fisherman who staged the first possession ceremony and who became the apical ancestor of the sorko.

ferrey: Khaya senegelensis, a plant used to combat witchcraft.

follo kadji: the unidentified root of a tree that is used during possession ceremonies.

fufu: a paste made from pounded cassava or plantain.

fula: a hat (lit). The term also corresponds to the initiation of a chief who receives his "hat" of authority.

Fulan: a cattle-herding pastoral people who are neighbors of the Songhay.

gani: to dance (lit.) The term also refers to a specific dance performed at possession ceremonies.

gao: Acacia albida, a tall tree common in the Sahel.

genji how: to attach or tie up the bush (lit.) This is the most important incantation in a sorcerer's repertoire; its aim is to harmonize the forces of the bush.

genji tambo: an unidentified plant used in sorko sorcery.

gezema: Boa senegelensis, a poisonous boa constrictor.

godji deli: an unidentified plant used as a sedative.

goronfol: Tribulus terrestris, a plant used in Sorko sorcery.

gunda beri: big belly (lit.), as well as the name for the great Sahelian famine of 1913–14.

guunu: the name of special sohanci who perform circumcisions. It is said that their fathers are descendants of Sonni Ali Ber and that their mothers are witches. This genealogy makes them alone powerful enough to perform the rites of manhood.

haasu kwarey: Securidaca longepedunculata. A tree the bark of which was pounded and eaten during famines.

Harakoy Dikko: the spirit queen of the Niger River and mother of the Tooru, nobles of the Songhay spirit world.

Hargay: spirits of the "cold" that precipate stillbirths, barrenness, and death.

Hausa: the language spoken by peoples living to the east and south of the Songhay.

Iblis: the devil who resides in the sixth level of hell, from the Arabic.

Iri Koy: our chief (lit.). The term denotes the High God who resides in the seventh heaven.

jumah: denotes the special afternoon prayer held in the Friday mosque and celebrating the Islamic sabbath.

kafia malam: an unidentified plant used in sorcery.

kobe: Ficus platyphylla, a tree used in sohanci sorcery.

komni tunda: an unidentified plant used to treat intestinal parasites.

korombey: Commiphora africana, a tree used in sohanci sorcery.

kosorey: Piliostigma reticulatum, a tree used in sohanci sorcery.

kram-kram: a spiny grass spore that burrows into the sand.

kusu: a magic paste that is eaten to increase a person's strength in the social or spirit worlds.

kwara tombo: an unidentified plant used in sorko sorcery.

Maalu (cirey): son of Harakoy Dikko, this spirit controls lightning.

marabout: tied to God (lit.). From the Arabic, the term denotes an Islamic cleric.

Moussa Nyori: son of Harakoy Dikko, this spirit controls the movements of clouds and snakes.

Ndebbi: the intermediary with the High God. Incantations are recited to Ndebbi, who relays the message to the High God. If the High God responds favorably to the incantation, a spell is cast. If he denies a sorcerer's request, the sorcerer's spell is powerless.

ngimgniti: a powder used in sorcery.

Nya Beri: the great mother (lit.), who is the mother of all the Hargay spirits. Knowing no fear, Nya Beri lives in cemeteries.

saa nya: an unidentified plant used by sorko.

Sadyara: the two-headed snake that guards Harakoy Dikko's spirit village under the Niger River.

Sangara: a village in Songhay country known for its sorcerers.

sherif: from the Arabic, a direct descendant of Mohammed the Prophet.

sibitah kadji: the root of an unidentified plant used by herbalists and sorcerers.

siria: Ficus deldekena, a tree used in sorko and sohanci sorcery.

sisiri: the chain of "power" that sohanci carry in their stomachs.

sohanci: patrilineal descendants of Sonni Ali Ber who practice sorcery.

Sonni Ali Ber: the king of the Songhay Empire from 1463 to 1491 and the ancestor of one group of Songhay sorcerers, the sohanci.

sorcery: the conscious use of specialized knowledge to precipitate change. In my view, sorcery is neither good nor evil; sorcerers use their knowledge and skill to develop their power and their reputations.

sorko: patrilineal descendants of Faran Make Bote who are praise-singers to the spirits and/or sorcerers.

sorko benya: lit., the sorko's slave; a non-sorko who is "pointed out" as having the capacities to learn the knowledge of the sorko.

soudure: refers to the period when last year's food is exhausted and the current crop is not ready to be harvested.

spirit sickness: an illness precipitated by a spirit possessing the body of its victim.

tamasheq: the language of the Tuaregs.

tooru: the nobles of the spirit world that control the major forces of the universe: water, wind, fire, clouds, thunder, and lightning.

Tuaregs: desert nomads who are neighbors to the Songhay.

wata gaya gaya: an unidentified plant used in possession ceremonies.

Youmbom: a lake near Wanzerbe famous for its enchanted crocodile.

Zerma: the "cross-cousins" of the Songhay. The Zerma live to the east of Songhay country. They speak Songhay and share Songhay culture but have a distinct social history.

zima: the priest or priestess of the possession troupe.

zongo: the section of a village or town set off for recently arrived foreigners.